CHEERS TO
TODAY

CHEERS TO TODAY

365 COCKTAILS

BECAUSE EVERY DAY IS A HOLIDAY

CHRIS VOLA

ILLUSTRATIONS BY MATTHEW LINZ

Countryman Press

An Imprint of W. W. Norton & Company
Independent Publishers Since 1923

FOR MOM

For information about permission to reproduce selections from this book, write to
Permissions, Countryman Press, 500 Fifth Avenue, New York, NY 10110

For information about special discounts for bulk purchases, please contact
W. W. Norton Special Sales at specialsales@wwnorton.com or 800-233-4830

Manufacturing by Versa Press
Book design by Allison Chi
Production manager: Devon Zahn

Countryman Press
www.countrymanpress.com

An imprint of W. W. Norton & Company, Inc.
500 Fifth Avenue, New York, NY 10110

www.wwnorton.com

978-1-68268-741-3 (pbk)

10 9 8 7 6 5 4 3 2 1

CONTENTS

INTRODUCTION

If you've taken more than a couple trips around the sun, you understand that life has few certainties. Besides the obvious constants—death, taxes, and the insatiable need for happy hour after an extended stint of drudgery—the world can feel overwhelmingly random and chaotic. But no matter what day of the year it is, one thing's guaranteed: It's a holiday somewhere.

A version of the word *holiday* first appeared in the Middle Ages as an amalgamation of the Old English words for "holy" and "day." As you might expect, the term referred to days set aside for religious observation, oftentimes to honor the many saints of the early Christian church. But yearly, spiritually centered occasions had been taking place for thousands of years before these somber events, with everyone from the ancient Mesopotamians and Egyptians to the Chinese and Celts holding boisterous festivals that thanked the gods for successful harvests, an abundance of children, and not striking everyone down in a sudden, vengeful apocalypse.

Modern secular holidays tend to eschew fire and brimstone in favor of guilt-free snacks, silly party hats, and booze, of course. It's been suggested that the ability to ferment directly contributed to the development of civilization as we know it. Party professionals recognize that celebrating a favorite holiday requires a delicious adult beverage or three. The most dedicated planners and longtime neurotic bartenders such as myself take it a step further, crafting their menus weeks before the festivities. But what about the "regular" times when you still feel like kicking back with a triumphant drink after a long day of making it through the grind? Isn't that worth celebrating, too?—especially nowadays.

Fortunately, as I've learned, there's no such thing as a regular day. Every page of the calendar is surprisingly chock full of less well known and occasionally downright obscure holidays. Some fete specific groups of people (Korean Americans Day) and world historical events (Italian Unification Day). Others honor deceased pop-culture icons (Steve Irwin Day, Kurt Cobain Day) or beloved regional foods (Kentucky Maple Day). Still more sound hilariously strange (International Kiss a Ginger Day).

Despite their obvious differences, these events and countless others like them have at least one point in common with their more hyped-up counterparts such as Thanksgiving, the Fourth of July, and Halloween: You can enjoy them better with cocktails!—and not just random drinks but ones with names, flavors, or histories that best embody the spirit of each observance. To appreciate each day properly and to its fullest, I've attempted to craft a perfect toast for hundreds of the zaniest, weirdest, and most historically significant holidays celebrated around the globe. This book features some of the best and oldest classic cocktails, variations on standbys such as the Manhattan and Margarita, dozens of innovative concoctions from contemporary bartenders, and several of my own creations.

Choosing which holiday and drink to select for a given day wasn't always the easiest task. Some selections are no-brainers: National Mint Julep Day and World Pisco Sour Day, for instance. But there are literally thousands of official (meaning: nationally sanctioned) and informal celebrations scattered throughout the year. February 1 alone has more than a dozen from which to pick, including Car Insurance Day, World Hijab Day, Change Your Password Day, and CBD Day. None of the first three screams "party time!" unless you derive inordinate joy from safe-driver discounts. CBD possesses some nifty stress-relief properties, but a cocktail including that bland substance more likely will put you to sleep than elevate your spirits. Luckily, February 1 is also G. I. Joe Day, the perfect occasion for sipping a spicy, gingery, fruity Toy Soldier while reminiscing about your action-figure glory days. Let's be honest, it's a lot more fun to raise a glass to a franchise loved by millions of children and nerdy adult collectors than a controversial religious garment or a secret word with letters, numbers, and at least one special character.

In *Cheers to Today*, fun is the name of the game. It's as important as ever to kick back with friends and loved ones (in person or electronically), pour some delicious drinks, and relish another 24 hours on this increasingly wacky planet. Appreciating a well-crafted cocktail every day can prove inspiring and invigorating on its own, but it's always more fun and slightly more socially acceptable when it has a great story behind it. Wherever and whenever this book finds you, don't forget to say cheers (*prost, salud, santé,* or *skol*) to today and every day!

BARWARE

BARSPOONS: There's a ton of barspoons out there, but you only need two: an elegantly thin, long-handled spoon with a teardrop-shaped bowl for stirring and a sturdier, utilitarian spoon for cracking and shaping ice. If you don't care about horrifying cocktail snobs, a long chopstick also works great in a pinch.

ICE MOLDS: Nothing will make your cocktails look more professionally crafted than a big, sexy block of ice. Invest in a few silicone ice cube molds, as well as ones that form rectangular blocks known as Collins spears, which are ideal for tall drinks.

JIGGER: When crafting cocktails, accuracy is crucial. Use a jigger or jiggers with 2-ounce, 1-ounce, ¾-ounce, and ½-ounce markings.

JUICER: A good electric or handheld juicer is a wise investment because your citrus always should be as fresh as possible. Be sure to strain all the pulp and seeds from your juice before fixing drinks.

MIXING GLASS: A pint glass works fine, but if you're looking to splurge on a fancy mixing glass, pick one with a sturdy base that can hold at least 500 milliliters of ice and booze.

MUDDLER: Avoid wooden muddlers and those with perforated ends because they tend to break more easily and are more annoying to clean. Heavy, smooth, and plastic are the key words here.

PEELER: Any inexpensive Y-shaped peeler will do. It offers more control than a straight vegetable peeler, and more control means less potential finger carnage.

SHAKERS: Most busy bartenders prefer a Boston shaker set with two metal tumblers of different sizes that fit together. This is due to their larger capacity and efficiency when working behind a lively bar. If you feel more comfortable with a classic three-piece shaker (with the built-in strainer) and you aren't churning out hundreds of cocktails every night, go for it.

STRAINER: Use a Hawthorne strainer for stirred and shaken drinks. This flat-topped favorite of industry professionals has a metal spiral around the edge that fits snugly into any mixing glass or shaker.

GLASSWARE

STEMMED COCKTAIL GLASS: Also known as a coupe, this longtime bartender favorite should be used for most drinks served without ice, such as a Gimlet or Manhattan. The ideal stemmed cocktail glass has a rounded bowl that can hold at least five fluid ounces. It should also have a (you guessed it) stem, which allows you to hold the glass without prematurely warming the drink.

TALL GLASS: Larger glassware comes in a variety of styles. Collins and Highball glasses are two popular choices. But for the purposes of this book, a tall glass is any that can accommodate a drink requiring ice and club soda or that uses a lot of crushed ice, such as a Mojito. A standard water glass from your kitchen will work just fine.

OLD-FASHIONED GLASS: Commonly referred to as a rocks glass or lowball glass, this short and stout tumbler is used primarily for spirit-forward drinks that, like its namesake, are served with ice cubes ("on the rocks"). Old-fashioned glasses traditionally hold between 6 and 10 fluid ounces.

DOUBLE OLD-FASHIONED GLASS: Slightly roomier (12 to 16 fluid ounces), this rocks glass is great for higher-volume stirred drinks, such as the Vieux Carré, as well as any shaken, citrusy cocktail that requires ice.

JULEP CUP: Traditionally made of silver, julep cups more commonly are found now in stainless steel or copper. All three metals do an excellent job of keeping juleps colder for longer by retaining the temperature of the ice. No one likes a glass of warm minty mush.

MUG: For steamy drinks such as the Hot Toddy and Irish Coffee, you want a hardy ceramic mug with a handle to prevent burning yourself. If you're one of the billions who regularly consume coffee or tea, you should be well-stocked already.

WINE GLASS: This household staple provides an attractive option for large, fizzy, spritz-style cocktails. It also can be used in place of a stemmed cocktail glass or a tall glass if you don't feel like doing the dishes.

INGREDIENTS

SPIRITS: Humorist David Sedaris writes that "no amount of physical contact could match the healing powers of a well-made cocktail." But where do those powers come from? Simply put, it's all about the spirits.

Also known as liquors, spirits form the potent backbone of most mixed drinks. They're created by fermenting various sugars with ethanol and carbon dioxide and then distilling them—which means separating the water—to up the alcohol content. Spirits have a variety of bases (agave, corn, sugarcane, wheat, etc.) and an entire world of flavors, but the important thing to know is that they're *strong*, usually around 70 to 80 percent alcohol by volume and sometimes significantly more. The most frequently featured liquors in this book include whiskey, rum, tequila, brandy, absinthe, gin, and vodka.

LIQUEURS: Spirits aren't the only high-proof alcoholic beverages, however. Many fall under the extremely broad category of liqueurs. It can get a little confusing, but basically a liqueur is any neutral spirit infused with sugars, fruits, herbs, barks, or spices. Many of these flavorful liquids are tamer than liquors, but they still pack a punch, averaging around 25 percent alcohol by volume.

Originally created in medieval times as herbal medicines, liqueurs are some of the most versatile ingredients. They can taste sweetly fruity like Cointreau, curaçao, Grand Marnier, and Midori; chocolaty like crème de cacao; or herbaceous like yellow and green Chartreuse and maraschino (not to be confused with neon-red maraschino cherries, which you should place only on whimsical tiki drinks and ice cream sundaes). On the other end of the flavor spectrum, Italian amari such as CioCiaro and Fernet-Branca possess extremely bitter notes that add a great deal of complexity to cocktails. Though they technically aren't liqueurs in the strictest sense of the word, sherries, vermouths, and other fortified wines infused with neutral spirits and botanicals basically serve the same function. If you prefer your cocktails with less of a kick, there are plenty that use only liqueurs for a lighter, hangover-averse drinking experience.

JUICES: With citrusy cocktails, freshness is *everything*, especially in the countless recipes that call for lime or lemon. Store-bought juices, even those that claim not to come from concentrate, don't measure up to freshly squeezed. At-home juicing is always tedious, time-consuming, and expensive. A fully squeezed lime or lemon usually yields just enough juice to make one drink, but it's well worth the effort. Buying all-natural orange, grapefruit, or pineapple juices from the grocery store won't ruin a drink, but there's still no substitute for the hard-earned good stuff.

BITTERS: According to Mark Bitterman, author of *Bitterman's Field Guide to Bitters and Amari*, "bitters are to cocktails as salt is to food." These boozy, proprietary blends of herbs, flowers, barks, roots, and berries have been used for centuries to improve and accentuate flavors already found in drinks and to add their own. There are dozens of bitters on the market today, but most of the drinks in this book (and classic cocktails in general) use one or more of the three most popular: Angostura, Peychaud's, and orange.

EGGS: If you've never subjected yourself to a *Rocky*-style training regimen, it might seem weird to drink an egg, but entire families of cocktails (namely sours and flips) highlight these frothy, flavorful orbs. Whether the recipe calls for the white or yolk—or, rarely, the whole shebang—medium-sized eggs are plenty big enough to get the job done. If you're mess-averse, you may want to use a pour carton for egg-white drinks instead of cracking fresh ones.

SWEETENERS: Health-conscious drinkers (oxymoron) tend to bristle at the mere mention of sugar, but if you want a perfectly balanced cocktail, you need a sweet element. The most iconic of these is the muddled sugar cube in an Old-Fashioned, but bartenders use a wide variety of simple and complex sweeteners, such as orgeat (a creamy almond-based syrup) and maple syrup. Those two are somewhat difficult to whip up yourself—unless you happen to live in a maple forest—but you easily can make the other sweeteners found in this book using the following recipes.

SYRUPS: You frequently will use these syrups (and hand-whipped cream) for the cocktails in this book.

CINNAMON SYRUP

1 cup water
1 cup superfine white sugar
3 crushed cinnamon sticks

In a medium saucepan, combine all ingredients and bring to a boil, stirring until the sugar dissolves completely. Simmer for two minutes, remove from heat, and strain into a glass container. Cover and store indefinitely.

GINGER SYRUP

Superfine white sugar
Fresh ginger

Peel the ginger, grate it, and squeeze the pulp between your fingers to release the juice. Combine the sugar and ginger juice in a nonreactive container and stir until the sugar has completely dissolved. Cover and refrigerate for up to five days.

HONEY SYRUP

3 parts honey
1 part hot water

Combine the ingredients and stir until well-blended. Cover and refrigerate for up to five days.

POMEGRANATE SYRUP

8 ounces pomegranate juice concentrate (such as FruitFast)
1 liter simple syrup

Combine ingredients and stir until well-blended to create a tangy, less sweet alternative to grenadine. Cover and refrigerate.

SIMPLE SYRUP

1 part superfine white sugar

1 part water

Combine ingredients and stir until the sugar dissolves. Do not boil. Cover and refrigerate for up to five days.

WHIPPED CREAM

6 ounces heavy cream

1 white sugar cube

2–3 small ice pebbles

In a squeeze bottle, combine all ingredients. Fasten the bottle's top and shake vigorously until the ice completely dissolves. Refrigerate for up to one week.

TECHNIQUES

MEASURING: To create consistently balanced and delicious cocktails, you have to measure or "jigger" the ingredients accurately, especially for recipes that use very small amounts of certain modifiers. When filling a jigger or pouring to reach a desired line, make sure that a rounded bubble of liquid rises out of the jigger or above the line. This is called a "meniscus," and it means you've got an accurate measurement.

SHAKING: Once you have measured your cocktail, you'll need to mix, chill, and dilute it. If the drink contains citrus or dairy, you're going to want to aerate it as well. The best way to accomplish all of these tasks is by shaking. If you're using a Boston shaker set, measure the ingredients in the smaller metal tumbler, then fill it with ice. Fill the larger tumbler about halfway with ice, then pour the contents of the smaller tumbler into it. Firmly close the smaller tumbler on top and shake vigorously—*as hard as you possibly can.* Seriously. Shaking a dozen drinks should feel like the Shake-Weight workout of a lifetime. Nobody likes a flat, room-temperature beverage.

DRY SHAKING: Also known as whipping, dry shaking refers to shaking a drink without ice for a few seconds. This technique is used when a recipe calls for an egg white or an egg yolk. It emulsifies the drink and gives it a delightfully frothy texture. Tall, citrusy drinks that require club soda, such as the Paloma, also should be dry shaken to avoid overdilution.

STIRRING: Spirit-forward drinks don't require the same kind of dilution and aeration as citrusy ones and should be treated more gently. For on-the-rocks cocktails such as the Negroni, simply pour the measured ingredients directly into the serving glass, add ice, and stir for a few seconds, being careful not to slosh any liquid from the glass or create any unwanted air bubbles. For drinks such as the Manhattan that are served up, measure and pour the ingredients into a mixing glass filled with ice. Stir in a calm, controlled fashion until the drink is very cold but not overdiluted.

STRAINING: Once your drink is sufficiently mixed and frosty, there's only one more step before you can enjoy it. To strain a stirred drink, simply place your Hawthorne strainer on the rim of the mixing glass and pour the cocktail into its chosen vessel. For shaken drinks, place some additional downward pressure on the strainer to reduce the open space between the rim of the shaker and the edge of the strainer, which will prevent bigger chunks of shaking ice from falling into the drink.

GARNISHING: For drinks that call for a citrus twist, express the oils from the peel before dropping it into the liquid to give your cocktail an aromatic boost. Hold the twist a few inches over the drink and gently pinch the long edges of the peel. A thin layer of oils should spray out and settle on the surface of the drink.

JANUARY

1	2	3	4	5	6	7
NEW YEAR'S DAY Gordon's Breakfast	NATIONAL MOTIVATION AND INSPIRATION DAY Act of Faith	NATIONAL FESTIVAL OF SLEEP DAY Night Cap	FREE FLOWER BASKET DAY Flower Shop	NATIONAL BIRD DAY Jungle Bird	APPLE TREE DAY Applejack Cocktail	TRICOLOR DAY Queen's Park Swizzle
8	**9**	**10**	**11**	**12**	**13**	**14**
NATIONAL ENGLISH TOFFEE DAY Toffee Negroni	NATIONAL APRICOT DAY Pendennis	NATIONAL BITTERSWEET CHOCOLATE DAY Right Hand	NATIONAL HOT TODDY DAY Hot Toddy	INTERNATIONAL KISS A GINGER DAY Ginger Rogers	KOREAN AMERICAN DAY Soju Martini	INTERNATIONAL KITE DAY Plastic Kite
15	**16**	**17**	**18**	**19**	**20**	**21**
NATIONAL STRAWBERRY ICE CREAM DAY Peach Blow Fizz	INTERNATIONAL HOT AND SPICY FOODS DAY Widow Maker	NATIONAL HOT BUTTERED RUM DAY Bear Trap No. 2	NATIONAL WINNIE THE POOH DAY Bee's Knees	POPCORN DAY Popcorn Old-Fashioned	NATIONAL COFFEE BREAK DAY Dominicana	NATIONAL HUGGING DAY Hanky Panky
22	**23**	**24**	**25**	**26**	**27**	**28**
NATIONAL COME IN FROM THE COLD DAY Base Camp	NATIONAL HANDWRITING DAY Fitzgerald	NATIONAL PEANUT BUTTER DAY Peanut Butter Cup	BURNS NIGHT Bobby Burns	NATIONAL SPOUSES DAY Remember the Alimony	NATIONAL PUNCH THE CLOCK DAY Blue Collar Cocktail	NATIONAL DAISY DAY Daisy de Santiago
29	**30**	**31**				
THOMAS PAINE DAY Good Fellow	NATIONAL CROISSANT DAY Blackberry Airmail	NATIONAL BACKWARD DAY Reverse Manhattan				

GORDON'S BREAKFAST

A new year means a fresh start, another chance for positive reinvention, a blank canvas with endless possibilities—as soon as you manage to drag your quasi-corpse from bed. After all, New Year's Day is also International Hangover Day, famous for Bloody Marys flowing faster than tears after a jilted midnight kiss. If you prefer foolproof hair of the dog without having to guzzle gobs of tomato juice, here's the Gordon's Breakfast. A lighter yet still mouthwateringly spicy rejuvenator from craft cocktail pioneer Sasha Petraske, this combination of gin, muddled lime, cucumber, and hot sauce tastes refreshing, clean, and tart enough to wash away the mental stench of every failed resolution.

2 ounces gin	4 heavy dashes Cholula hot sauce
¾ ounce simple syrup	1 dash Worcestershire sauce
4 lime wedges	1 pinch salt, for garnish
3 cucumber slices	1 pinch cracked black pepper, for garnish

Combine ingredients in a shaker. Muddle, fill the shaker with cracked ice, and shake vigorously three to four times. Dump the entire contents of the shaker into a double Old-Fashioned glass. Garnish with salt and cracked black pepper.

National Motivation and Inspiration Day

ACT OF FAITH

You've put the decorations away, you've scarfed down the last leftovers, and your hangover has disappeared (mostly). Time to be a real human again! Dreamed up by motivational speaker Kevin McCrudden, National Motivation and Inspiration Day is all about starting the year right by maximizing your potential. Do those productive activities you've been putting off, reconnect with people who inspire you, or create a resolution that you—gasp—might follow through on.

Though making positive personal changes can feel daunting, all you really need is a little faith in yourself. The Act of Faith, first served by Dan Greenbaum at Brooklyn's Diamond Reef in 2017, is an unlikely, exquisitely spirit-forward blend of bold rums and sherry that inspires by-the-books bartenders to think outside the box.

1½ ounces Jamaican rum

½ ounce blackstrap rum

½ ounce Pedro Ximénez sherry

¼ ounce Angostura bitters

1 orange twist, for garnish

Combine ingredients in a double Old-Fashioned glass. Add ice and stir for five or six seconds. Garnish with an orange twist.

National Festival of Sleep Day

NIGHT CAP

Sleep does a body good—like, really, really good. A full night's rest reduces stress, lowers the risk of diabetes and heart disease, and improves brain function and mood. Intentionally held at the tail end of the holiday season, National Festival of Sleep Day encourages the approximately 70 percent of Americans who suffer from insufficient shut-eye to develop better bedtime habits.

Unfortunately, limiting late-night boozing is one of the keys to achieving your best rest, but there's nothing wrong with a before-bed tipple or two to calm the nerves and ease the mind. For snoozers in 1930s Havana, Cuba, the Night Cap at Sloppy Joe's Bar was one of the most popular and yummiest tickets to slumberland. An egalitarian blend that highlights cognac's effortlessly smooth nose, gin's calming botanicals, interesting chocolate notes, and an elegant and citrusy finish, this classic should not be slept on.

¾ ounce cognac	¾ ounce crème de cacao
¾ ounce gin	¾ ounce fresh lime juice

Combine ingredients in an ice-filled shaker. Shake vigorously and strain into a stemmed cocktail glass.

Free Flower Basket Day

FLOWER SHOP

Most people love the excitement that comes with giving and receiving unexpected gifts. For many of us, nothing brightens an indoor space or garden like a basket of beautiful flowers, which makes Free Flower Basket Day a no-brainer! Surprise loved ones, friends, or coworkers today with an arrangement of their favorite seasonal buds.

Sadly, allergies mean that many of us can't enjoy the splendor of freshly picked flowers, but fortunately many of the most succulent floral beauties come in liquid form—including the Flower Shop, which blossomed in the mind of bartender Mitchell Taylor at Attaboy Nashville in 2018. Gin, ginger, citrus, and fragrant elderflower create a veritable potpourri for the palate. This bright, brisk, sweet bouquet is better served in a glass than a basket, however.

1½ ounces gin

¾ ounce ginger syrup

½ ounce elderflower liqueur

½ ounce fresh lime juice

Club soda, to top

1 piece candied ginger,
    for garnish

 Combine the gin, ginger syrup, elderflower liqueur, and lime juice in a shaker. Whip shake (no ice) and pour into a tall glass filled with ice. Top with club soda and garnish with a piece of candied ginger.

JUNGLE BIRD

*Today is for the birds . . . literally! In 2002, conservation organizations
Born Free USA and the Avian Welfare Coalition founded National Bird
Day to recognize the more than 10,000 bird species flying—and in some
cases swimming—on every corner of the planet.*

*Few cocktails, avian related or otherwise, soar to the heights of the
Jungle Bird, a 1970s tiki classic first served at the Aviary Bar in Kuala
Lumpur and recorded in John Poister's* The New American Bartender's
Guide *(1989). Revived by New York City bartenders in the early 2000s, its
bittersweet notes of molasses, citrus, and aromatic herbs fuse to create a
libation as delightfully unique as a multicolored bird of paradise, with the
unexpectedly powerful grace of a blue-footed booby. If the bird is indeed
the word, this one's worth more than a few sentences.*

1½ ounces blackstrap rum
1½ ounces fresh pineapple juice
¾ ounce Campari

¾ ounce fresh lime juice
½ ounce simple syrup
1 thin orange slice, for garnish

Combine ingredients in an ice-filled shaker. Shake vigorously and
strain into a double Old-Fashioned glass over ice. Garnish with an
orange slice.

TURN THE PAGE TO
SEE THE ILLUSTRATION
FOR THIS DRINK.

Jungle Bird
PAGE 21

JANUARY 6
Apple Tree Day

APPLEJACK COCKTAIL

If an apple a day keeps the doctor away, imagine what a whole tree can do! People have cultivated apples for thousands of years in Asia and Europe, but Rev. William Braxton planted the first North American apple orchard in Boston in 1625.

Fermented apples hold a high place in alcohol history, with the Greeks and Romans perfecting hard cider by 55 BCE. In recent times, the most appley adult beverage for your sipping pleasure is unquestionably the Applejack Cocktail, a slightly lighter take on the Prohibition-era Applejack Rabbit, which first appeared in the 1927 edition of Here's How *by Judge Jr. Featuring Laird's Applejack brandy from one of America's oldest licensed distilleries as well as fresh cider, this fruity refresher doesn't fall far from the tree.*

---

2 ounces Laird's Applejack	**½ ounce fresh apple cider**
½ ounce fresh lemon juice	**½ ounce simple syrup**

Combine ingredients in an ice-filled shaker. Shake vigorously and strain into a stemmed cocktail glass.

QUEEN'S PARK SWIZZLE

Feeling patriotic today? You should, because January 7 is all about hoisting the flag and giving a hearty salute to the Red, White, and . . . Green? Not especially popular in America, Fiesta del Tricolore (Tricolor Day) is a major holiday in Italy, where it celebrates the three colors that compose that nation's national flag.

The Queen's Park Swizzle, the liquid jewel of Trinidad's Queen's Park Hotel, is layered, utterly refreshing and minty, and always photogenic. It's one red, white, and green tradition to which you're going to want to pledge your allegiance immediately.

---

2 ounces white rum

1 ounce fresh lime juice

¾ ounce simple syrup

6 to 8 fresh mint leaves

1 brown sugar cube

2 dashes Angostura bitters

2 dashes Peychaud's bitters

1 sprig mint, for garnish

Muddle the rum, lime juice, simple syrup, mint leaves, and sugar cube in a Collins glass. Fill the glass two-thirds of the way with crushed ice. Add the bitters and stir briefly with a swizzle stick. Fill the glass to the top with crushed ice. Garnish with a mint sprig.

TOFFEE NEGRONI

If you've chomped a Heath Bar, you understand the buttery, sugary, crispy perfection of English toffee. British candymakers have been producing various toffees for more than 200 years, but the confection most of us know and love is a distinctly American invention made by caramelizing a mixture of sugar or molasses and butter until it hardens and topping it with almonds. Give into temptation today with a toffee spree. Find a recipe for toffee-covered cake or cookies or splurge for a toffee-infused milkshake. Come on, you know you want to!

If you prefer a boozier route for satisfying your sweet tooth, you're also in luck. Many potations, such as the fittingly named Toffee Negroni, mimic the flavors of our favorite treats without as much sugar—or condescending stares from health nuts. Though it doesn't contain any candy, this impressively balanced combination of molasses-rich aged rum, nutty fino sherry, and aromatic Aperol checks all the boxes of English toffee's flavor profile—and then some. It's an (almost) guilt-free way to satisfy your inner candy monster.

1½ ounces aged rum	¾ ounce Aperol
¾ ounce fino sherry	1 orange twist, for garnish

Combine ingredients in a double Old-Fashioned glass. Add ice and stir for five or six seconds. Garnish with the orange twist.

PENDENNIS

Sometimes it's tough to be an apricot. Often overshadowed in the velvety fruit world by its sweeter, juicier cousins, the peach and nectarine, this tart and slightly firm fuzzball has a lot more to offer than just constipation relief. Apricots, both raw and dried, are antioxidant and vitamin powerhouses, contain lots of magnesium and fiber, and boast a unique flavor that lends itself well to favorites both savory and sweet, such as granola, salads, or jams. Snack on some of these low-calorie delights today and see for yourself why the apricot is one of the most versatile fruits Mother Nature has to offer.

Apricot liqueurs went out of fashion for much of the 20th century, but they've experienced a resurgence in recent years thanks to pre-Prohibition favorites such as the Pendennis, the earliest mention of which you can find in the 1915 supplement to William Boothby's The World's Drinks and How to Mix Them. *Yet even this classic has fallen prey to apricot bias, with many bartenders now mistakenly—or perhaps maliciously?—making it with peach liqueur. We're here to set the record straight: Golden-hued, tangy, subtle, and effortlessly thirst-quenching, a Pendennis without apricot is no Pendennis at all.*

---

2 ounces gin

¾ ounce apricot liqueur

¾ ounce fresh lime juice

1 barspoon cane syrup

2 dashes Peychaud's bitters

Combine ingredients in an ice-filled shaker. Shake vigorously and strain into a stemmed cocktail glass.

RIGHT HAND

You might think of chocolate as a saccharine, milky, generally unhealthy confection, but that's not always the case. Raw cacao seeds, from which producers make chocolate, are nutrient-rich but intensely bitter. They require heavy processing, liquefying, and infusing with sugar, vanilla, spices, and sometimes dairy products before resembling anything close to their final form.

If you're of the "here for a good time, not a long time" ilk and still want to enjoy the depth of flavor that bittersweet chocolate offers, there's the Right Hand. The flagship cocktail of a family of drinks developed at New York City's Milk & Honey in the mid-2000s, this rum-forward Boulevardier improvisation delivers multiple levels of herbal sharpness from Campari and chocolate bitters, which also help to bring out the notes of vanilla and cocoa that naturally occur in the best Italian vermouths. Why bite into a bittersweet chocolate bar when you can drink one?

1½ ounces aged rum
¾ ounce Campari
¾ ounce sweet vermouth

2 dashes chocolate bitters, such as Scrappy's
1 orange twist, for garnish

Combine ingredients in a mixing glass filled with cracked ice. Stir with a long-handled spoon for 30 seconds and strain into a stemmed cocktail glass. Garnish with the orange twist.

HOT TODDY

Who knew that taking your medicine could be fun and delicious?

Used for restorative purposes, hot drinks featuring liquor, water, and spices were well established in British-controlled India by the 18th century and later appropriated by the colonists (because the British). But not until the mid-1800s, when Irish physician Robert Bentley Todd treated cold and flu patients with a steamy mixture of brandy, sugar, and cinnamon, did the Hot Toddy become popular with Western imbibers.

The modern, Americanized version of the cocktail initially featured rum, and doctors touted it as a stimulating cure-all for everything from minor aches and coughs to fever and deafness. Originally prescribed to adults and children, the Hot Toddy does provide an excellent jolt of vitamin C from lemon juice; soothing, antiviral properties from honey; and the numbing effect of alcohol.

---

2 ounces brown spirit of choice
1 ounce water
¾ ounce fresh lemon juice

¾ ounce honey syrup
1 pinch cinnamon, for garnish
1 lemon wedge, for garnish

In a small saucepan over medium-low heat, combine the spirit, water, lemon juice, and honey syrup and heat until steaming. Pour into a mug and garnish with the freshly grated cinnamon and the lemon wedge.

International Kiss a Ginger Day

GINGER ROGERS

Molly Ringwald, Prince Harry, Jessica Rabbit, the entire Weasley family—everyone's got a crush on at least one redhead, real or fictional. International Kiss a Ginger Day is the perfect time to show some love for this too-often maligned demographic.

Crafted by New York City's Bryan Miller, ostensibly in honor of the Golden Age film star of the same name, this sharp and spicy number's chock-full of highly complementary (and complimentary) black rum, cognac, citrus, bitters, and, yes, lots of ginger—with a tawny hue that can't be faked. Sorry, Scarlett Johansson.

1 ounce black rum, preferably
  Goslings
1 ounce cognac
¾ ounce fresh lemon juice

¾ ounce ginger syrup
2 dashes Peychaud's bitters
1 piece candied ginger,
  for garnish

Combine the rum, cognac, lemon juice, ginger syrup, and bitters in an ice-filled shaker. Shake vigorously and strain into a coupe. Garnish with the candied ginger.

Korean American Day

SOJU MARTINI

Shortly after the establishment of peaceful relations between Korea and the United States in 1882, the first recorded Korean immigrants arrived on American shores. Since then, many have followed in their footsteps, adding unique traditions, philosophies, cuisine, and music to America's proverbial melting pot.

As far as drinking goes, it doesn't get more Korean than soju. American bartenders recently discovered that this spirit works nicely as a base in cocktails, such as the Soju Martini. Elusively seductive elderflower liqueur embellishes soju's faintly sweet and subtly floral notes, while Cointreau gives the drink a pleasantly dry, orange-forward finish. It makes a wonderful introduction to a liquor enjoyed by millions, especially if pounding a bottle's worth of shots isn't your idea of a digestif.

2 ounces soju

½ ounce St-Germain

½ ounce Cointreau

1 lemon twist, for garnish

Combine the soju, St-Germain, and Cointreau in a mixing glass filled with cracked ice. Stir with a long-handled spoon for 30 seconds and strain into a stemmed cocktail glass. Garnish with the lemon twist.

International Kite Day

PLASTIC KITE

If some jerk tells you to go fly a kite—which would be weird because most people haven't used that phrase unironically in decades—smile, nod, and whip out your favorite flier because it's International Kite Day!

Your fondest memories of kite-flying might involve the simple, plastic-and-string, diamond-shaped models of your youth. A toy-themed take on the Paper Plane, the Plastic Kite has everything to help you soar far above the threshold of sobriety. It's spicy, smoky, citrusy, and infused with energy-supplying Amaro Averna to provide as many second (and third) winds as necessary.

¾ ounce mezcal

¾ ounce Ancho Reyes

¾ ounce Amaro Averna

¾ ounce fresh lemon juice

Combine ingredients in an ice-filled shaker. Shake vigorously for 25 to 30 seconds and strain into a stemmed cocktail glass.

National Strawberry Ice Cream Day

PEACH BLOW FIZZ

It might seem odd to celebrate National Strawberry Ice Cream Day in the dead of winter, but there's nothing like a blast of refreshing berry sweetness to remind you to look forward to warmer months ahead.

This classic brings its dessert-drink A game with more than a hint of strawberry and creamy goodness, as well as warming notes of juniper and a frothy texture that's the next best thing to biting into an actual berry.

2 ounces gin
¾ ounce fresh lemon juice
¾ ounce simple syrup
½ ounce heavy cream

2 strawberries, halved
1 egg white
Club soda, to top
½ strawberry, for garnish

Combine the gin, lemon juice, simple syrup, cream, halved strawberries, and egg white in a shaker. Shake without ice (to emulsify the egg white) for 10 seconds, then add ice and shake vigorously. Strain into a tall glass filled with ice. Top with club soda and garnish with half of a strawberry.

International Hot and Spicy Foods Day

WIDOW MAKER

Craving curry? Salivating for Szechuan? Champing at the bit for some chili peppers? International Hot and Spicy Foods Day has you covered.

Highlighting intense flavors without allowing them to overpower other ingredients can prove an extremely difficult task, and no drink performs it better than the Widow Maker from Little Branch's Luis Gil, which turns up the heat with poblano chilis, habanero bitters, and cayenne pepper, all wonderfully balanced by palate-cleansing pineapple and orgeat. Mouthwateringly aromatic, smoky, hot, sour, sweet, bitter, and pungent, this modern tiki masterpiece tastes anything but boring.

1½ ounces mezcal

1 ounce fresh pineapple juice

½ ounce Ancho Reyes Verde

½ ounce orgeat

½ ounce fresh lime juice

2 dashes habanero bitters

1 pinch cayenne pepper, to top

Combine the mezcal, juices, Ancho Reyes Verde, orgeat, and bitters in an ice-filled shaker. Shake vigorously for 25 to 30 seconds and strain over ice into a double Old-Fashioned glass. Top with cayenne pepper.

BEAR TRAP NO. 2

"Hot buttered rum." If those three words—preferably spoken slowly in a Barry White baritone—don't cause you to salivate immediately, you're officially dead inside . . . or you care about your health. In which case, why are you reading this book?

The Bear Trap No. 2, the sequel to a version first served at Long Island City's Dutch Kills Bar in the late 2000s, is hot buttered rum on steroids. This dense, savory, sweet, smooth, and steamy potion adds honey syrup and apple cider to an already seductive base of rum, butter, and cinnamon, the finest restorative mix in a long line of bone-heating palate pleasers. It won't help you win any weight-loss competitions, but there's nothing tastier to keep you warm on a chilly night on the prairie or when the heat mysteriously dies in your apartment.

1½ ounces Goslings Black Seal rum

1½ ounces fresh apple cider

½ ounce honey syrup

1 teaspoon butter

1 pinch freshly grated cinnamon, for garnish

1 apple slice, for garnish

 In a small saucepan over medium-low heat, combine the rum, cider, honey syrup, and butter and heat until steaming. Pour into a mug and garnish with the freshly grated cinnamon and the apple slice.

National Winnie the Pooh Day

BEE'S KNEES

"Rivers know this: There is no hurry. We shall get there someday."

It's rare to confuse an Eastern philosopher with a fictional talking teddy, but Winnie the Pooh is no ordinary bear. Pooh's adventures in the Hundred Acre Wood with pals Piglet, Eeyore, and Christopher Robin appeared in dozens of books, plays, films, and television shows, as well as Benjamin Hoff's best-selling introduction to Taoism, The Tao of Pooh, cementing the bumbling, red-shirted furball's status as one of the 20th century's most recognizable—and lovably profound—anthropomorphic animals.

If one thing can disrupt Pooh's Zen-like calm, it's the prospect of getting his paws on a jar of honey. Frank Meier's Bee's Knees has enthralled real-life honey hoarders since at least 1921, when it debuted in Paris on the menu of the Ritz's Café Parisian. This straightforward Gin Sour variation features just three ingredients, yet its simple construction, like the best of Pooh's memorable observations ("It isn't much good having anything exciting, if you can't share it with somebody"), belies a richness of spirit hard to duplicate.

2 ounces gin	**¾ ounce fresh lemon juice**
	¾ ounce honey syrup

Combine ingredients in an ice-filled shaker. Shake vigorously and strain into a stemmed cocktail glass.

POPCORN OLD-FASHIONED

Step aside, snap and crackle. Today's all about the pop! National Popcorn Day recognizes a savory treat devoured for at least 500 years. Aztecs used popcorn in headdresses worn during ceremonies honoring Tlaloc, their god of maize and fertility. Since the development of commercial popping machines in the 1800s, popcorn has become the go-to snack for sports-loving and movie-going Americans, who consume 3.25 billion gallons of the fluffy kernels each year. Whether you prefer your popcorn plain, buttered, candied, caramelized, or tossed with nuts and chocolate, there's no wrong way or time to scarf a fistful of corny goodness.

If you're feeling more adventurous, why not drink your popcorn? It might sound a little weird, but the Popcorn Old-Fashioned adapts a recipe from inventive London restaurant Sexy Fish. The hodgepodge of classic flavors tastes distinctly smoky, buttery, and slightly sweet, with a vegetal finish.

2 ounces popcorn-infused whisky	2 dashes Angostura bitters
1 barspoon cane syrup	1 lemon twist, for garnish
1 barspoon absinthe	1 orange twist, for garnish

Combine the whisky, cane syrup, absinthe, and bitters in an Old-Fashioned glass. Add ice and stir for five or six seconds. Garnish with the lemon and orange twists.

POPCORN-INFUSED WHISKY

30 grams popcorn	10 ounces Japanese whisky or blended scotch

Add the popcorn to your favorite whisky, freeze overnight, and strain through a coffee filter the following morning.

DOMINICANA

Can't make it through the morning without a steaming or icy infusion of lifesaving caffeine bliss? You're not alone. Though not mandated by law, coffee breaks have become an integral part of most workplaces. If your boss doesn't allow a quick pick-me-up, explain that the National Coffee Association encourages coffee breaks to encourage productivity and camaraderie in the office. It's worth a shot!

People have been combining coffee and alcohol for at least 1,200 years, back to when Ethiopian goat herders discovered that fermenting coffee berries made for quite a groovy time. Today, menus everywhere feature caffeinated concoctions such as the Espresso Martini, the most famous "Martini" variation that has absolutely nothing to do with an actual Martini. If you're looking for a deeper, more interesting take on boozy coffee, try the Dominicana, first served by Sasha Petraske at Milk & Honey in 2001. Rich, cream-covered, and supremely decadent, this one's better as an after-work treat—unless your morning really sucks, then, hey, why not?

1½ ounces aged rum
1½ ounces Caffé Lolita

2 dashes Angostura bitters
2 dashes chocolate bitters
Hand-whipped cream float

Combine the rum, Caffé Lolita, and bitters in a mixing glass filled with cracked ice. Stir with a long-handled spoon for 30 seconds and strain into a stemmed cocktail glass. Top with the whipped cream.

TURN THE PAGE TO
SEE THE ILLUSTRATION
FOR THIS DRINK.

Dominicana
PAGE 37

HANKY PANKY

Today takes embracing the day to another level because it's National Hugging Day! Created in 1986 by Michigan pastor Kevin Zaborney, this holiday celebrates an age-old way to show affection.

For those who hug, it's well known that playfully locking shoulders frequently can lead to more, um, intimate activities. Legendary bartender Ada Coleman first served the Hanky Panky, an ode to tomfoolery (both romantic and otherwise), at London's Savoy Hotel around 1903. A sultry blend of gin and vermouth to cool things down after they get hot and heavy, with a minty blast of Fernet-Branca to keep breath fresh during close encounters, this sexy number makes the perfect companion for an epic cuddling session.

1½ ounces gin
1½ ounces sweet vermouth

¼ ounce Fernet-Branca
1 orange twist, for garnish

Combine the gin, vermouth, and Fernet-Branca in a mixing glass filled with cracked ice. Stir with a long-handed spoon for 30 seconds and strain into a stemmed cocktail glass. Garnish with the orange twist.

National Come in from the Cold Day

BASE CAMP

In the Northern Hemisphere, the end of January is one of the most frigid times of the year, statistically speaking. Wintertime activities such as skiing, sledding, skating, and building snowmen can be lots of fun, but nothing's better than heading inside, kicking off all those layers of outerwear, and cozying up next to a roaring fire with a few close friends and a mug of hot cocoa.

Sometimes the elements can feel so brutal, though, that getting the chill out of your bones requires a much stronger beverage. Celebrate National Come in from the Cold Day the right way, with a Base Camp, created by Matty Clark at Manhattan's Attaboy in 2017. This spicy, savory Old-Fashioned variation—also a play on Clark's similarly delectable Sherpa—features the best warming properties of scotch and bourbon, embellished with cacao and notes of cinnamon, clove, and nutmeg. Strong enough to appease the most weather-hardened adventurers, it's a delight for whiskey lovers in all climates.

1½ ounces bourbon
¼ ounce Islay scotch
¼ ounce crème de cacao

¼ ounce St. Elizabeth Allspice Dram
2 dashes orange bitters
1 lemon twist, for garnish

Combine the bourbon, scotch, crème de cacao, allspice dram, and bitters in an Old-Fashioned glass. Add ice and stir for five or six seconds. Garnish with the lemon twist.

National Handwriting Day

FITZGERALD

In an era when most written communication is done hastily with thumbs and an emoji can carry the same weight as a sentence, working on your handwriting can seem impractical, if not a total waste of time. But even as we stray further into the digital realm, there's still something to be said about putting pen or pencil to paper.

Before typewriters—and later, word processors—were readily available, most authors painstakingly wrote their great books by hand, including F. Scott Fitzgerald's The Great Gatsby. *Completing such a carpal tunnel–inducing task deserves an appropriately celebratory beverage, and the author-inspired Fitzgerald from Dale DeGroff is more than up to snuff. This stripped-down Sour features gin—though it works well with just about any spirit—fresh lemon juice, and simple syrup, with a hearty dose of Angostura bitters to add depth and roundness. Enjoy a couple of these and you might be inspired to jot down a few bons mots, even if it's just signing the bar tab.*

---

2 ounces gin or your favorite
   liquor
¾ ounce fresh lemon juice

¾ ounce simple syrup
3 dashes Angostura bitters,
   to top

Combine the gin, lemon juice, and simple syrup in an ice-filled shaker. Shake vigorously for 25 to 30 seconds and strain into a stemmed cocktail glass. Top with the bitters.

JANUARY 24
National Peanut Butter Day

PEANUT BUTTER CUP

Whether smooth or chunky, or infused with chocolate or jelly, no pantry is complete without a jar of rich, gooey, delicious peanut butter. Unless you have a peanut allergy, that is. Sadly, many people's bodies have never allowed them to experience buttery bliss. Until today. The Peanut Butter Cup, created by New York City's Cervantes Ramirez, faithfully recreates peanut butter's unique flavor characteristics without any peanuts. It's unclear how this miraculous alchemy works (we're no scientists), but the sumptuous, silky combination of bourbon, CioCiaro, cacao, honey, cream, egg yolk, and champagne is a worry-free liquid introduction to a food that's a regular part of millions of lives—and an unbelievably extra way to wash down a PB&J.

1 ounce bourbon

½ ounce Amaro CioCiaro

½ ounce crème de cacao

½ ounce honey syrup

½ ounce heavy cream

1 egg yolk

Champagne, to top

 Combine the bourbon, Amaro CioCiaro, crème de cacao, honey syrup, heavy cream, and egg yolk in a shaker. Shake without ice (to emulsify the egg yolk) for 10 seconds, then add ice and shake vigorously. Strain into a fizz glass and top with champagne.

Burns Night

BOBBY BURNS

Regarded as the national poet of Scotland and a major influence on romanticism, liberalism, and socialism, Robert Burns is still revered in his home country, where a truly epic feast takes place each year on his birthday. Burns loved the Scottish "water of life" so much that a cocktail, first appearing in Harry Craddock's The Savoy Cocktail Book *(1930), was created in his name. A smoky, slightly sweeter take on a Manhattan, the Bobby Burns is as eloquent as an ode recited in the Scots language by a master poet. But have too many of these peaty, boozy tipples before dinner arrives and you might be addressing the haggis face-first.*

1½ ounces blended scotch

1 ounce sweet vermouth

½ ounce Islay scotch

2 dashes Angostura bitters

1 brandied cherry, for garnish

Combine the scotches, vermouth, and bitters in a mixing glass filled with cracked ice. Stir with a long-handled spoon for 30 seconds and strain into a stemmed cocktail glass. Garnish with the brandied cherry.

REMEMBER THE ALIMONY

You can be in love without being married, but it's hard to have a successful marriage without love. If you're one of the more than 60 million spouses in America, take a few moments of your hectic life to show just how much your other half means to you and reflect on your journey together.

Unfortunately, "'til death do us part" doesn't always work out. That's why it's vital not to rush into matrimony or you might have to deal not only with getting your heart broken but also your wallet. Dan Greenbaum implores us to remember the alimony, or the financial support you could be forced to give your spouse in the event of a separation. It's also the name of a fantastically rich sipper that he created at New York City's The Beagle in 2012. This marriage of nutty amontillado aherry and bittersweet Cynar is as complex and complementary as the most successful partnerships. Negroni-esque in body, its alcohol content is low enough for you to keep your head during the big decisions—like, you know, spending the rest of your life with one person.

1¼ ounces amontillado sherry

1¼ ounces Cynar

¾ ounce gin

1 orange twist, for garnish

 Combine the sherry, Cynar, and gin in a double Old-Fashioned glass. Add ice and stir for five or six seconds. Garnish with the orange twist.

BLUE COLLAR COCKTAIL

Many of America's greatest monuments and institutions might take their names from wealthy benefactors, but those patrons didn't build them. National Punch the Clock Day honors the indispensable and too-often underappreciated achievements of the working class.

An honest eight-plus hours of labor rarely comes easy, but a relaxing after-work beverage always should, especially one as potent and replenishing as the Blue Collar Cocktail, concocted by Michael Madrusan at Milk & Honey in 2008. A subtle, herbaceous play on a Manhattan, the flavor profile belies its salt-of-the-earth sensibilities.

2 ounces rye whiskey

½ ounce sweet vermouth

¼ ounce maraschino liqueur

¼ ounce Amaro CioCiaro

2 dashes orange bitters

1 lemon twist, for garnish

Combine the rye, vermouth, maraschino liqueur, Amaro CioCiaro, and bitters in a mixing glass filled with cracked ice. Stir with a long-handled spoon for 30 seconds and strain into a stemmed cocktail glass. Garnish with the lemon twist.

DAISY DE SANTIAGO

If you have seen Disney's animated Alice in Wonderland *or listened to the grumblings of a curmudgeonly gardener, you know that weeds get a bad rap. But not all of these invasive plants are nuisances. Daisies, for example, are prized not only for their attractive white and yellow flowers but also are considered a symbol of innocence, simplicity, virtue, and childhood.*

The flower shares its name with a loosely related family of drinks that dates to the late 1800s. One of the most fragrant of these is the Daisy de Santiago, which Charles H. Baker describes as "a lovely thing introduced to us through the gracious offices of the late Facundo Bacardi" in his 1939 collection, Jigger, Beaker, and Glass: Drinking around the World. *Elegant in nose, stately in appearance, and topped with just the right botanicals, this is one daisy you'll want for a centerpiece.*

2 ounces white rum
1 ounce fresh lime juice

¼ ounce simple syrup
¼ ounce yellow Chartreuse
1 sprig fresh mint, for garnish

Combine the rum, lime juice, and simple syrup in an ice-filled shaker. Shake vigorously and strain into a large wine glass filled with cracked ice. Top with the yellow Chartreuse and garnish with the mint sprig.

GOOD FELLOW

Corset-maker, journalist, philosopher, political theorist, activist, pro-
pagandist, patriot. Those are just a few of the roles that describe Revo-
lutionary War–era polymath Thomas Paine, who was born on this date
in 1732.

Championing revolutionary causes such as democracy, liberty, and
equality generally are seen as positive character traits unless you're
really into dictatorships for some reason. Meaning that Thomas Paine,
by all accounts, was a swell guy, a good fellow, if you will. The latter
term shares its name with a complex, zesty sipper first served at New
York City's Gramercy Tavern in 2012. On the drier side yet still fruity
and as nutty as British loyalists considered Paine, this provocative Old-
Fashioned riff has all the smoke you need to stoke the passion for what-
ever noble cause lies dearest to your heart.

---

2 ounces blended scotch	**¼ ounce walnut liqueur**
½ ounce oloroso sherry	**1 dash orange bitters**
¼ ounce pear liqueur	**1 orange twist, for garnish**

Combine the scotch, sherry, pear liqueur, walnut liqueur, and
bitters in a double Old-Fashioned glass. Add ice and stir for
five or six seconds. Garnish with the orange twist.

National Croissant Day

BLACKBERRY AIRMAIL

Golden. Flaky. Buttery. Crispy. Perfection. The croissant has been a top choice of pastry aficionados since at least 1839, when it appeared on the menu at a Parisian bakery owned by former Viennese military officer August Zang. Quickly spreading throughout Paris and beyond, these crescent-shaped delicacies have become far more than just a simple breakfast staple, and enthusiasts often enhance them with sweeteners such as blackberries and honey.

The Blackberry Airmail, based on a drink first described in W. C. Whitfield's Here's How: Mixed Drinks *(1941), features both delightful flavors. Berry-fresh, delicately airy, and topped with a generous dose of champagne, it's the perfect companion for a night on the town or a croissant-fueled boozy brunch.*

---

1 ounce white rum
½ ounce fresh lime juice

½ ounce honey syrup
4 blackberries
Champagne, to top

Combine the rum, lime juice, honey syrup, and three blackberries in an ice-filled shaker. Shake vigorously and strain into a stemmed cocktail glass. Top with champagne and garnish with another blackberry.

REVERSE MANHATTAN

Today's the perfect opportunity to shake things up—by doing everything backward! Start a book from the last page. Eat ice cream for breakfast. Like Leonardo da Vinci, write your letters backward.

Some of the most time-honored cocktails have benefited from the occasional switcheroo. The Reverse Manhattan, popular with the low-ABV set, flips the traditional two-to-one whiskey-to-vermouth ratio with surprisingly enjoyable results. Taking rye out of the spotlight gives the drink's often overlooked herbal and bittersweet notes a chance to shine, especially when using a richer vermouth such as Punt e Mes, Carpano Antica, or a blend of the two, if you're feeling extra fancy. This drink serves as an excellent reminder that nothing's set in stone, not even the supposedly perfect recipes of the past.

2 ounces Italian vermouth

1 ounce rye whiskey

2 dashes Angostura bitters

1 brandied cherry, for garnish

Combine the vermouth, whiskey, and bitters in a mixing glass filled with cracked ice. Stir with a long-handled spoon for 30 seconds and strain into a stemmed cocktail glass. Garnish with a brandied cherry.

FEBRUARY

			1	2	3	4
			G.I. JOE DAY Toy Soldier	GROUNDHOG DAY Young American	TAKE A CRUISE DAY Death in the Gulf Stream	LIBERACE DAY Eastside Royale
5	6	7	8	9	10	11
DISASTER DAY Hurricane	KENTUCKY MAPLE DAY Kentucky Maple	WORLD PISCO SOUR DAY Pisco Sour	OPERA DAY Crimes of Passion	NATIONAL TOOTHACHE DAY Dr. Henderson	ALL THE NEWS THAT'S FIT TO PRINT DAY Journalist	NATIONAL PEPPERMINT PATTY DAY Grasshopper
12	13	14	15	16	17	18
DARWIN DAY Philosopher's Grog	INTERNATIONAL CONDOM DAY Between the Sheets	VALENTINE'S DAY Pink Lady	REMEMBER THE *MAINE* DAY Remember the *Maine*	NATIONAL ALMOND DAY Charo's Kick	MY WAY DAY Sea Way	DRINK WINE DAY Goldfinch
19	20	21	22	23	24	25
NATIONAL LASH DAY Hawkeye	KURT COBAIN DAY Nirvana	NATIONAL GRAIN-FREE DAY Bramble	NATIONAL MARGARITA DAY Margarita	PINOCCHIO DAY Pleasure Island	WORLD BARTENDER DAY Negroni	NATIONAL PISTOL PATENT DAY .38 Special
26	27	28	29			
NATIONAL PISTACHIO DAY Broadway Diner	NATIONAL KAHLÚA DAY Holy Mole	NATIONAL FLORAL DESIGN DAY Water Lily	LEAP DAY Leap Year			

G.I. Joe Day

TOY SOLDIER

In an action-figure industry dominated by laser-wielding aliens, super-heroes, and sentient shape-shifting cars, G.I. Joe has always been a patri-otic breath of fresh air. The Toy Soldier, adapted from a drink created by Michael McCollum at Nashville's Bastian, takes the classic Mule arche-type and reimagines it for a flashier era. Smoky mezcal and silky pine-apple collide like a battle between the Joes and the Cobras, with tequila and ginger doing the heavy lifting to bring everything to a delicious res-olution. One sip from this war-inspired bad boy and you'll immediately become a pacifist.

1½ ounces tequila blanco
½ ounce mezcal
¾ ounce fresh pineapple juice
¾ ounce fresh lime juice
¾ ounce ginger syrup

¼ ounce St. Elizabeth Allspice Dram
Club soda, to top
1 piece candied ginger, for garnish

Combine the tequila, mezcal, juices, ginger syrup, and allspice dram in a shaker. Whip shake (no ice) and pour into a tall glass filled with ice. Top with club soda. Garnish with the piece of candied ginger.

YOUNG AMERICAN

Who needs scientists when you have a chunky rodent to foretell the weather?

Since 1887, residents of Punxsutawney, Pennsylvania, have held fast to the tradition that, if a local groundhog named Punxsutawney Phil emerges from hibernation today and sees his shadow (due to clear weather), he will run back into his burrow and wintry conditions will continue for six more weeks. Groundhog Day also was immortalized in the 1993 Bill Murray film of the same name, in which Punxsutawney weatherman Phil Connors gets stuck in a time loop and must relive February 2 repeatedly. The Young American's sweet vermouth base, amplified by Italian amari Campari and Aperol, makes for an unapologetically bittersweet and herbaceous experience you'll want to recreate again and again. Bright and cheerful for toasting to an early spring, it also has enough of a kick to fortify you if the weather doesn't cooperate.

1½ ounces sweet vermouth	1 barspoon absinthe
½ ounce Campari	Club soda, to top
½ ounce Aperol	1 grapefruit twist, for garnish

 Combine the vermouth, Campari, Aperol, and absinthe in a double Old-Fashioned glass. Add ice and stir for five or six seconds. Top with club soda. Garnish with the grapefruit twist.

DEATH IN THE GULF STREAM

A refreshing breeze at your back, the glint of sun on the waves, and all the water slides, ziplining, simulated surfing, rock-wall climbing, and endless buffets that you and your sunburned family can handle.

There's nothing better than kicking back on deck in a lounge chair and enjoying a cold drink. Ernest Hemingway, who spent countless hours afloat on modern cruising hot spots in the Caribbean Sea, would agree. One of his favorite nautical refreshers was Death in the Gulf Stream, a charmingly tart—if ominously named—potable that legendary spirits writer Charles H. Baker claims "cools the blood and inspires renewed interest in food, companions, and life." That's just about everything you could want in a cruise or a drink.

2 ounces genever	4 dashes Angostura bitters
1 ounce fresh lime juice	1 mint sprig, for garnish
½ ounce simple syrup	1 lime wedge, for garnish

Combine the genever, lime juice, and simple syrup in a double Old-Fashioned glass. Fill the glass two-thirds of the way with crushed ice. Add the bitters and stir briefly with a swizzle stick. Fill the glass to the top with crushed ice. Garnish with the mint sprig and lime wedge.

EASTSIDE ROYALE

Before Elton John or Freddie Mercury, the most dashingly flamboyant front man to tickle the ivories was "Mr. Showmanship" himself, Władziu Valentino Liberace. Today, toast to a man who lived his life the way he wanted, haters and conservative aesthetics be damned.

Nothing says excess quite like champagne, which happened to be Liberace's beverage of choice. Chances are he would have loved the Eastside Royale, a bubbly, vegetal take on George Delgado's modern classic. A haughty diva featuring bright notes of juniper, cucumber, and mint, it's tasty enough to make anyone feel like pop-culture royalty. Have one sip and you soon will find yourself wanting to laugh all the way to the bar to fix yourself round two.

---

1 ounce gin
½ ounce fresh lime juice
½ ounce simple syrup
3 or 4 fresh mint leaves

2 thin cucumber slices
Champagne, to top
1 thin cucumber slice,
   for garnish

 Combine the gin, lime juice, simple syrup, mint leaves, and cucumber slices in an ice-filled shaker. Shake vigorously and strain into a stemmed cocktail glass. Top with champagne and garnish with another cucumber slice.

Disaster Day

HURRICANE

Held on the anniversary of an earthquake that rocked Pompeii in 62 CE (which preceded the massive volcanic eruption that buried the Roman city a few years later), Disaster Day encourages us to learn about past calamities and take steps, where possible, to avoid future ones.

In storm-afflicted New Orleans, not all hurricanes are to be feared. Served in the French Quarter since the 1940s, the Hurricane cocktail is a powerful tiki blend featuring two full servings of light and dark rum, rounded out with a fruity mélange that hides its bark, if not its bite. One round is as calming as the proverbial eye of the storm, but anything more and you risk inciting a Category-5 hangover.

2 ounces light rum

2 ounces dark rum

1 ounce orange juice

¾ ounce passion fruit syrup

½ ounce fresh lime juice

½ ounce cane syrup

¼ ounce pomegranate syrup

1 thin orange slice, for garnish

1 brandied cherry, for garnish

Combine the rums, juices, passion fruit syrup, cane syrup, and pomegranate syrup in a shaker. Pour into a tall glass or mug filled two-thirds of the way with crushed ice. Add a straw and top with more crushed ice. Garnish with the orange slice and the brandied cherry.

KENTUCKY MAPLE

Kudos to the first prehistoric oddball who saw brown gunk flowing from a maple tree and licked it. Celebrate that good work by dousing your pancakes, waffles, or French toast in gooey, syrupy bliss or participate in a Super Troopers–style chugging contest.

Better yet, savor the maple's unique flavor as part of a boozy ensemble. Mixologists only recently started highlighting maple syrup as a sweetener in cocktails, but you can enjoy plenty of maple-powered modern classics, such as this hearty take on the Pélerin from Nicole Lebedevitch of Food & Wine. *In addition to its delightfully smooth blend of syrup, citrus, and bourbon—another of the United States's most delectable exports—an infusion of allspice gives the drink a decidedly autumnal vibe. That season has a strong association with sap production, but you can and should shake up this all-American nugget of golden goodness whenever the craving strikes.*

1½ ounces Kentucky straight
  bourbon
1 ounce fresh lemon juice

¾ ounce pure maple syrup
¼ ounce St. Elizabeth Allspice
  Dram
2 dashes Angostura bitters

Combine all ingredients in an ice-filled shaker. Shake vigorously and strain into a stemmed cocktail glass.

FEBRUARY 7
World Pisco Sour Day

PISCO SOUR

For such a charmingly smooth spirit, pisco has a surprisingly turbulent history. First produced in Peru and Chile using grapes brought across the Atlantic by Spanish conquistadors, the brandy's country of origin is unknown, though both South American nations fiercely claim it as their own. This uncertainty has led to a centuries-long conflict highlighted by bitter trade wars and even the occasional patriotic act of booze-related violence.

Almost single-handedly responsible for introducing pisco to the rest of the world, the modern version of the Pisco Sour has changed very little since the 1920s, when bartenders began topping it with bitters and cinnamon. This curiously sharp, foamy, tangy, and sublimely refreshing drink is still so locally important that the Peruvian government recently declared it part of Peru's National Cultural Patrimony, a decision that predictably enraged Chileans.

2 ounces pisco
¼ ounce simple syrup
⅛ ounce fresh lemon juice
⅛ ounce fresh lime juice

1 egg white
1 dash Angostura bitters, to top
1 pinch freshly grated cinnamon, for garnish

Combine the pisco, simple syrup, juices, and egg white in a shaker. Shake without ice (to emulsify the egg white) for 10 seconds, then add ice and shake vigorously. Strain into a stemmed cocktail glass and top with the bitters. Garnish with the freshly grated cinnamon.

CRIMES OF PASSION

One of opera's defining characteristics is the sheer power of its singers, whose voices can fill an entire theater, belting out thrilling lyrics about love, heartbreak, and cunning deception. Though its name might evoke the actions of some of the stage's greatest heroes and villains, the Crimes of Passion—invented by Hunter Orahood at Attaboy in 2018—is all about squashing the drama. A smooth and smoky base of tequila and mezcal blends with silky-tart passion fruit and decadent honey to calm the jitters of the most high-strung characters. But avoid drinking one of these during a performance, as opera singers' vocal abilities have been known to shatter glass. Ruining a drink this good would be a truly criminal act.

1½ ounces tequila

¾ ounce fresh lime juice

¾ ounce passion fruit syrup

½ ounce mezcal

¼ ounce honey syrup

1 pinch cayenne pepper, for garnish

Combine the tequila, lime juice, passion fruit syrup, mezcal, and honey syrup in an ice-filled shaker. Shake vigorously for 25 to 30 seconds and strain into a stemmed cocktail glass. Garnish with the cayenne pepper.

DR. HENDERSON

Before the advent of modern anesthesia, the much more lit medical practitioners of the 19th century prescribed alcohol for nearly every procedure, from tooth extractions to amputations. While that's thankfully not the case today, pain sufferers still swear by numerous boozy home remedies, including the Dr. Henderson. This minty, medicinal-tasting concoction, attributed to the physician father of chef Fergus Henderson, is best known as an excellent hangover cure, but its numbing and cooling properties might be just the thing for minor tooth irritation. Described unflatteringly as "toothpaste for the liver," it still beats a root canal.

2 ounces Fernet-Branca　　　　**1 ounce crème de menthe**

Combine both ingredients in a double Old-Fashioned glass. Add ice and stir for five or six seconds.

All the News That's Fit to Print Day

JOURNALIST

In America's earliest newsrooms, sensationalism and misinformation ran rampant, so much so that New York Times *owner Arthur S. Ochs created the slogan "All the News That's Fit to Print" to declare his paper's impartiality and to throw some passive-aggressive shade at his competitors.*

As relentless as journalists can be when pursuing the truth, many are equally dogged in the search for a stiff drink. That was certainly the case in the 1930s, when the Journalist emerged as the favorite Martini variation of New York City newspaper employees. Featuring two vermouths, curaçao, bitters, and a dash of citrus, it's a blend as sharp as the finest investigative reporting, with a dry, hard-nosed finish impossible to fake. Simply put, it's all the stuff that's fit to drink.

---

2 ounces gin
½ ounce dry vermouth
½ ounce sweet vermouth

2 dashes curaçao
2 dashes fresh lemon juice
1 dash Angostura bitters
1 lemon twist, for garnish

Combine the gin, vermouths, curaçao, lemon juice, and bitters in a mixing glass filled with cracked ice. Stir with a long-handled spoon for 30 seconds and strain into a stemmed cocktail glass. Garnish with the lemon twist.

FEBRUARY 11
National Peppermint Patty Day

GRASSHOPPER

Get the sensation! *Any candy connoisseur who grew up in the 1970s, '80s, or '90s will recognize that slogan as referring to the kingpin of chocolaty, minty confections: the York Peppermint Pattie! York's catchy commercials may have hooked more recent generations looking to satisfy their sweet teeth, but the pleasantly pungent treat has a much longer history, dating to 1840, when the Quiggin family began producing "mint cakes" on the Isle of Man.*

The refreshing yet indulgent flavor combination of chocolate and mint isn't just reserved for sweets. Hailing from New Orleans's French Quarter, the Grasshopper has been brightening the after-dinner cocktail scene since at least 1918. Featuring crème de menthe, cacao, and fresh mint for an extra kick, it's a lusciously cooling and, yes, sensational palate cleanser. Indulge in a Grasshopper tonight, and—if you're feeling crazy—a peppermint patty on the side. Your taste buds will thank you.

1¼ ounces crème de cacao
1 ounce crème de menthe

1 ounce heavy cream
3 or 4 fresh mint leaves

Combine all ingredients in an ice-filled shaker. Shake vigorously for 25 to 30 seconds and strain into a stemmed cocktail glass.

PHILOSOPHER'S GROG

Curiosity may have killed the cat, but it also led Charles Darwin to change the course of scientific history. Fascinated by life in all its many forms, the English naturalist and geologist set sail on the HMS Beagle *in 1831, embarking on a five-year voyage to study animals and plants on five continents. To combat seasickness, Darwin and his crewmates concocted a stomach-settling potation they called Philosopher's Grog, composed of ingredients brought from England and picked up on their adventures. In this modernized version, sweet and supple South American liquors pisco and cachaça easily mingle with gin's juniper-forward bouquet, scurvy-preventing lime juice, and a hint of bubbly to combat the most egregious acts of gluttony.*

1 ounce gin
¾ ounce fresh lime juice
½ ounce cachaça
½ ounce pisco
½ ounce simple syrup

¼ ounce Licor 43
Splash of champagne
1 pinch freshly grated cinnamon,
    for garnish
1 lime wedge, for garnish

Combine the gin, lime juice, cachaça, pisco, simple syrup, and Licor 43 in a shaker. Pour into a tall glass filled two-thirds of the way with crushed ice. Add a splash of champagne and top with more crushed ice. Garnish with the cinnamon and lime wedge.

BETWEEN THE SHEETS

Created by the AIDS Healthcare Foundation, International Condom Day promotes one of the most effective and easily available methods of contraception. Condoms can prevent pregnancy and STDs, as well as slow the spread of potentially life-threatening viruses such as HIV and HPV. When things get heated in the bedroom (or a secluded corner of your local watering hole), remember that safer is always sexy.

Few aphrodisiacs stoke the libido like a well-made libation. The Between the Sheets, a sultry little Sidecar riff that gained notoriety during Prohibition for its popularity among sex workers, has been known to provoke such risqué reactions. With a seductive coupling of white rum and cognac, it's fair to assume that sharing one or two of these with a special new friend might take you from the bar to the bedsheets faster than you can say "Check, please!" Just be sure to use a condom when you get there.

1 ounce Cointreau

¾ ounce aged rum

¾ ounce cognac

½ ounce fresh lemon juice

1 lemon twist, for garnish

Combine the Cointreau, rum, cognac, and lemon juice in an ice-filled shaker. Shake vigorously for 25 to 30 seconds and strain into a stemmed cocktail glass. Garnish with the lemon twist.

PINK LADY

*Originally the date of Lupercalia, a pagan fertility festival, February 14
has evolved into a commercial juggernaut in which exchanging cards,
gifting candy, and unencumbered smooching have become the norm for
star-crossed and Tinder-matched lovers. But if you're not into the PDA,
don't stress. Treat yourself to a solo night out at all your favorite spots
because Valentine's Day is about loving the most important people in
your life—including you. Just don't forget to make reservations before it's
too late!*

*If you did, there's no plan B like ordering take-out, firing up Netflix,
and whipping up a couple of passion-provoking cocktails, such as the silky
and sumptuous Pink Lady. Though its true origins are uncertain, it's
thought to have been inspired by Ivan Caryll's 1911 Broadway musical of
the same name. Long belittled by misogynistic barflies as a strictly female
potable, the dry yet fruity, surprisingly strong Gin Sour riff now attracts
fans of all genders as much for its Insta-friendly rose hue as its intriguing
flavor profile. One sip and you'll understand: This is one romance meant
to last.*

---

1 ounce gin
1 ounce applejack

¾ ounce fresh lemon juice
¾ ounce pomegranate syrup
1 egg white

Combine all ingredients in a shaker. Shake without ice
(to emulsify the egg white) for 10 seconds, then add ice and
shake vigorously for 25 to 30 seconds. Strain into a stemmed
cocktail glass.

REMEMBER THE *MAINE*

In a hypothetical list ranking the most memorable wars fought by the United States, the Spanish-American War probably wouldn't land anywhere near the top. But central to the conflict was the explosion and sinking of the American battleship USS Maine *in Havana Harbor, which ethically challenged yellow journalists blamed on Spain despite little to no evidence. The tragedy instantly helped sway American public opinion in favor of war and gave rise to the popular cheer "Remember the Maine! To hell with Spain!"*

The Remember the Maine, a highlight of Charles H. Baker Jr.'s The Gentleman's Companion (1939), has enough rye whiskey to satisfy proud patriots, as well as Cherry Heering and anise from Europe and Angostura bitters from the Caribbean, making the drink worthy of its internationally significant namesake. Take it easy with this too-easily-quaffed, absinthe-tinged whiskey battleship, or you most definitely won't remember the Maine—or anything else, for that matter.

2 ounces rye whiskey	2 dashes Angostura bitters
¾ ounce sweet vermouth	1 barspoon absinthe
¼ ounce Cherry Heering	1 lemon twist, for garnish

Combine the whiskey, vermouth, Cherry Heering, bitters, and absinthe in a mixing glass filled with cracked ice. Stir with a long-handled spoon for 30 seconds and strain into a stemmed cocktail glass. Garnish with the lemon twist.

CHARO'S KICK

Native to Iran, almond trees are prized worldwide for their healthy, hearty seeds, which are technically not true nuts, but drupes (whatever, nerds). These brown kernels of goodness have countless culinary applications, appearing as the central ingredient in cookies, confections, pastries, pastas, curries, and cakes. But for our money, the best way to enjoy the benefits of almonds—which are full of vitamins, fiber, and magnesium—is how nature intended: raw and by the handful.

Almonds have been used in beverages since at least the 13th century, when recipes for almond milk began appearing in Middle Eastern cookbooks. While almond milk might not sound like an ideal cocktail component, orgeat—a richer, sweeter almond syrup—most certainly is. Popular in rum-forward tiki drinks for decades, it's also excellent in agave-based drinks such as the Charo's Kick, from Anthony Schmidt at San Francisco's Noble Experiment. This smoky-sweet number is equally imbued with tequila and mezcal, as well as a balanced dose of brightly sour citrus, all of which bring out orgeat's nuttiest properties. It's a decidedly well-rounded almond candy for those seeking more than just a sugar rush.

1½ ounces tequila reposado	¾ ounce fresh lemon juice
½ ounce mezcal	¾ ounce orgeat

 Combine all ingredients in an ice-filled shaker. Shake vigorously for 25 to 30 seconds and strain into a stemmed cocktail glass.

My Way Day

SEA WAY

*The classic cocktail world's unofficial rules have stifled many a mixolo-
gist's creativity. As in, never combine certain spirits, use lime and lemon
only in specific proportions, cocktail umbrellas are only for tiki drinks
and not apron flair pieces, etc. But often the best magic happens when
flouting those laws, as when Michael Madrusan whipped up the Sea Way
at Little Branch in 2009, much to his coworkers' dismay. Strange bedfellows Islay scotch and tequila effortlessly combine in a peaty, peppery,
fruity Old-Fashioned variation that shouldn't taste as good as it does. A
truly fine example of not giving a you-know-what for a holiday that's all
about originality.*

1½ ounces tequila
½ ounce Cherry Heering

¼ ounce Islay scotch
2 dashes orange bitters
1 lemon twist, for garnish

Combine the tequila, Cherry Heering, and bitters in an
Old-Fashioned glass. Add ice and stir for five or six seconds,
then top with the scotch. Garnish with the lemon twist.

GOLDFINCH

Today, pop the cork on your favorite bottle, visit a vineyard, or learn about the complex and fascinating history of winemaking. If you're one of the world's millions of wine aficionados, Drink Wine Day is a great excuse to do what you'd be doing anyway.

Wine plays a much bigger role in cocktails than you may realize, mainly in the form of distilled or fortified grape-based spirits including cognac, port, Madeira, and vermouth. Two of these boozier wines feature heavily in the Goldfinch, created by Brooklyn's Lauren Schell. Cocchi Americano's tart, zesty, and lightly honeyed notes blend exquisitely with the aromatic nuttiness of amontillado sherry for a pleasantly dry, appetite-inducing quaff—and a lovely companion for another February 18 celebration: National Crab-Stuffed Flounder Day. Just a suggestion!

1 ounce amontillado sherry
1 ounce Cocchi Americano
¼ ounce fresh lemon juice

½ ounce simple syrup
Club soda, to top
1 long grapefruit twist,
  for garnish

Combine the sherry, Cocchi Americano, lemon juice, and simple syrup in a shaker. Whip shake (no ice) and strain into a tall glass filled with ice. Top with club soda and garnish with the grapefruit twist.

National Lash Day

HAWKEYE

Cosmetic company House of Lashes created National Lash Day to celebrate lashes of all shapes and sizes, encouraging participants to post pictures of their lashes before and after gussying them up because apparently that's a thing on social media. Not excited about showing some love to the lash? Just be thankful you don't live in a world where no one has them. That alone should be reason to celebrate.

A sexy pair of lashes can be an irresistible aphrodisiac. Add an eye-catching cocktail to the mix, and you've got the total package. They don't come much more stunning than the Hawkeye, first served by Lew Caputa at Las Vegas's Electra Cocktail Club in 2018. Exquisitely bold and unapologetically smoky, this Pineapple Daiquiri offshoot radically combines mezcal with black and overproof rums, performing a striking, multifaceted balancing act that unleashes the brightness of all three spirits without giving anything away. Which is nothing to bat an eye at.

1 ounce mezcal
½ ounce Goslings Black Seal rum
½ ounce overproof aged rum,
    such as Smith & Cross

¾ ounce fresh pineapple
    juice
¾ ounce fresh lime juice
½ ounce cane syrup

Combine all ingredients in an ice-filled shaker. Shake vigorously for 25 to 30 seconds and strain into a stemmed cocktail glass.

Kurt Cobain Day

NIRVANA

Come as you are or as you were. Either way, dig out your old CDs and flannel shirts today and prepare to mosh in honor of one of music's most talented, tortured souls.

Since his death in 1994, thousands of Cobain's fellow musicians and ravenous fans have paid tribute to their fallen hero. No homage is nearly as tasty as the Nirvana, a brooding, herbaceous Manhattan riff created by Jamie Boudreau at Vessel in Seattle, just a short distance from the venues where the band made its name. Hard-hitting overproof whiskey serves as the front man for an assault on the palate, backed by a trio of pitch-perfect liqueurs. You'll want to put this bittersweet and bracingly honest single on repeat.

---

2 ounces overproof rye whiskey

½ ounce Amer Picon

¼ ounce Bénédictine

¼ ounce maraschino liqueur

1 orange twist, for garnish

Combine the whiskey, Amer Picon, Bénédictine, and maraschino liqueur in a mixing glass filled with cracked ice. Stir with a long-handled spoon for 30 seconds and strain into a stemmed cocktail glass. Garnish with the orange twist.

BRAMBLE

No grains? No gluten? No problem. Mexican American food brand Siete established National Grain-Free Day to recognize the difficulties of living with dietary restrictions.

In the cocktail world, dietary restrictions aren't as big of an issue. Grain-based spirits such as whiskey and gin are safe for those with celiac disease because the distillation process removes any gluten. For a truly grain-free experience, stick with tequila (agave), white rum (sugarcane), or potato vodka. Any of these works amazingly in a Bramble, which became a hit at Fred's Bar in London in the 1980s. Likened by many to an alcoholic snow cone, this icy, blackberry-infused, sweet-and-sour blast is lauded as one of the most egalitarian potations around, and for good reason. The only way you won't be able to handle one of these is if you're allergic to deliciousness.

**2 ounces grain-free spirit
of choice**

¾ ounce fresh lemon juice
¾ ounce simple syrup
5 blackberries

 Combine the spirit, lemon juice, and simple syrup in a shaker. In a double Old-Fashioned glass, muddle four blackberries, then fill the glass two-thirds of the way with crushed ice. Add the contents of the shaker and top with crushed ice. Garnish with another blackberry.

MARGARITA

Few cocktails are as recognizable as the Margarita. Extolled for decades by everyone from chilled-out rockers such as Jimmy "Margaritaville" Buffett to Cinco de Mayo–inspired revelers looking to get soused south-of-the-border style to the no-sugar set who demand their Margs "skinny," there's no shortage of love for this enduringly popular potable.

A far cry from the frozen, salt-rimmed, fruit-infused varieties offered at most bars and restaurants today, the original three-ingredient Margarita emerged in the early 20th century, though its origins still remain a mystery. Some cocktail historians believe it first was served in Tijuana to American tourists during Prohibition as a tequila-forward version of the Daisy. (Margarita is the Spanish word for "daisy.") Others have argued that it's an alternate name for the Picador, which appeared in William Tarling's Café Royal Cocktail Book (1937). Dozens of bartenders from Mexico, California, Texas, and even Syracuse, New York, have claimed the Margarita as their own invention over the years.

1½ ounces tequila	½ ounce fresh lime juice
1 ounce Cointreau	1 lime wedge, for garnish

Combine the tequila, Cointreau, and lime juice in an ice-filled shaker. Shake vigorously for 25 to 30 seconds and strain into a double Old-Fashioned glass over ice. Garnish with the lime wedge.

PLEASURE ISLAND

If you think about it, fairy tales can be pretty messed up. The Adventures of Pinocchio—an 1883 novel by Italian writer Carlo Collodi that Walt Disney Pictures later adapted into a 1940 animated film—is one of the darkest.

One of the book's many frightening moments involves Pinocchio dropping out of school and journeying to Pleasure Island, a cursed amusement park where wayward boys engage in every form of excess while unknowingly transforming into donkeys later sold into slavery or "discarded." A far cry from its source, the Pleasure Island cocktail, from the folks at the Disney Cocktails Instagram account, is an indulgent sipper without the danger of a bewitching. With Italian Campari and frothy egg white highlighting this brightly succulent, bittersweet sour, it's easy to get carried away.

1½ ounces navy-strength gin
¾ ounce Campari
¾ ounce fresh lemon juice
½ ounce simple syrup

1 dash orange bitters
1 egg white
1 thin orange slice,
   for garnish

Combine the gin, Campari, lemon juice, simple syrup, bitters, and egg whites in a shaker. Shake without ice (to emulsify the egg white) for 10 seconds, then add ice and shake vigorously. Strain into a stemmed cocktail glass. Garnish with the orange slice.

World Bartender Day

NEGRONI

After sampling countless concoctions, it takes a little pizzazz to stimulate a bartender's palate. This is why many industry veterans opt for a Negroni. This simple-to-make yet beguilingly complex classic allegedly was created in Florence, Italy, in 1919 at the behest of Count Camillo Negroni, who requested a stronger version of an Americano cocktail (page 354). Since then, the zesty, bitter, medicinal, and artfully layered combination of gin, Campari, and sweet vermouth has soothed the bodies and invigorated the minds of countless drink makers. Endlessly fascinating from first sip to last, it's also strong enough to ward off the existential dread of dealing with customers who think life behind the bar is one constant Coyote Ugly.

1 ounce gin

1 ounce sweet vermouth

1 ounce Campari

1 orange twist, for garnish

Combine the gin, vermouth, and Campari in a double Old-Fashioned glass. Add ice and stir for five or six seconds. Garnish with the orange twist.

TURN THE PAGE TO
SEE THE ILLUSTRATION
FOR THIS DRINK.

Negroni
PAGE 75

.38 SPECIAL

Guns make for be a touchy subject. Regardless of your feelings about them, it's impossible to ignore the impact that Samuel Colt's pistol has had on modern history.

Pistols had been in use since the 16th century, but a slight upgrade from an outside-the-box thinker forever changed how people thought about guns. The same might be said about the Revolver, a modern Old-Fashioned spin-off from San Francisco's Jon Santer. With a simple substitution of coffee liqueur for sugar, this boozier, subtly bright sipper becomes a powerfully mysterious force worthy of multiple rounds. It's a simple but effective precursor to many of the excellent spirit-forward, whiskey-cacao sippers that appeared in the mid-2000s and beyond.

2 ounces bourbon

½ ounce Caffé Lolita

3 dashes orange bitters

1 orange twist, for garnish

Combine the bourbon, Caffé Lolita, and bitters in an Old-Fashioned glass. Add ice and stir for five or six seconds. Garnish with the orange twist.

BROADWAY DINER

In Arabic, the word for pistachio loosely translates to "smiling nut." In China, it's "happy nut." If you've had the pleasure of chomping down on the smoothly textured, slightly earthy seeds from the pistachio tree, you probably will find those descriptions particularly apt. The demand for these nutrient-dense nuggets is so great that America produces more than 300 million pounds of them each year, mostly in California.

The pistachio's inherent sweetness also lends itself nicely to rich desserts and cordials. The Broadway Diner, named for a restaurant on Manhattan's Upper West Side that serves a mean pistachio ice cream sundae, provides all the velvety, creamy goodness with only a fraction of the calories—just kidding! Port wine and aged rum not only allow the pistachio syrup to shine but also embellish it with their own nutty undertones. Overdo it on these decadent adult smoothies and you may need to revert to a plant-based diet for a while.

---

1 ounce aged rum
1 ounce port
¾ ounce heavy cream
¾ ounce pistachio syrup

1 dash Peychaud's bitters
1 egg yolk
1 pinch finely grated nutmeg,
  for garnish

Combine the rum, port, heavy cream, pistachio syrup, bitters, and egg yolk in a shaker. Shake without ice (to emulsify the egg yolk) for 10 seconds, then add ice and shake vigorously. Strain into a stemmed cocktail glass and garnish with the grated nutmeg.

HOLY MOLE

In the world of coffee liqueurs, it's Kahlúa and then everyone else. Kahlúa is a staple of both the liquor cabinet and the kitchen, where it's often used as an adult topping on cakes and ice cream, a warming addition to a morning cup of joe, or an ingredient in cakes and cookies.

Delicious desserts notwithstanding, it's often assumed that Kahlúa's place in the cocktail world is similarly relegated to creamy, potentially cloying concoctions including the Mudslide or Moose Milk. The Holy Mole originally appeared in Kelly "Hiphipahula" Reilly and "Trader" Tom Morgan's The Home Bar Guide to Tropical Cocktails *(2019) as a tribute to the Mole Poblano—a savory-sweet, peppery sipper that's been called the national dish of Mexico—and as a nod to Kahlúa's Mexican origins. Notes of oak, vanilla, almond, and chocolate fuse effortlessly in this tiki-influenced flavor saver. It's a perky, nutty, intriguing beige bombshell that you don't have to wait for dessert to enjoy.*

1 ounce bourbon	½ ounce orgeat
1 ounce fresh lemon juice	3 dashes chocolate bitters
¾ ounce Kahlúa	1 lemon twist, for garnish

Combine the bourbon, lemon juice, Kahlúa, orgeat, and bitters in a shaker. Pour into a double Old-Fashioned glass and fill with crushed ice. Garnish with the lemon twist.

WATER LILY

National Floral Design Day, created to honor floral design pioneer Carl Rittner, celebrates the many ways this vital cultural art form enriches our lives. Spend today flexing your floral design muscles. Create your own floral paintings and textiles, add a flowery touch to a home renovation, or simply bring home a bouquet to brighten your favorite living space. But please leave your grandma's bell-bottoms in the attic where they belong.

Flower-based liqueurs first became widespread in the late 19th century, so it was only a matter of time before cocktail-minded bartenders caught on to their uniquely delicious properties. However, it took another hundred years or so for floral cocktails to reach the level of popularity they enjoy today. One of the first and finest examples of this modern movement is the Water Lily, concocted by Richard Boccato at Little Branch in 2007. Its artfully balanced notes of violet and orange have been known to turn taste buds into a garden of earthly delights. Svelte, purple-hued, and irresistibly fragrant, this arrangement's design is nearly flawless.

¾ ounce gin
¾ ounce Cointreau

¾ ounce crème de violette
¾ ounce fresh lemon juice
1 orange twist, for garnish

Combine the gin, Cointreau, crème de violette, and lemon juice in an ice-filled shaker. Shake vigorously for 25 to 30 seconds and strain into a stemmed cocktail glass. Garnish with the orange twist.

LEAP YEAR

Most of us consider the 365-day Gregorian calendar the most accurate way to count the days, but it's not perfect. It takes Earth approximately 365 days, 5 hours, 48 minutes, and 45 seconds to circle the sun. To account for that overtime, we add an extra day to the calendar, February 29, nearly every four years. It's a little confusing and slightly unfortunate for anyone born on this rare date, but it sure beats the ancient Chinese and Roman calendars that occasionally had to add an entire leap month to realign the solar cycle.

Over time, the date has become a magnet for wacky superstitions and traditions. In many European countries, it's common for women to propose to men on this day, and any bachelor who refuses must gift his proposer 12 pairs of gloves. Still, February 29 offers a great quadrennial opportunity to celebrate with a beverage. No drink is more a propos than Harry Craddock's Leap Year, a Savoy Cocktail Book standout that effortlessly marries citrus and sweet vermouth with a dryly fruity, Curaçao-backed finish. You may not want to wait until the next leap year to enjoy this super-delicious rarity.

1½ ounces gin
½ ounce sweet vermouth

½ ounce curaçao
½ ounce fresh lemon juice
1 lemon twist, for garnish

 Combine the gin, vermouth, curaçao, and lemon juice in an ice-filled shaker. Shake vigorously for 25 to 30 seconds and strain into a stemmed cocktail glass. Garnish with the lemon twist.

MARCH

			1 NATIONAL HORSE PROTECTION DAY Caballo Blanco	**2** NATIONAL BANANA CREAM PIE DAY Bourbon Banana Flip	**3** INTERNATIONAL IRISH WHISKEY DAY Irish Carry-On	**4** NATIONAL BACKCOUNTRY SKI DAY Moose Jaw
5 NATIONAL ABSINTHE DAY Sea Fizz	**6** DAY OF THE DUDE White Russian	**7** ALEXANDER GRAHAM BELL DAY Tattletale	**8** BE NASTY DAY Ramos Gin Fizz	**9** NATIONAL NAPPING DAY Siesta	**10** MARIO DAY Italian Rivalry	**11** JOHNNY APPLESEED DAY McIntosh
12 NATIONAL ALFRED HITCHCOCK DAY White Lady	**13** NATIONAL JEWEL DAY Bijou	**14** LEARN ABOUT BUTTERFLIES DAY Mariposa	**15** IDES OF MARCH Rome with a View	**16** NATIONAL ARTICHOKE HEARTS DAY Moai Spritz	**17** ST. PATRICK'S DAY Shamrock	**18** GODDESS OF FERTILITY DAY Aphrodite
19 NATIONAL POULTRY DAY Speckled Hen	**20** UN FRENCH LANGUAGE DAY Vieux Carré	**21** NATIONAL FLOWER DAY Honeysuckle	**22** NATIONAL GOOF OFF DAY Accidental Hipster	**23** NATIONAL PUPPY DAY Bulldog Cooler	**24** NATIONAL CHEESESTEAK DAY Fish House Punch	**25** MARYLAND DAY Preakness
26 NATIONAL LIVE LONG AND PROSPER DAY Vulcan Nerve Pinch	**27** INTERNATIONAL WHISK(E)Y DAY Don Lockwood	**28** NATIONAL RESPECT YOUR CAT DAY Tequila Bearcat	**29** SMOKE AND MIRRORS DAY Houdini	**30** NATIONAL DOCTORS DAY Penicillin	**31** EIFFEL TOWER DAY Café de Paris	

CABALLO BLANCO

Created by animal activist Colleen Page in 2005, National Horse Protection Day raises awareness of abused and neglected horses, especially older ones whose time on the farm, racetrack, or calvary has come to an end. If you love equines, today's a great opportunity to volunteer at a horse rescue, donate to a worthy horse charity, or spread awareness about the plight of too many of our hooved homeys.

Working to improve the lives of legendary animals is enough to generate a stallion-sized thirst. Enter the Caballo Blanco, which is Spanish for "white horse." A sultry, smoky, fruity, south-of-the-border riff on the classic scotch-based White Horse (duh), it's got a hefty helping of energetic citrus and ginger, as well as a plentiful dose of mezcal to numb the pain of hours spent in the saddle. Enjoy these in moderation or you may suddenly find yourself chattering like Mr. Ed.

2 ounces mezcal
1 ounce fresh pineapple juice
¾ ounce ginger syrup
½ ounce fresh lime juice

2 dashes Angostura bitters
Club soda, to top
1 piece candied ginger,
   for garnish
1 thin orange slice, for garnish

Combine the mezcal, pineapple juice, ginger syrup, lime juice, and bitters in a shaker. Whip shake (no ice) and strain into a tall glass filled with ice. Top with club soda. Garnish with the piece of candied ginger and the orange slice.

BOURBON BANANA FLIP

In the 19th century, pastry chefs introduced the supremely delectable banana cream pie to high society as a delicacy because of the difficulties of importing bananas at the time. Once the exotic fruits became readily available, this Midwestern invention quickly spread across America. Servicepeople consistently have ranked it their favorite dessert since the 1950s. (If you have served in the armed forces or sampled one of those ready-to-eat ration packs, you know that most military food isn't considered mouthwatering cuisine!)

This tropical take on a New York Flip from Sam Ross is everything to love about a cream pie minus the crust, with just enough bourbon and nutmeg to make things interesting without losing those uniquely delightful notes of banana.

1½ ounces bourbon
¾ ounce banana liqueur
¾ ounce simple syrup

½ ounce heavy cream
1 egg yolk
1 pinch finely grated nutmeg,
    for garnish

Combine the bourbon, banana liqueur, simple syrup, heavy cream, and egg yolk in a shaker. Shake without ice (to emulsify the egg yolk) for 10 seconds, then add ice and shake vigorously. Strain into a stemmed cocktail glass and garnish with the nutmeg.

IRISH CARRY-ON

Raise your glasses, practice your best Irish drinking toasts, and have some craic (a fun time) because it's International Irish Whiskey Day!

Irish whiskey traditionally has been consumed straight from the bottle, either for sipping or shooting, but it's also the base spirit in a growing number of modern cocktails rapidly becoming classics. The Irish Carry-On, created by Chris Covey at Little Branch in 2019, is a delightfully balanced Old-Fashioned variation with a finish that sings like the finest Irish ballads. Its subtly sweet, herbal, and chocolate components, rather than masking the whiskey's flavor, accentuate its woodsy, fruity, and grainy properties—an excellent introduction to this still-too-underappreciated spirit. Sláinte!

2 ounces Irish whiskey	2 dashes chocolate bitters
¼ ounce Cynar	1 pinch salt
¼ ounce honey syrup	1 lemon twist, for garnish

Combine the whiskey, Cynar, honey syrup, bitters, and salt in an Old-Fashioned glass. Add ice and stir for five or six seconds. Garnish with the lemon twist.

National Backcountry Ski Day

MOOSE JAW

This holiday celebrates off-the-grid adrenaline seekers who prefer to live life without a trail map. Hiking, snowmobiling, or helicoptering to the most remote parts of mountains, backcountry skiers enjoy some of the most spectacular vistas and pristine runs imaginable, as well as fun little life-threatening dangers including unpredictable weather, avalanches, and crevasses. If you participate in this fast-growing sport, take lots of pics and humblebrag on social media—preferably after you finish defying death.

Regardless of your outdoor sports ability level, there's nothing like a cocktail after a long day of hitting the slopes, especially one as apropos as the Moose Jaw. With warming apple brandy and whisky from the snowy north, this slightly sour Jack Rose variation drinks as smooth as an untouched layer of fresh powder, taking your après-ski to uncharted heights. An exhilarating, wintry dash of peppermint schnapps will have you coming back for more, but, as any extreme backcountry skier will tell you, make sure you can handle it first.

1 ounce Canadian whisky
1 ounce applejack
¾ ounce fresh lemon juice

¾ ounce pomegranate syrup
1 barspoon peppermint schnapps

Combine all ingredients in an ice-filled shaker. Shake vigorously for 25 to 30 seconds and strain into a double Old-Fashioned glass over ice.

National Absinthe Day

SEA FIZZ

For more than a century, absinthe has received an undeserved amount of hate. Whether that's due to its association with mentally unwell artists such as Vincent van Gogh—who hacked off his own ear while trying to wean himself off the stuff—or its potential though unproven hallucinogenic properties, the overproof French spirit was so demonized in its native Europe that America banned it from 1912 to 2007.

If you're looking for a less aggressive introduction to absinthe's unique flavor profile, there's no better option than a Sea Fizz, which first appeared in David A. Embury's The Fine Art of Mixing Drinks *(1948). Its well-balanced doses of citrus, egg white, and sugar brighten and smooth the botanicals, so you probably won't be seeing any of the infamous green fairies that allegedly have plagued the visions of absinthe imbibers for centuries—even after a couple of rounds. Some absinthes boast up to 74 percent alcohol by volume, though, so it's still wise to take it slow.*

1¼ ounces absinthe
¾ ounce fresh lemon juice

¾ ounce simple syrup
1 egg white
Club soda, to top

Combine ingredients in a shaker. Shake without ice (to emulsify the egg white) for 10 seconds, then add ice and shake vigorously. Strain into a fizz glass and top with club soda.

Day of the Dude

WHITE RUSSIAN

Sometimes there's a man, and today that man is the Dude, or his Dude-ness, or Duder, or El Duderino if you're not into the whole brevity thing. On this date in 1998, Gramercy Pictures released The Big Lebowski, *the magnum comedic opus of film directors Joel and Ethan Coen, which introduced the world to the aforementioned Jeffrey "Dude" Lebowski (played by Jeff Bridges), an amateur bowler and consummate slacker from Los Angeles with a heart of gold and a penchant for doing a J.*

If the Dude loved anything more than a rug that could tie a room together, it was knocking back White Russians, which he did nine times during the film. Introduced in the 1960s, this vodka, coffee, and dairy sipper surged in popularity after The Big Lebowski's *release, and for good reason. Cozy as a winter blanket and as silky and unassuming as a Lebowski retort, there's nothing better for kicking back with the Coen brothers and embracing your inner Dude. If that doesn't sound like a good time . . . well, you know, that's just, like, your opinion, man.*

---

2 ounces vodka

1 ounce Kahlúa

Heavy cream or whole milk, to taste

Combine the vodka and Kahlúa in a double Old-Fashioned glass with ice. Top with cream or milk and stir.

TATTLETALE

Once upon a time, phones didn't exist. That is, until 1876, when Scottish-born inventor Alexander Graham Bell received the first US patent for a device that could replicate the human voice intelligibly into a second device at a distance. Bell's original telephone was crude by today's standards, but other like-minded inventors—several of whom sued him—rapidly developed the instrument that has become an indispensable part of billions of lives.

Gossip has formed part of phone culture since the beginning, and nothing aids idle chatter like a hearty, tongue-loosening adult beverage. Sam Ross's Tattletale, first served at Milk & Honey in 2010, features two single-malt whiskies from Bell's native Scotland, as well as a dollop of honey to soothe the vocal cords after a long chitchat. If you're prone to running your mouth (or thumbs), ask a friend to hide your phone after knocking back a couple of these spirit-forward sippers.

1½ ounces Highland single-malt scotch

¾ ounce Islay scotch

1 barspoon honey syrup

2 dashes Angostura bitters

1 lemon twist, for garnish

1 orange twist, for garnish

Combine the scotches, honey syrup, and bitters in an Old-Fashioned glass. Add ice and stir for five or six seconds. Garnish with the lemon and orange twists.

RAMOS GIN FIZZ

This New Orleans classic dates to the 1880s, when Henry C. Ramos invented it at his Imperial Cabinet Saloon. Most bartenders loathe this sumptuous, floral, gorgeously frothy, uniquely delectable, nine-ingredient showstopper for the disruptive, labor-intensive process that goes into making it. Remember, there's a difference between being nasty and just plain cruel. If you must request a Ramos from a defenseless spirits professional, do it when business is slow.

1½ ounces navy-strength gin
½ ounce heavy cream
½ ounce simple syrup
¼ ounce fresh lemon juice
¼ ounce fresh lime juice

2 drops orange blossom water
1 drop vanilla extract
   (optional)
1 egg white
Club soda, to top

Combine the gin, cream, simple syrup, citrus, orange blossom water, vanilla extract, and egg white in a shaker. Shake without ice (to emulsify the cream and egg white) for 10 seconds, then add ice and shake extremely vigorously for at least another minute, the longer the better. Strain into a fizz glass and top with club soda. Lift the glass and use a muddler to tap the base gently to remove any air bubbles that may have formed along the rim. Place the glass in a freezer for two to three minutes. Remove and drizzle club soda directly into the center of the glass until the foam rises to form a perfectly fluffy top.

SIESTA

Take a break from the rat race for a few minutes of shut-eye. You've earned it. Even if you haven't, sneak in a quick nap anyway. Boston University professor William Anthony and his wife, Camille, created National Napping Day, first celebrated in 1999, to promote the importance of getting enough sleep.

Residents of Spain and other Spanish-speaking countries have been taking advantage of napping's benefits for centuries, with businesses and restaurants shutting down each day for an early afternoon "siesta." Mexico officially abolished the siesta in 1944, but, like tequila, it's still a cultural cornerstone. The Siesta, created by Katie Stipe at New York City's Flatiron Lounge in 2006, is the liquid embodiment of this practice. Featuring palate-cleansing citrus, relaxing notes of agave, and the stomach-soothing properties of Campari and Angostura bitters, it's perfect after a big meal, when the urge to nap feels strongest.

1½ ounces tequila
½ ounce Campari
½ ounce fresh grapefruit juice
½ ounce fresh lime juice
½ ounce simple syrup
2 dashes Angostura bitters
1 grapefruit twist, for garnish

Combine the tequila, Campari, juices, simple syrup, and bitters in an ice-filled shaker. Shake vigorously for 25 to 30 seconds and strain into a stemmed cocktail glass. Garnish with the grapefruit twist.

ITALIAN RIVALRY

Created by Nintendo game designer Shigeru Miyamoto, Mario debuted in 1981 in the arcade classic Donkey Kong *as a carpenter dodging ape-thrown projectiles. He switched careers and journeyed to the Mushroom Kingdom, where he's been stomping Bowser and his minions, saving Princess Peach, ingesting magical stars and fungi, riding pet dinosaurs and go-carts, and having a swell time ever since.*

Besides giant reptiles and angry ghosts, Mario's biggest competition is with his taller, slimmer brother (and some say superior character), Luigi. We don't know what either of these fictional handymen would drink, but it's a good bet that Joshua Perez's Italian Rivalry would top the list. With a robust, fireball-like blast of Amaro Montenegro and with cognac and bourbon serving as Player 1 and Player 2, everyone's a winner. Exactly the power-up you need for another lengthy adventure in the Nintendo universe.

1 ounce bourbon

1 ounce cognac

½ ounce Amaro Montenegro

1 brown sugar cube

1 lemon twist, for garnish

1 orange twist, for garnish

Combine the bourbon, cognac, Amaro Montenegro, and sugar cube in an Old-Fashioned glass. Muddle the sugar cube, then add ice and stir for five or six seconds. Garnish with the lemon and orange twists.

Johnny Appleseed Day

McINTOSH

Most of the heroes in American folklore—Paul Bunyan, John Henry, Molly Pitcher—are either fictional composites of historical figures or pure fantasy. A select few, such as Johnny Appleseed, were real people who lived up to their legends, and then some.

During his lifetime, Johnny Appleseed was held in perhaps highest esteem by booze-starved pioneers who used his precious apples to get wasted on hard cider. The McIntosh cocktail doesn't contain any, but its hefty dose of fresh cider is enhanced by an even greater helping of bourbon, that most patriotic of spirits. Invigorating notes of ginger and citrus provide more than a hint of Johnny's indefatigable spirit. It's as American as apple pie, a phrase that wouldn't exist without you-know-who.

---

2 ounces bourbon
1 ounce fresh apple cider
¾ ounce ginger syrup
½ ounce fresh lime juice

2 dashes Angostura bitters
Club soda, to top
1 piece candied ginger, for garnish
1 thin apple slice, for garnish

Combine the bourbon, apple cider, ginger syrup, lime juice, and bitters in a shaker. Whip shake (no ice) and pour into a tall glass filled with ice. Top with club soda and garnish with the piece of candied ginger and apple slice.

WHITE LADY

If you're of a certain generation and harbor irrational fears of murderous birds, voyeuristic neighbors, or shower stabbings, Alfred Hitchcock is probably to blame.

No stranger to the bottle, Hitchcock highlighted booze in many of his films, notably champagne in, um, Champagne, and practically everything behind the bar in North by Northwest. *Infamous for using alcohol to fuel his creativity—often from his 1,600-bottle wine cellar—the London native remained partial to gin when it came to cocktails. His favorite was the White Lady, a Prohibition-era classic first served by Harry MacElhone in 1919. Sleek and shapely as a cinematic starlet, it's got the same rich depth as so many of Hitchcock's masterpieces. Calm the nerves with one and you might be able to watch* The Birds *without freaking out each time a pigeon peers in your rear window.*

1½ ounces gin
1 ounce Cointreau

½ ounce fresh lemon juice
1 egg white

 Combine all ingredients in a shaker. Shake without ice (to emulsify the egg white) for 10 seconds, then add ice and shake vigorously for 30 seconds. Strain into a stemmed cocktail glass.

Naitonal Jewel Day

BIJOU

Sure, diamonds are a girl's best friend, but don't forget the dozens of other precious and semiprecious stones that have been enthralling humans since we decided that we like shiny things. National Jewel Day specifically celebrates the jewelers whose artistry transforms gemstones into pieces of fine art and high fashion coveted by just about everyone.

The Martini is one of the jewels of the cocktail world, and few if any Martini variations drink as glamorously as the Bijou, the French word for "jewel." This spirit-forward stunner from Harry Johnson, the "father of professional bartending," boasts a trifecta of palate pleasers, with decadent green Chartreuse and sumptuous sweet vermouth doing most of the heavy lifting. Unlike most gems, this one won't keep you transfixed for long—mostly because your glass will be empty faster than you can say "Diamonds are forever."

1½ ounces gin	¾ ounce green Chartreuse
¾ ounce sweet vermouth	2 dashes orange bitters
	1 lemon twist, for garnish

Combine the gin, vermouth, Chartreuse, and bitters in a mixing glass filled with cracked ice. Stir with a long-handled spoon for 30 seconds and strain into a stemmed cocktail glass. Garnish with the lemon twist.

Learn about Butterflies Day

MARIPOSA

Even if bugs aren't your thing, it's hard to hate on butterflies. These strikingly beautiful, polychromatic fliers not only offer a feast for the eyes, but, as pollinators, they also are partially responsible for the feast on your table. The journey from humble caterpillar to majestic butterfly is one of nature's most astonishing transformations. A similar example of cocktail evolution, the Mariposa (Spanish for "butterfly") began its life as a simple combination of tequila and coffee. Adding a significant dose of chili-flavored Ancho Reyes, as well as subtler notes of anise and orange, allowed the drink to shed its bittersweet cocoon and ascend to the upper echelons of agave-forward sippers. Unlike most brightly colored insects, this spicy, complex butterfly is as delicious as it is eye-catching.

1½ ounces tequila reposado
½ ounce Ancho Reyes
½ coffee liqueur
2 dashes absinthe

1 dash orange bitters
1 orange twist, for garnish
1 brandied cherry,
    for garnish

Combine the tequila, Ancho Reyes, coffee liqueur, absinthe, and bitters in an Old-Fashioned glass. Add ice and stir for five or six seconds. Garnish with the orange twist and the brandied cherry.

ROME WITH A VIEW

Absolute power corrupts absolutely. Just ask your boy Gaius Julius Caesar. Since Caesar's assassination in 44 BCE, the Ides of March have warned those with powerful aspirations about the pitfalls of wealth, fame, and generally being a massive dick. It's also sometimes known as Brutus Day, as a reminder always to prepare for betrayal and subterfuge, even from those you trust the most.

As enthralling as ancient Roman politics, the Rome with a View from Milk & Honey's Michael McIlroy crosses an Americano and a Rickey and features one of Italy's favorite aperitifs. It's a great companion for observing political intrigue or calming the nerves after going down a Wikipedia hole researching the grisly deaths that befell the rest of the Roman emperors. As Shakespeare wrote in the play Julius Caesar, *"Beware the Ides of March." That is, unless you've got a delightfully bright Rome with a View or two to see you through this historically ominous day.*

1 ounce dry vermouth
1 ounce Campari
1 ounce fresh lime juice

¾ ounce simple syrup
1 thin orange slice,
   for garnish

Combine the vermouth, Campari, lime juice, and simple syrup in shaker. Whip shake (no ice) and pour into tall glass filled with ice. Garnish with the orange slice.

TURN THE PAGE TO
SEE THE ILLUSTRATION
FOR THIS DRINK.

National Artichoke Hearts Day

MOAI SPRITZ

Try to have a heart today. An artichoke heart, that is!

Artichokes are the primary ingredient in Cynar, an Italian amaro lauded by bartenders for its beguiling and fragrant properties. Bitter yet bright, medicinal yet approachable, it's an essential component of numerous cocktails, including the Moai Spritz, otherwise known as a tiki Mimosa. A far more interesting take on the classic Aperol or wine spritz, this savory bubbler expertly combines refreshingly nutty and herbaceous elements that, like the best artichoke dip, will have you coming back for more. If munching its heart is the best way to enjoy an artichoke, then downing a Moai Spritz comes a very close second.

1 ounce Cynar

½ ounce aged rum

½ ounce velvet falernum

2 ounces champagne

Club soda, to top

1 long lemon twist, for garnish

Combine the Cynar, rum, and velvet falernum in a wine glass filled with cracked ice. Add the champagne and top with club soda. Garnish with the lemon twist.

SHAMROCK

How does a minor feast day commemorating the exploits of one country's patron saint (who wasn't even born in that country) transform into a massive rager that—erroneously—has become synonymous with all things Ireland? As usual, blame Americans.

The most "authentic" aspect of today's St. Patrick's Day festivities is perhaps the shamrock, considered a sacred plant in Ireland long before Patrick used its three leaves to explain the Holy Trinity to Christian converts. It's also the name of a delightful Irish whiskey sipper that offers a drier, more serene version of the classic Tipperary. Bold, herbaceous, and of course featuring green Chartreuse as a nod to Patrick's Gaelic roots, it's a classy yet still green-tinged antidote to the day's usual debauchery.

---

2 ounces Irish whiskey

½ ounce dry vermouth

½ ounce green Chartreuse

2 dashes orange bitters

1 brandied cherry, for garnish

 Combine the whiskey, vermouth, Chartreuse, and bitters in a mixing glass filled with cracked ice. Stir with a long-handled spoon for 30 seconds and strain into a stemmed cocktail glass. Garnish with the brandied cherry.

APHRODITE

Having trouble propagating your houseplants? Looking to add another little screaming, stinking addition to your family? No worries. Grab an appropriate offering and head down to your local pagan temple because today is Goddess of Fertility Day.

A playful, seductive riff on the classic sherry-forward Adonis, the Aphrodite cocktail from Christine Gallary proffers a rich, creamy, caramel-tinged nectar guaranteed to bring fertile vibes to the hearts and loins of even the most frigid cocktail lover. Its low alcohol content makes it a great choice if you have to get up early to work on your crops or want to stay "up" all night trying to make babies. It's also a much better offering than the boring seashells and perfume that Aphrodite usually receives.

1 ounce oloroso sherry

1 ounce dry vermouth

1 ounce sweet vermouth

2 dashes orange bitters

1 orange twist, for garnish

Combine the sherry, vermouths, and bitters in a double Old-Fashioned glass. Add ice and stir for five or six seconds. Garnish with the orange twist.

SPECKLED HEN

Which came first, the chicken or the egg? Give your brain a rest from the age-old question because National Poultry Day celebrates both! This holiday honors all the delectable fowls we love (to cook), including turkeys, ducks, geese, and even the occasional pheasant.

While chowing down on an omelet, chicken Parmesan, or duck confit today, don't forget that poultry is also an essential component in many of the best cocktails. One of these, the Speckled Hen, is a surprising riff on a traditional Gin Sour that's perfect for stimulating the palate after a poultry-laden feast. With a fluffy texture and a cocky cucumber and pepper garnish, it's a bird with plumage as appealing as its taste. If you prefer your feathered friends (and their embryos) alive and clucking, forgo the froth and enjoy this bright and savory flier sans egg white.

---

2 ounces gin
¼ ounce fresh lemon juice
¼ ounce simple syrup
3 thin cucumber slices

1 egg white
1 thin cucumber slice, for garnish
1 pinch cracked black pepper,
  for garnish

Combine the gin, lemon juice, simple syrup, cucumber slices, and egg white in a shaker. Shake without ice (to emulsify the egg white) for 10 seconds and then add ice and shake vigorously. Strain into a stemmed cocktail glass, garnish with the cucumber slice, and top with the cracked black pepper.

VIEUX CARRÉ

*Greet everyone today with a hearty "Bonjour" today because—*sacré bleu*—it's UN French Language Day. Established in 2010 by the United Nations Department of Public Information to celebrate multilingualism and cultural diversity, the event coincides with the founding date of La Francophonie, an organization composed of countries and regions where a significant portion of the population speaks French and promotes French cultural values. The Vieux Carré, meaning "old square" or "old neighborhood," is an iconic New Orleans cocktail first served by Walter Bergeron at the Hotel Monteleone in the 1930s. With a base that's equal parts rye and cognac, this elegant and boozy, savory and bittersweet tipple combines French ingredients with those from the Americas and Italy, perfectly encapsulating the unique mélange of the French Quarter and the willingness of French culture to adapt as it expands across the globe.*

1 ounce rye whiskey

1 ounce cognac

¼ ounce sweet vermouth

¼ ounce Bénédictine

2 dashes Angostura bitters

2 dashes Peychaud's bitters

1 lemon twist, for garnish

1 brandied cherry, for garnish

 Combine the whiskey, cognac, sweet vermouth, and bitters in a double Old-Fashioned glass. Add ice and stir for five or six seconds. Top with Bénédictine and garnish with the lemon twist and brandied cherry.

HONEYSUCKLE

Ah yes, early spring. The weather warms, birds return from their winter roosts, grass begins to grow, and, most excellently, the year's first flowers start to bloom. National Flower Day, founded to coincide with the start of the season, celebrates the more than 400,000 species of flowering plants found throughout the world. March 21 also marks the beginning of Aries, the first astrological sign of the zodiac, whose flower is the honeysuckle. If you can't find any of these pink and white, oval-shaped beauties to add to a floral arrangement, try the Honeysuckle cocktail, which first appeared in David A. Embury's 1948 classic, The Fine Art of Mixing Drinks. *Even if you do find the flowers, try the drink anyway! Its three ingredients form a luscious and fragrant Honey Daiquiri variation with all the sweetness that those born in March under the Aries sign supposedly possess. Simple yet succulent, this is one boozy flower you're not going to want to stare at for too long.*

---

2 ounces white rum

1 ounce fresh lime juice
¾ ounce honey syrup

Combine all ingredients in an ice-filled shaker. Shake vigorously for 25 to 30 seconds and strain into a stemmed cocktail glass.

ACCIDENTAL HIPSTER

Seriously: why so serious?

According to the American Medical Association, feeling frazzled and anxious too often is the number-one killer on the planet, with more than 60 percent of human disease and illness attributed to chronic stress. Meaning: it's not only good to chill out every once in a while, it's vital to your health! National Goof Off Day encourages everyone to relax and embrace that silliness. Some cocktail bartenders—usually self-described "mixologists" with bespoke suspenders and ambiguous facial hair—have a reputation for taking themselves a little too seriously. But on a slow night, even the sternest bar professional likes to play around a little. Often that's when cocktail magic happens. Like when San Francisco bartender Chris Tunstall jokingly decided to make the most "hip" drink possible by casually throwing together whatever obscure ingredients he had lying around. The result, the Accidental Hipster, features a bold, herbaceous blend of palate-pounding service-industry favorites, including Fernet-Branca and maraschino liqueur. It's a sneakily strong potation guaranteed to put you in a goofy mood, regardless of how cool you think you might be.

¾ ounce overproof rye, such as Rittenhouse

¾ ounce Fernet-Branca

¾ ounce maraschino liqueur

¾ ounce fresh lemon juice

1 brandied cherry, for garnish

Combine the rye, Fernet-Branca, maraschino liqueur, and lemon juice in an ice-filled shaker. Shake vigorously for 25 to 30 seconds and strain into a stemmed cocktail glass. Garnish with the brandied cherry.

National Puppy Day

BULLDOG COOLER

If you're a canine enthusiast, it's only natural to sneak a break from less important matters (work, marriage, kids, etc.) to scroll mindlessly through the endless array of doggo photos that make social media somewhat tolerable. But today, feel free to indulge unapologetically in cuteness overload because it's National Puppy Day!

It's hard to find a breed of puppy cuter than a bulldog or a cocktail more refreshing than the Bulldog Cooler, which first appeared in Herbert Jenkins's A Lifetime Collection of 688 Cocktails *(1934). Like its lovable, slobbery namesake, the drink's bark is equal to its gingery, citrusy bite. Notes of orange and juniper will ease the inevitable tribulations of puppy training, which probably will take dog years from your life, no matter how chill you claim to be.*

2 ounces gin
1 ounce fresh orange juice
¾ ounce ginger syrup
½ ounce fresh lime juice

1 dash Angostura bitters
Club soda, to top
1 piece candied ginger,
   for garnish
1 thin orange slice, for garnish

Combine the gin, orange juice, ginger syrup, lime juice, and bitters in a shaker. Whip shake (no ice) and pour into a tall glass filled with ice. Top with club soda and garnish with the piece of candied ginger and the orange slice.

FISH HOUSE PUNCH

Sometimes switching it up a little can yield spectacular results. Like when 1930s Philadelphia hot dog vendors Pat and Harry Olivieri tried a new sandwich using finely chopped steak and onions. Their creation, the cheesesteak, became an immediate success and an inextricable part of Philly's culinary culture.

You don't need to be anywhere near the East Coast to enjoy a real Fish House Punch, however. Philadelphia's oldest signature cocktail has been satiating spirits lovers since 1732. It allegedly caused George Washington's most epic hangover, reportedly keeping the commander-in-chief in bed for three days. Perfect for washing down a beefy meal, this silky-smooth, fruity, and refreshing sipper packs enough of a sneak-up-on-you, Philly-sized punch that, like an oh-so-heavy cheesesteak, will make you think twice before you order seconds.

1 ounce peach liqueur
¾ ounce Jamaican amber rum
¾ ounce cognac

½ ounce fresh lemon juice
Club soda (optional)
1 lemon wedge, for garnish

 Combine the peach liqueur, rum, cognac, and lemon juice in a shaker. Whip shake (no ice) and pour into a tall glass filled with crushed ice. Dilute with club soda if necessary. Garnish with the lemon wedge.

PREAKNESS

For one of the smallest states in America, Maryland lays claim to an inordinate amount of history and unique culture. "Maryland is for crabs," the state's unofficial motto goes, but it's also famous for horse racing. The biggest of these events, the Preakness Stakes, forms part of the sport's hallowed Triple Crown and has been run every year since 1873 at Baltimore's Pimlico Race Course. It's important enough to have inspired a Prohibition-era Manhattan riff brightened with Bénédictine—those monastery origins recalling the Catholic faith of Lord Baltimore, Maryland's first provincial English ruler—and lemon zest from a garnish the same color as Maryland's state flower, the black-eyed Susan. Have a Preakness or two with your crabcakes tonight but avoid equestrian events until the morning.

---

2 ounces rye whiskey
¾ ounce sweet vermouth
¼ ounce Bénédictine

2 dashes Angostura bitters
1 dash orange bitters
1 lemon twist, for garnish

Combine the whiskey, vermouth, Bénédictine, and bitters in a mixing glass filled with cracked ice. Stir with a long-handled spoon for 30 seconds and strain into a stemmed cocktail glass. Garnish with the lemon twist.

VULCAN NERVE PINCH

Mr. Spock's favorite proverb from his home world was "Live long and prosper," a phrase encouraging all of us humanoids to improve our health and happiness however we see fit. His signature move was the Vulcan nerve pinch, a pressure-point technique that immediately rendered any foe unconscious. The Vulcan Nerve Pinch cocktail probably won't knock you out—depending on your tolerance level—but it does stun the senses with the fiery flavors of three different chili peppers and a dollop of cayenne.

1½ ounces aged rum
1 ounce fresh lime juice
½ ounce Ancho Reyes Verde
½ ounce simple syrup

3 thin cucumber slices
2 dashes Cholula hot sauce
1 dash Worcestershire sauce
Club soda, to top
1 pinch cayenne pepper, to top

Combine the rum, lime juice, Ancho Reyes Verde, simple syrup, two cucumber slices, hot sauce, and Worcestershire sauce in an ice-filled shaker. Shake vigorously for 25 to 30 seconds and strain into a tall glass filled with ice. Top with club soda and cayenne pepper. Garnish with the additional cucumber slice.

DON LOCKWOOD

"Too much of anything is bad, but too much good whiskey is barely enough."

International Whisk(e)y Day uses the parentheses to accommodate Scottish, Canadian, and Japanese imbibers who prefer their whisky sans the e. But no matter how you spell it, all varieties of the world's most popular spirit contain ellagic acid, a powerhouse antioxidant known for its cancer-fighting abilities, as well as decongestive benefits and pain-killing properties to soothe sore throats. Those are more than enough reasons to raise a glass—or three—today. No cocktail allows a whiskey's unique tasting notes to shine like an Old-Fashioned, and no Old-Fashioned variation straddles both ends of the whiskey spectrum as elegantly as the Don Lockwood, from Abraham Hawkins at Long Island City's Dutch Kills Bar. Two very different whiskeys (or whiskies) from both sides of the Atlantic fuse to create a crowd-pleaser that's equal parts smoky, earthy, caramelly, oaky—and 100 percent irresistible.

1 ounce Islay scotch	2 dashes Angostura bitters
1 ounce bourbon	2 dashes chocolate bitters
⅛ ounce maple syrup	1 orange twist, for garnish

Combine the scotch, bourbon, maple syrup, and bitters in an Old-Fashioned glass. Add ice and stir for five or six seconds. Garnish with the orange twist.

TEQUILA BEARCAT

One of the reasons feline fanatics think most cats are so special is that you usually have to earn a cat's respect before it warms up to you . . . if it warms up at all. Today's about winning over your favorite finicky furballs by giving them all the appreciation they deserve. Unlike easily won-over dogs, they can be aloof, fickle, and downright disdainful toward their human housemates. But as every cat lover knows, inside even the orneriest old tom lives a precious little kitty just begging to have his tummy scratched. Okay, maybe not. The Tequila Bearcat, however, will make you feel warm and fuzzy when your pet can't be bothered. A delicious blend of tequila and strawberries, with notes of almond and Peychaud's bitters for added depth, it tastes sweet as your cat can behave when you show the proper respect—or when it just want some kibbles.

2 ounces tequila

¾ ounce fresh lemon juice

¾ ounce orgeat

2 strawberries, halved

4 dashes Peychaud's bitters

1 whole strawberry, for garnish

Combine the tequila, lemon juice, and orgeat in a shaker. In a double Old-Fashioned glass, muddle the halved strawberries, then fill the glass two-thirds of the way with crushed ice. Add the contents of the shaker and then add the bitters. Top with crushed ice. Garnish with a whole strawberry.

HOUDINI

If you were hoping that Smoke and Mirrors Day had to do with cigars and bathroom selfies, sorry to burst your bubble. Today's holiday—named after the classic illusion that makes an object appear to hover in space— honors magicians and all the mind-bending stunts they pull off, from simple card tricks to making the Statue of Liberty vanish. (Seriously, look it up.)

Even if magic's never been your cup of tea, you probably have heard of Harry Houdini. The Austrian-born escape artist famously incorporated handcuffs and straightjackets into his jaw-dropping routines, many of which no one has duplicated. For one-of-a-kind cocktail magic, try this mysterious potion still mixed in his name. A Martini variation conjured by Kevin Martin at Boston's Eastern Standard in the early 2000s, the Houdini is malty and botanical-heavy, with illusory notes of citrus from the twist. This liquid performance finishes with a flourish that doesn't require a trapdoor or a rabbit in a hat, thankfully.

1½ ounces genever	¼ ounce Bénédictine
¾ ounce Cocchi Americano	1 lemon twist, for garnish

Combine the genever, Cocchi Americano, and Bénédictine in a mixing glass filled with cracked ice. Stir with a long-handled spoon for 30 seconds and strain into a stemmed cocktail glass. Garnish with the lemon twist.

PENICILLIN

Hypochondriacs rejoice! National Doctors Day honors the routine heroics of the physicians who have dedicated their professional lives to the pursuit of wellness, research, and—most importantly—compassion for others, even those poor, easily swayed souls who have gone down one too many WebMD rabbit holes.

If visiting a doctor's office was as pleasant as drinking a Penicillin, the world would be a much healthier place. Sam Ross's ubiquitous whisky reviver, named after one of 20th-century medicine's most important breakthroughs, has inspired numerous riffs and reinterpretations and established a ravenous following. Fortified by life-giving citrus and ginger, as well as two varieties of scotch—"Grandpa's cough medicine"—it's tough to beat this monument of 21st-century ingenuity. If you're looking to start a career in cocktail bartending, make sure you know how to make one of these, or you might get berated worse than an intern on Grey's Anatomy.

2 ounces blended scotch
¼ ounce fresh lemon juice
⅜ ounce honey syrup

⅜ ounce ginger syrup
¼ ounce Islay scotch
1 piece candied ginger,
   for garnish

Combine the blended scotch, lemon juice, honey syrup, and ginger syrup in an ice-filled shaker. Shake vigorously for 25 to 30 seconds and strain into a double Old-Fashioned glass over ice. Float the Islay scotch. Garnish with the piece of candied ginger.

TURN THE PAGE TO
SEE THE ILLUSTRATION
FOR THIS DRINK.

Penicillin
PAGE 117

Eiffel Tower Day

CAFÉ DE PARIS

"I should be jealous of the tower," Gustave Eiffel wrote about the colossal monument that still bears his name. *"She is more famous than I am."*
*Regardless of whether its architect envied his creation (he did have a
habit of referring to himself as a genius, so probably), the Eiffel Tower is
as popular today as it was when first unveiled in 1889. If you happened to
be in the 1920s, taking in a view of the Tower while seated at a nearby bar
or restaurant, it's very possible you'd be sipping on a Café de Paris. Harry
Craddock invented this silky-smooth Prohibition-era sipper in London,
but it quickly spread to France, where its uniquely complex, anisette-
tinged flavor profile made it a favorite of the Parisian artistic community.
Its intriguing, texturally intricate combination of gin, cream, egg white,
and absinthe is as unforgettable as seeing the Eiffel Tower in person.*

2 ounces gin	½ ounce simple syrup
½ ounce heavy cream	¼ ounce absinthe
	1 egg white

Combine all ingredients in a shaker. Shake for 10 seconds without ice
(to emulsify the egg white), then add ice and shake vigorously. Strain
into a stemmed cocktail glass.

APRIL

						1 APRIL FOOL'S DAY El Presidente
2 CHILDREN'S BOOK DAY Mr. Grinch	3 NATIONAL PONY EXPRESS DAY Home on the Range	4 NATIONAL VITAMIN C DAY Northside Special	5 NATIONAL DANDELION DAY Dandelion	6 ARMY DAY Commando	7 NATIONAL BEER DAY Michelada	8 ZOO LOVERS DAY Tiger's Eye
9 CHERISH AN ANTIQUE DAY Sazerac	10 GOLFER'S DAY Hole in the Cup	11 NATIONAL SUBMARINE DAY Yellow Submarine	12 NATIONAL LICORICE DAY Tritter Rickey	13 NATIONAL SCRABBLE DAY Bird Is the Word	14 NATIONAL EX-SPOUSE DAY Haitian Divorce	15 NATIONAL *TITANIC* REMEMBRANCE DAY Iceberg
16 WORLD VOICE DAY Harry Nilsson	17 INTERNATIONAL HAIKU POETRY DAY Japanese Maple Cocktail	18 INTERNATIONAL AMATEUR RADIO DAY Columbia Cocktail	19 NATIONAL AMARETTO DAY Godmother	20 420 Brooklynite	21 QUEEN ELIZABETH'S BIRTHDAY Dubonnet Cocktail	22 EARTH DAY Captain Planet
23 ST. GEORGE'S DAY White Dragon 30 INTERNATIONAL JAZZ DAY Chet Baker	24 NEW KIDS ON THE BLOCK DAY Star Cocktail	25 EAST MEETS WEST DAY Shangri-La	26 REMEMBER YOUR FIRST KISS DAY Kissy-Face	27 BABE RUTH DAY Great Bambino	28 NATIONAL SUPERHERO DAY Rum Runner	29 INTERNATIONAL DANCE DAY One Dance

EL PRESIDENTE

*Forget about the Ides of March (page 99). Beware the First of April!
There are no treats—but plenty of tricks—on April Fool's Day, an ode to
good-natured mischief and tomfoolery celebrated since at least the late
14th century. If you've been served a shot of vodka (or even worse, water)
when you asked for tequila, you know that bartenders can be some of the
cruelest pranksters of all. But not all booze-related trickery has to end in
disappointment. When expats in early-1900s Cuba tried to keep things
American and ordered a familiar Manhattan, they often received the
similar-looking El Presidente instead. The semidry, slightly sweet, and
full-bodied rum sipper, though quite different from its whiskey-based
cousin, was a hit with bamboozled customers, who eventually brought
the recipe stateside to even greater acclaim. In this rare case, the trick
became a treat.*

1½ ounces aged rum
1½ ounces blanc vermouth

¼ ounce curaçao
1 barspoon grenadine
1 orange twist, for garnish

Combine the rum, vermouth, curaçao, and grenadine in
a mixing glass filled with cracked ice. Stir with a long-
handled spoon for 30 seconds and strain into a stemmed
cocktail glass. Garnish with the orange twist.

APRIL 2
Children's Book Day

MR. GRINCH

Few characters are as recognizable to readers of all ages as Mr. Grinch, the fiendish furball who first appeared in Dr. Seuss's 1957 best-seller, How the Grinch Stole Christmas! *He's also the curmudgeonly yet ultimately endearing inspiration for the Mr. Grinch, a fruity and citrusy concoction that has just the right amount of complexity to satisfy a mature palate, with more than a little melon-tinged sweetness to thrill one's inner child. Bright green and highlighted by red bitters that allude to the Grinch's uplifting character arc, it's a delightfully low-ABV adventure for fans of any genre.*

2 ounces Midori
¾ ounce fresh lemon juice
¼ ounce Licor 43

3 dashes Angostura bitters
3 dashes Peychaud's bitters
1 brandied cherry, for garnish

Combine the Midori, lemon juice, and Licor 43 in a shaker. Pour into a double Old-Fashioned glass filled two-thirds of the way with crushed ice. Add bitters and top with more crushed ice. Garnish with the brandied cherry.

HOME ON THE RANGE

Wanted: Young, skinny, wiry fellows not over eighteen. Must be expert riders, willing to risk death daily. Orphans preferred.

That job description wouldn't entice too many members of Gen Z, but for thousands of teens in 1860, the Pony Express represented an unparalleled chance for an adrenaline rush—and a hefty paycheck. For a brief time, this horseback mail service was the fastest way to send messages across the vast American frontier—assuming that the riders didn't fall victim to bandits, die at the hands of justifiably pissed-off American Indians, or succumb to the elements.

Nowhere was frontier life more idealized than in the lyrics to the classic tune "Home on the Range," which eventually became the unofficial anthem of pioneers. This subtly sweet, boozier Old-Fashioned variation would have been ideal for Pony Express employees looking to brace themselves for another day in the saddle, if they weren't too busy literally riding for their lives.

2 ounces bourbon	**2 dashes Angostura bitters**
½ ounce sweet vermouth	**1 lemon twist, for garnish**
½ ounce Cointreau	**1 orange twist, for garnish**

Combine the bourbon, vermouth, Cointreau, and bitters in a double Old-Fashioned glass. Add ice and stir for five or six seconds. Garnish with the lemon and orange twists.

NORTHSIDE SPECIAL

Of all the nutrients commonly consumed by people, vitamin C might be the most well known, and for good reason. Not only effective for warding off colds, this powerhouse supplement also is clinically proven to reduce blood pressure, improve heart health, protect skin, and decrease inflammation. Before the advent of (boring) modern medicine, the most commonly prescribed cold remedy came in the form of a few jolly gulps of rum. The medicinal value of getting plastered probably isn't that high, but a reasonable amount of booze does help to relieve stress and stabilize blood pressure. Originally popularized in Jamaica during the early 20th century—and first appearing in print in David A. Embury's 1948 classic The Fine Art of Mixing Drinks—*the Northside Special combines the best health benefits of both rum and citrus juices. A fantastically energetic blend of orange, lemon, and molasses, it's tastier than a Flintstone Vitamin and a whole lot more fun.*

---

2 ounces Goslings Black Seal rum
1½ ounces orange juice
½ ounce fresh lemon juice

½ ounce simple syrup
Club soda, to top
1 thin orange slice, for garnish

 Combine the rum, juices, and simple syrup in a shaker. Whip shake (no ice) and pour into a tall glass filled with ice. Top with club soda and garnish with the orange slice.

DANDELION

Dandelions and the wine distilled from their petals rarely go into cocktails, but quite a few drinks have taken inspiration from the flower's bitterly herbaceous flavor profile. Nick Caruana's Dandelion is perhaps the most fragrant of these, a riff on the classic Chrysanthemum that harnesses the potentially volatile combination of both yellow and green Chartreuse—mysterious liqueurs with earthy and nutty notes that have led some to speculate that dandelion might be one of their secret ingredients—to wildly successful results. But go overboard on this potent ode to plant life and your head soon will feel like a dandelion flower unceremoniously popped from its stem.

2 ounces dry vermouth
¾ ounce yellow Chartreuse
¼ ounce green Chartreuse
3 dashes absinthe
1 lemon twist, for garnish

Combine the dry vermouth, yellow Chartreuse, green Chartreuse, and absinthe in an ice-filled mixing glass. Stir for 30 seconds and strain into a stemmed cocktail glass. Garnish with the lemon twist.

COMMANDO

An army can contain dozens of branches and factions, but the most heralded troops are usually the commandos. These elite squadrons— including the US Army Rangers—specialize in the most dangerous and crucial missions, which often involve frontline combat.

A New York City classic from Lucius Beebe's The Stork Club Bar Book *(1946), the Commando makes a powerful addition to any tactical cocktail operation. Delightfully dry with hints of orange and anise, this bourbon-led platoon will give you the liquid fortitude to take on injustice, like an overcharge on a bar tab, wherever it lurks.*

1½ ounces bourbon

¾ ounce Cointreau

¾ ounce fresh lime juice

¼ ounce simple syrup

1 dash absinthe

 Combine all ingredients in an ice-filled shaker. Shake vigorously for 25 to 30 seconds and strain into a stemmed cocktail glass.

National Beer Day

MICHELADA

One of the best remedies for combating the effects of a night of too many ales or lagers is also one of the simplest: more beer! Mexicans have been adding a spicy twist to their hair of the dog for decades with the Michelada, a Pilsner-based Bloody Mary variation most often made with lime juice and a variety of spicy, savory sauces. Little Branch's simple yet oh-so-satisfying version from Luis Gil features paradoxically stomach-settling hot sauce and as much cayenne pepper as you need to sweat out whatever ails you. It's a great recipe to have on hand, especially if you celebrate the joys of beer more than once a year.

1 ounce fresh lime juice
¾ ounce Worcestershire sauce
¾ ounce hot sauce, such as Cholula
1 pinch black pepper

Cayenne pepper, to taste
Salt, for rim
12-ounce can or bottle of light, Pilsner-style beer, such as Modelo

Combine the lime juice, Worcestershire sauce, hot sauce, black pepper, and cayenne pepper in a shot glass. Rim a tall glass with salt and fill it two-thirds of the way with cracked ice. Pour half of the shot glass's contents into the glass and top with beer. Add the remaining contents of the shot glass to taste.

TIGER'S EYE

This holiday celebrates the conservation efforts of zoo employees who work tirelessly to ensure that thousands of endangered species continue to share the planet with the wildest animals of all: us. Siberian tigers are some of the most popular big cats found in zoos around the world. Thanks to breeding programs at some of these facilities, this extremely rare mammal is making a slow but steady comeback in the wild. It's an achievement worth toasting, preferably with a Tiger's Eye from Dale DeGroff. Created for the American Museum of the Cocktail in 2006, this auburn-hued, pisco-based marriage of orange, grape, and vanilla has a nose and finish both as striking as a tiger's markings—but without the bite. A silent yet delicious killer that will sneak up on you if you're not careful.

1½ ounces pisco
1 ounce Cointreau
¾ ounce fresh lime juice

½ ounce Licor 43
½ ounce orange juice
1 orange twist, for garnish

Combine the pisco, Cointreau, juices, and Licor 43 in an ice-filled shaker. Shake vigorously for 25 to 30 seconds and strain into a double Old-Fashioned glass over ice. Garnish with the orange twist.

Cherish an Antique Day

SAZERAC

Marie Kondo acolytes might have you think otherwise, but some posses-sions are indispensable, especially ones with an extensive (family) history. National Cherish an Antique Day encourages you to find a new appreci-ation for items passed down from elder family members. If you enjoy (or have been dragged on) antiquing trips, you know that objects from the past don't come cheap. But antique cocktails are a different story. Thanks to preserved recipe books, we easily and accurately can experience many of the most beloved drinks from centuries past, including the Sazerac. This Old-Fashioned cousin arose in antebellum New Orleans around 1840 and quickly defined the Crescent City's burgeoning cocktail scene. A timeless combination of whiskey, sugar, French absinthe, and gentian- and anise-infused bitters from local apothecary Antoine Peychaud, it offers a living window into a fascinating culture and era.

2 ounces overproof rye whiskey
¼ ounce absinthe

4 dashes Peychaud's bitters
1 white sugar cube
1 lemon twist, for garnish

Fill an Old-Fashioned glass with crushed ice and add the absinthe. Allow the glass to chill while preparing the rest of the drink. Next, add the sugar cube to a mixing glass and douse it with the bitters. Muddle the sugar cube, add the whiskey, and fill the mixing glass with cracked ice. Stir with a long-handled spoon for 25 seconds. Empty the Old-Fashioned glass of crushed ice and absinthe. Strain the contents of the mixing glass into the Old-Fashioned glass. Garnish with the lemon twist.

HOLE IN THE CUP

Get out and hit the links today—and not the ones in your social media feeds. Since it emerged on the moors of Scotland in the 15th century, golf has enthralled and infuriated millions of players on every continent. Notoriously difficult yet able to be enjoyed by athletes of all ages, the "gentleman's game" is one of the best ways to enjoy nature, burn some calories, spend quality time with friends or associates, and (paradoxically) lower stress. Clubhouse bars are the perfect place to wind down, complain about all the putts you "almost" made, and settle any hard-won bets with your buddies. It's even better if you're sipping a Hole in the Cup, a spectacular variation on Sasha Petraske's Gordon's Cup from Lauren McLaughlin, first served at Brooklyn's Fresh Kills. Its combination of tequila, pineapple, and absinthe is as rare as a hole in one and no less gratifying.

1½ ounces tequila
1 ounce fresh pineapple juice
¾ ounce fresh lime juice

½ ounce simple syrup
1 barspoon absinthe
4 thin cucumber slices

Combine the tequila, juices, simple syrup, absinthe, and three cucumber slices in a shaker. Muddle the cucumbers, then fill the shaker with cracked ice. Shake four or five times and then dump the entire contents of the shaker into a double Old-Fashioned glass. Garnish with another cucumber slice.

YELLOW SUBMARINE

Submarines have come a long way since Connecticut inventor David Bushnell's Turtle *attempted to make waves in the American War of Independence, failed all its missions, and nearly killed its pilot. No longer wooden death traps, today's nuclear-powered subs cost millions of dollars and feature stealth technology, state-of-the-art life support systems, futuristic weaponry, and advanced tracking capabilities.*

Sure, it's amazing to explore the ocean's depths with relative ease, but not many people want to be cooped up in a submersible for an extended period. A nod to the eponymous song and its big-time banana flavor profile, the Yellow Submarine from Colleen Graham is a rare spirit-forward sipper that's both satisfyingly tropical and sneakily boozy. Beware of getting the bends if you accidentally "submerse" a few of these too quickly.

1½ ounces vodka

¾ ounce white rum

¾ ounce banana liqueur

1 banana slice, for garnish

Combine the vodka, rum, and banana liqueur in a mixing glass filled with cracked ice. Stir with a long-handled spoon for 30 seconds and strain into a stemmed cocktail glass. Garnish with the banana slice.

TRITTER RICKEY

You may love licorice or hate it, but it's hard to ignore this aromatic root's uniquely pungent flavor. Especially popular in Nordic countries, licorice extract serves as a main ingredient in hard candies and chocolates. Practitioners of traditional herbal medicine also praise its immune-boosting, anti-inflammatory properties when consumed in moderation. But where's the fun in that?

If you don't have a sweet tooth or an interest in shamanism, you still can experience this salty, sour, sweet sensation with a cocktail infused with absinthe, an anise-based spirit with an uncannily similar flavor profile. Named for Little Branch patron Michael Tritter, the Tritter Rickey offers a refreshing, herbaceous twist on the classic Gin Rickey that every licorice enthusiast should try. But if you consider licorice a punishment rather than a cause for celebration, there's no harm in enjoying this minty cooler sans absinthe.

2 ounces gin	**¼ ounce absinthe**
1 ounce fresh lime juice	**6 mint leaves**
¾ ounce simple syrup	**1 sprig fresh mint, for garnish**

 Combine the gin, lime juice, simple syrup, absinthe, and mint leaves in an ice-filled shaker. Shake vigorously for 25 to 30 seconds and strain into a tall glass filled with ice. Garnish with the mint sprig.

BIRD IS THE WORD

Happy National Scrabble Day! If you're keeping score, those four words are worth 44 points in the world's most popular language-related board game. Created in 1938 by architect Alfred Mosher Butts, Scrabble continues to enthrall countless wordsmiths online and in heated real-life battles. Even if you don't have the largest vocabulary, the game can improve concentration and communication skills, lower blood pressure (yeah, right), and boost the immune system. Which might ease the sting the next time a friend or family member who happens to be a walking thesaurus demolishes you.

To succeed at Scrabble, always remain calm. Some recommend yoga for this, but we prefer a cocktail—especially one as lexically leaning as the Bird Is the Word, bartender Fraser Campbell's spin on the classic Last Word. Our adaptation features a harmoniously assembled pairing of big herbaceous flavors with fruity, citrusy undertones. "Bird" (7 points) might not help you win the game, but this tequila-feathered friend will have you feeling as light as a zephyr (23 points).

1½ ounces tequila

¾ ounce yellow Chartreuse

¾ ounce fresh lemon juice

½ ounce apricot brandy

1 lemon twist, for garnish

Combine the tequila, yellow Chartreuse, lemon juice, and apricot brandy in an ice-filled shaker. Shake vigorously for 25 to 30 seconds and strain into a stemmed cocktail glass. Garnish with the lemon twist.

HAITIAN DIVORCE

About 50 percent of first marriages are doomed to fail, with an even higher divorce rate for second and third marriages. As messy as breakups can be, it's never good to hold on to all the anger and bitterness that often go with them. National Ex-Spouse Day encourages forgiveness among the recently separated, to inspire them to let go of the past and move on in a healthy way.

Chock-full of mezcal, rum, and the always versatile Pedro Ximénez sherry, this smoky-smooth, supremely funky blend of seemingly disparate spirits proves that opposite ingredients sometimes do attract, but they always need to be in the right proportions for the union to work. As a bonus, if you drink enough of these lime-scented beauties, you probably will forget that you were married in the first place!

1½ ounces aged rum

¾ ounce mezcal

½ ounce Pedro Ximénez sherry

3 dashes Angostura bitters

1 lime twist, for garnish

1 orange twist, for garnish

 Combine the rum, mezcal, sherry, and bitters in a double Old-Fashioned glass. Add ice and stir for five or six seconds. Garnish with the lime twist and the orange twist.

ICEBERG

It was the greatest ship ever conceived, a marvel of 20th-century engineering built to be unsinkable. Until it wasn't. Considered the safest vessel on the ocean, the Titanic *carried only enough lifeboats for about half the passengers onboard, a deadly oversight when the ship struck an iceberg just five days into its maiden transatlantic voyage. To avoid similarly disastrous acts of hubris, it's important to keep a clear head, and it doesn't get more coldly refreshing than the Iceberg, created at Little Branch in 2021. Featuring frigid vodka, an arctic blast of peppermint, and a snow-like dollop of cream peeking out above its icy depths, this is one stately monument of cocktail creativity that's impossible to miss.*

2 ounces vodka
½ ounce peppermint schnapps
½ ounce crème de cacao (white)
Hand-whipped cream, to top
1 mint leaf, for garnish

Combine the vodka, peppermint schnapps, and crème de cacao in an ice-filled mixing glass. Stir with a long-handled spoon for 30 seconds and strain into a stemmed cocktail glass. Float the cream. Garnish with the mint leaf.

TURN THE PAGE TO
SEE THE ILLUSTRATION
FOR THIS DRINK.

Iceberg
PAGE 135

HARRY NILSSON

Dust off those windpipes and let out a healthy shout—where appropriate—because it's World Voice Day!

With abilities that far surpass mere communication, a select few singers can raise their singing to the level of fine art. One of these troubadours was the criminally underrated singer-songwriter Harry Nilsson, a tenor with a three-and-a-half-octave range whose greatest fame came in the 1970s with hits including "Coconut," in which a doctor prescribes a drink of lime and coconut for a stomachache. Inspired by the man and his words, Attaboy's Andrew Rice devised the Harry Nilsson cocktail, a Piña Colada riff with a personality all its own. Breezy and potent, with the Caribbean flavors that Nilsson often favored in his music, this one will have you crooning in no time.

---

2 ounces aged rum
2 ounces fresh pineapple juice
¼ ounce coconut syrup
Splash of blackstrap rum

Splash of heavy cream
1 lime wedge
1 pinch grated nutmeg,
  for garnish

Combine the rums, pineapple juice, coconut syrup, cream, and lime wedge in an ice-filled shaker. Shake vigorously for 25 to 30 seconds and strain into a double Old-Fashioned glass over ice. Garnish with the grated nutmeg.

JAPANESE MAPLE COCKTAIL

Haiku are easy / But sometimes they don't make sense / Refrigerator

For many brown liquor aficionados, Japan's barley-based whisky is pure liquid poetry. The Japanese Maple Cocktail, a stimulating Sour riff from Damian Windsor at Los Angeles's The Roger Room, highlights that spirit's oaky, slightly sweet, and herbaceous properties and embellishes them with a sinuous, frothy finish. Like haiku poetry, the cocktail draws influences from natural elements, the citrus and maple syrup putting you in a Zen-like mode of contemplation . . . or just getting you pleasantly puckered, which is perfectly fine as well.

2 ounces blended Japanese
  whisky
¾ ounce fresh lemon juice

½ ounce maple syrup
2 dashes orange bitters
1 egg white

Combine all ingredients in a shaker. Shake without ice (to emulsify the egg white) for 10 seconds, then add ice and shake vigorously. Strain into a stemmed cocktail glass.

International Amateur Radio Day

COLUMBIA COCKTAIL

Not all wave surfing requires a board. Amateur (or "ham") radio oper-
ators have been taking to the airwaves since the early 1900s, building a
wireless, noncommercial communications network that extends around
the globe and that millions of enthusiasts access on a regular basis. The
first American ham radio organization, the Wireless Telegraph Club,
formed in 1908 at Columbia University and still exists today. Around the
same time, prototypes of the school's signature drink, the Columbia Cock-
tail, began to appear in New York City bars. Eventually making its way
into Trader Vic's Bartender's Guide *(1947), this charming, berry-infused*
Rum Sour variation is perfect for soothing the vocal cords after a long
radio-gab session. Enjoy it as a brisk, fruity ode to a non-digital form of
entertainment that, like the cocktail, has stood the test of time.

2 ounces light rum

¾ ounce fresh lemon juice

¾ ounce simple syrup

6 raspberries

Combine the rum, lemon juice, simple syrup, and five raspberries in an ice-filled shaker. Shake vigorously for 25 to 30 seconds and strain into a stemmed cocktail glass. Garnish with
the remaining raspberry.

GODMOTHER

In Italian, amaretto means "a little bitter," but its sweetness and exotic aroma define this nutty, fruity liqueur more than anything. Originally produced in Saronno, Italy, in the 16th century, the secret blend of almond and brandy was commercialized by the Disaronno family, who began exporting it to America in the early 1900s. The two most popular amaretto-based cocktails are the Amaretto Sour and the Godfather. The former can taste cloying, and the latter's smoky overtones tend to suffocate amaretto's flavor rather than enhance it. If you're looking for an undiluted amaretto experience with a boozier kick, try the Godmother instead. This exceedingly simple after-dinner delight has been embellishing nightcap repertoires for decades, and it's no surprise why. As a neutral spirit, vodka tones down the liqueur's sweetness and graciously allows all the best notes of almond, cherry, and apricot to shine. This fairy godmother might send you to dreamland faster than you anticipate.

---

2 ounces vodka   **1 ounce amaretto**

Combine both ingredients in a double Old-Fashioned glass. Add ice and stir for five or six seconds.

BROOKLYNITE

Smoke 'em if you got 'em, heady people, because it's 4:20 somewhere! Today's holiday—named for a popular code word and time of day for smoking marijuana—celebrates all things cannabis, a plant humans had been consuming freely since prehistory until a few government buzzkills in the 1930s decided they didn't like people having fun. Oh, and something about evil jazz musicians.

Confronting the blatant hypocrisy of federal marijuana legislation sometimes requires something stronger than a pleasant toke. For that, there's the Brooklynite, a laid-back Daiquiri riff from Trader Vic's Bartender's Guide (1972). Featuring delectable amber rum from Jamaica— where Rastafarianism and reggae are synonymous with marijuana use—this sweet, citrusy, and far too easily quaffed tiki gem can soothe even the most bong-charred throat. Alcohol, like weed, can impair short-term memory, so stock up on munchies before shaking up a few of these.

---

2 ounces Jamaican
amber rum
1 ounce fresh lime juice

¾ ounce honey syrup
2 dashes Angostura bitters
1 lime wedge, for garnish

Combine the rum, lime juice, honey syrup, and bitters in an ice-filled shaker. Shake vigorously for 25 to 30 seconds and strain into a stemmed cocktail glass. Garnish with the lime wedge.

DUBONNET COCKTAIL

God save the queen and anyone who tries to go drink-for-drink with the world's oldest monarch. The always popular queen's drinking habits are debatable, but it's well known that her favorite tipple is a gin and Dubonnet, otherwise known as a Dubonnet Cocktail. First appearing in Jacques Straub's Drinks *(1914), this dry, mildly bitter blend of fortified wine, spices, and juniper has a flavor profile as complex as a head of state's day-to-day engagements, with a regal finish that might give you royal aspirations of your own. But don't excommunicate your local watering hole if they can't make one of these because finding a bottle of Dubonnet behind a bar is as rare as a woman reigning for seven decades.*

1½ ounces Dubonnet

1½ ounces London dry gin
1 orange twist, for garnish

Combine the Dubonnet and gin in a mixing glass filled with cracked ice. Stir with a long-handled spoon for 30 seconds and strain into a stemmed cocktail glass. Garnish with the orange twist.

APRIL 22
Earth Day

CAPTAIN PLANET

Many 1990s kids got their first taste of conservationism by watching Captain Planet and the Planeteers, *an animated series in which five teens receive elemental rings that, when combined, summon the ecologically friendly superhero Captain Planet. The cocktail that shares its name with him features components that align with each Planeteer's ring—bourbon (earth), tequila (fire), vodka (wind), passion fruit (heart), and club soda (water)—as well as natural ingredients such as ginger and lime juice. Effortlessly smooth yet highly potent, fruity yet brisk, it's a surprising example of what happens when disparate elements combine to help the greater good or get you buzzed.*

¾ ounce bourbon

¾ ounce tequila

¾ ounce vodka

½ ounce passion fruit syrup

½ ounce ginger syrup

½ ounce fresh lime juice

2 dashes Angostura bitters

Club soda, to top

1 piece candied ginger,
   for garnish

Combine the bourbon, tequila, vodka, passion fruit syrup, ginger syrup, lime juice, and bitters in a shaker. Whip shake (no ice) and pour into a tall glass filled with ice. Top with club soda. Garnish with the piece of candied ginger.

WHITE DRAGON

Historians know little about St. George's life, except that he was probably a Roman soldier in the third century who was martyred shortly before the empire embraced the Christian faith. Monks soon spread tales of his legendary (alleged) exploits, particularly the story of him traveling to Libya and defeating a murderous dragon that had been terrorizing a city, killing it in return for that city's conversion to Christianity. Although dragons may have lost some of their cultural cachet in recent years—thanks, Game of Thrones, ugh—the White Dragon is one liquefied beast you're going to want to sink your fangs into. Created by bartending icon Jim Meehan as a tequila-based reimagining of the classic White Lady and originally featuring Casa Dragones Tequila Blanco, this sublimely velvety sipper is a much smoother, well-balanced tipple than its frightening moniker implies. Allow the St. George vibes to flow into you while drinking a few of these, providing you with the courage to exterminate whatever (metaphorical) monsters have been giving you grief.

1¼ ounces tequila blanco

¾ ounce Cointreau

¾ ounce fresh lime juice

1 egg white

1 orange twist, for garnish

Combine the tequila, Cointreau, lime juice, and egg white in a shaker. Shake without ice (to emulsify the egg white) for 10 seconds, then add ice and shake vigorously. Strain into a stemmed cocktail glass. Garnish with the orange twist.

STAR COCKTAIL

The godfathers of all modern boy bands, New Kids on the Block caused pop-music pandemonium in the late 1980s and early '90s with an MTV-friendly image and sugary hits such as "Please Don't Go Girl" and "I'll Be Loving You (Forever)." One of the most popular classics in George A. Kappeler's still-influential 1895 bartending guide, Modern American Drinks, *the Star Cocktail has enthralled generations of drinkers long past its pre-Prohibition heyday. Silky and sweet without being saccharine, the combination of apple brandy and Italian vermouth performs like the verse and chorus of a catchy hit single that deserves to be played again and again. Like the New Kids, it's truly got "The Right Stuff."*

1½ ounces apple brandy, such as calvados or applejack

1½ ounces sweet vermouth
3 dashes Peychaud's bitters
1 lemon twist, for garnish

Combine the brandy, vermouth, and bitters in an ice-filled mixing glass. Stir with a long-handled spoon for 30 seconds and strain into a stemmed cocktail glass. Garnish with the lemon twist.

SHANGRI-LA

May 8, 1945, also known as Victory in Europe Day, marks when World War II ended in the European theater of war. But perhaps the most strikingly symbolic example of Nazi Germany's defeat had occurred two weeks earlier, on April 25. On that day, the American-led Western Front of the Allied forces met the mostly Soviet Eastern Front on the Elbe River near Berlin, uniting two massive armies and virtually crushing the Axis powers' final, desperate hopes.

As far as cocktails are concerned, regulations don't block combining like-minded elements from far-flung locales. In fact, it's encouraged. There's no tastier example of harmony between Asian and European ingredients than the Shangri-La, invented by Sam Ross at Attaboy in 2015. Japanese whisky's brooding, malty overtones embrace the sweet yet complex notes of fig and grape found in Spain's Pedro Ximénez sherry. If this cross-cultural sensation had been served at 20th-century peace treaties, we might not have had any more wars.

2¼ ounces blended Japanese whisky

½ ounce Pedro Ximénez sherry
3 dashes chocolate bitters
1 orange twist, for garnish

Combine the whisky, sherry, and bitters in an Old-Fashioned glass. Add ice and stir for five or six seconds. Garnish with the orange twist.

Remember Your First Kiss Day

KISSY-FACE

Maybe it was painfully awkward. Maybe it was everything that your pubescent heart and mouth wanted. Maybe there was too much tongue. Whatever the case, a first kiss is a milestone that's hard to forget.

Few experiences can thrill like a first kiss, except perhaps for the first time a new favorite cocktail graces your lips. Created by Zachary Gelnaw-Rubin at Harlem bar Lion Lion in 2018, the Kissy-Face is a fruity, chocolaty take on the salted Margarita that's like a big wet smooch to the palate. Notes of tequila, apricot, cacao, and lemon lock together for a mouthfeel guaranteed to kindle any romance. Make one to share with that special someone in your life and you might get to first base—and then some!

1½ ounces tequila
½ ounce crème de cacao

½ ounce apricot liqueur
½ ounce fresh lemon juice
Salted rim, for garnish

Combine the tequila, crème de cacao, apricot liqueur, and lemon juice in an ice-filled shaker. Shake vigorously for 25 to 30 seconds and strain into a stemmed cocktail glass with a salted rim.

GREAT BAMBINO

The Sultan of Swat, the Caliph of Clout, the Behemoth of Bust, the Great Bambino, a man of countless nicknames and seemingly infinite power when swinging a bat, George Herman "Babe" Ruth was baseball's most iconic figure, both on and off the field.

You don't have to be a Yankees or Red Sox fan to appreciate the Babe's mind-blowing achievements. You don't even have to like baseball to enjoy Sam Ross's Great Bambino, first served at Las Vegas's The Dorsey in 2018. Consisting of bourbon, which Ruth often drank during games to revive himself from his well-publicized benders, with the fastball-like zip of Fernet-Branca and an intriguing blend of pear juice and citrus, it's as satisfying as mashing a baseball into the upper deck. A fascinating tipple worthy of a man who single-handedly changed an entire sport.

1½ ounces bourbon

1 ounce pear juice

½ ounce Fernet-Branca

½ ounce fresh lemon juice

½ ounce orgeat

1 pinch freshly grated cinnamon, for garnish

1 thin pear slice, for garnish

Combine the bourbon, pear juice, Fernet-Branca, lemon juice, and orgeat in a shaker. Whip shake (no ice) and pour into a double Old-Fashioned glass two-thirds of the way filled with crushed ice. Add a straw and top with more crushed ice. Garnish with the grated cinnamon and pear slice.

National Superhero Day

RUM RUNNER

During the dark days of Prohibition, bootleggers were the ultimate champions of justice for many a thirsty soul. Also known as rum runners, these brave vigilantes risked their health and freedom to deliver cheap booze, often by boat, to speakeasies throughout America. Bartender Deke Dunne pays homage to their vital work with the Rum Runner, created at Allegory at the Eaton Hotel in Washington, DC. The alchemy of bourbon, aged rum, and biscotti liqueur imbue this oaky, honeyed, and insatiably warming Old-Fashioned variation with a larger-than-life personality. Though you might feel like you've gained super abilities after downing more than a couple of these, keeping your wits about you while drinking in moderation is the greatest power of all.

1 ounce bourbon

1 ounce aged rum

¼ ounce demerara syrup

1 barspoon biscotti liqueur, such as Faretti

1 pinch salt

1 orange twist, for garnish

Combine the bourbon, aged rum, demerara syrup, biscotti liqueur, and salt in an Old-Fashioned glass. Add ice and stir for five or six seconds. Garnish with the orange twist.

TURN THE PAGE TO
SEE THE ILLUSTRATION
FOR THIS DRINK.

Rum Runner
PAGE 149

ONE DANCE

"The dance can reveal everything mysterious that is hidden in music, and it has the additional merit of being human and palpable," poet Charles Baudelaire wrote. *"Dancing is poetry with arms and legs."*

For better or worse, nothing has convinced more people to get out on the dance floor than alcohol. Here to continue that proud and hilarious tradition is the One Dance from Chantelle Gabino. Energetically floral, cooling, and as smooth as a pirouette, it's the perfect ice-topped refreshment for when the booty just won't shake anymore. Luckily, a few sips of one of these will have you back on your feet and making an idiot of yourself on your friends' feeds in no time.

1½ ounces gin
¾ ounce Lillet
½ ounce elderflower liqueur, such as St-Germain

½ ounce fresh lemon juice
2 dashes celery or Angostura bitters
1 lemon wedge, for garnish

Combine the gin, Lillet, elderflower liqueur, and lemon juice in a shaker. Dump into a double Old-Fashioned glass filled two-thirds of the way with crushed ice. Add bitters and swizzle briefly. Add a straw and top with crushed ice. Garnish with the lemon wedge.

CHET BAKER

Love jazz or hate it, this enduring genre's impact on modern music cannot be understated.

It's no secret that many of the most celebrated jazz musicians throughout history have been equally notorious for their love of spirits (as well as any number of more volatile substances). One of the most notable of these hard-partying hepcats was trumpeter Chet Baker, a troubled virtuoso who played alongside the greatest jazz legends for more than three decades until an untimely fall from a hotel balcony. His namesake drink, first served at Milk & Honey in 2005, is as smooth and sophisticated as a funky trumpet solo, as catchy as one of the all-time standards performed by a true master. Just don't let the subtly sweet notes of honey and vermouth fool you into thinking that this crowd-pleaser doesn't pack a baritone saxophone-sized wallop, or you may, like poor Chet, find yourself on the wrong side of a window ledge.

---

2 ounces aged rum	2 dashes Angostura bitters
2 barspoons sweet vermouth	2 dashes orange bitters
1 barspoon honey syrup	1 orange twist, for garnish

Combine the rum, vermouth, honey syrup, and bitters in an Old-Fashioned glass. Add ice and stir for five or six seconds. Garnish with the orange twist.

MAY

1	2	3	4	5	6
NATIONAL EGG MONTH Sevilla	WILDFIRE COMMUNITY PREPAREDNESS DAY Firefighter's Sour	NATIONAL PARANORMAL DAY Tombstone	INTERGALACTIC STAR WARS DAY Rancor's Toothpick	CINCO DE MAYO Tijuana Lady	INTERNATIONAL NO DIET DAY French Kiss

7	8	9	10	11	12	13
COSMOPOLITAN DAY Debutante	NATIONAL COCONUT CREAM PIE DAY Another Time	INTERNATIONAL MIGRATORY BIRD DAY Migration	MOTHER'S DAY Cork County Bubbles	NATIONAL EAT WHAT YOU WANT DAY Red Grass-hopper	INTERNATIONAL NURSES DAY Painkiller	WORLD COCKTAIL DAY Old-Fashioned

14	15	16	17	18	19	20
UNDER-GROUND AMERICA DAY Coal Miner	NATIONAL DINOSAUR DAY Dino Sour	INTERNATIONAL PICKLE DAY Pickled Surfer	NATIONAL WALNUT DAY The Board-room	INTERNATIONAL MUSEUM DAY Artist's Special	PLANT SOMETHING DAY Garden Grove	WORLD BEE DAY Beekeeper's Daughter

21	22	23	24	25	26	27
EAT MORE FRUITS AND VEGETABLES DAY Pimm's Rangoon	NATIONAL MARITIME DAY Deep Blue Sea	WORLD TURTLE DAY Tortuga	VICTORIA DAY Full Windsor	AFRICA DAY African Flower	NATIONAL PAPER AIR-PLANE DAY Paper Plane	NATIONAL GRAPE POPSICLE DAY Enzoni

28	29	30	31			
NATIONAL BURGER DAY Ross Collins	IRON MAN DAY Tony Stark	NATIONAL MINT JULEP DAY Mint Julep	WHAT YOU THINK UPON GROWS DAY Ninth Wonder			

National Egg Month

SEVILLA

Omne vivum ex ovo. If your Latin is lacking, physician William Harvey's famous 17th-century maxim translates roughly to: "All life comes from the egg." Eating cooked eggs is one thing, but for those not named Rocky Balboa, the thought of drinking a raw egg can be extremely unsettling. Which is a shame because many of the oldest and best cocktails feature egg whites, yolks, or, more rarely, both. One of these whole-egg master-pieces is the Sevilla, an adaptation of a classic from Harry Craddock's Savoy Cocktail Book (1930). Its delicately nutty and fruity balance of white rum and port allows the egg white's texture and the yolk's flavor to take center stage. If you're still a little apprehensive, we promise that, once you've had a round or two of this rich and earthy concoction, you'll be feeling "sunny side up"—or possibly scrambled.

1 ounce white rum	**½ ounce simple syrup**
1 ounce port	**1 whole egg**

Combine all ingredients in a shaker. Shake without ice (to emulsify the egg) for 10 seconds, then add ice and shake vigorously. Strain into a stemmed cocktail glass.

Wildfire Community Preparedness Day

FIREFIGHTER'S SOUR

Harnessing the power of fire is one of humanity's greatest achievements. It's also insanely dangerous. Wildfire Community Preparedness Day, sometimes called National Fire Day, encourages you to learn about the risks of all manner of sizzling predicaments, from wildfires to home electrical fires, and most importantly how to survive them. Because the ability to spit fire rhymes won't help in the event of an actual blaze.

Luckily, if flames get out of hand, thousands of trained professionals are ready to respond at a moment's notice. Raise a glass to these brave people with a Firefighter's Sour, a tart and cooling riff on a classic first mentioned in Hugo Ensslin's Recipes for Mixed Drinks *(1917). White rum takes the reins here, but the bright citrus, tasty pomegranate, and extinguisher-like foam provide the refreshment to douse any boozy craving that might set a fire in your belly.*

---

2 ounces white rum

1 ounce fresh lime juice

½ ounce pomegranate syrup

¼ ounce cane syrup

1 egg white

1 thin orange slice, for garnish

Combine the rum, lime juice, pomegranate syrup, cane syrup, and egg white in a shaker. Shake without ice to emulsify the egg white for 10 seconds, then add ice and shake vigorously. Strain over ice into a double Old-Fashioned glass. Garnish with the orange slice.

TOMBSTONE

October is officially spooky season, but haunting is a year-round activity, which is why it makes ghoulishly good sense that today is National Paranormal Day. It's the perfect time to round up a posse of like-minded ghost hunters and explore the strangest occurrences that science can't explain. Break out a Ouija board for a good, old-fashioned séance, spend the night in a location known for its poltergeists, or search the sky for strange lights that may be trying to contact you from the other side.

Few places are better conduits of paranormal energy than graveyards. The Tombstone—an Old-Fashioned variation from Dave Wondrich, first described in his seminal 2007 book, Imbibe!—*is a wonderfully balanced sipper powerful enough to ward off spirits or to invite them to come hang out, depending on how you're feeling. Whether you're psyching yourself up for a long night of delving into the world's creepiest mysteries or just trying to freak yourself out in front of the TV watching* Paranormal Activities, *this whiskey-forward wonder is guaranteed to provide a much-needed jolt of stone-cold courage.*

---

2 ounces bourbon	2 dashes peach bitters
1 barspoon cane syrup	2 dashes Angostura bitters
	1 lemon twist, for garnish

 Combine the bourbon, cane syrup, and bitters in an Old-Fashioned glass. Add ice and stir for five or six seconds. Garnish with the lemon twist.

Intergalactic Star Wars Day

RANCOR'S TOOTHPICK

May the Fourth be with you, young Padawans! It's time for a journey to everyone's favorite long-ago and faraway galaxy.

Many of the most memorable moments in Star Wars *involve the delightfully monstrous aliens that populate Lucas's fictional universe. Among the nastiest of these are the reptilian carnivores known as rancors. One of them lives in the dungeons of gangster Jabba the Hutt's palace and nearly has Luke for breakfast in* Return of the Jedi. *The Rancor's Toothpick, created by Timothy Miner at Brooklyn's Long Island Bar, is as darkly mysterious as a Sith Lord, minus any evil intentions. This calming blend of bourbon, Cynar, and vermouth is potent enough to pacify the most colossal grumps without (spoiler alert) having to smash their heads with a portcullis.*

1½ ounces overproof bourbon

1 ounce Cynar

1 ounce sweet vermouth

2 dashes mole bitters

1 orange twist, for garnish

Combine the bourbon, Cynar, sweet vermouth, and bitters in a double Old-Fashioned glass. Add ice and stir for five or six seconds. Garnish with the orange twist.

TIJUANA LADY

Let's get one thing straight: Cinco de Mayo is not Mexican Independence Day, which falls on September 16. Today's festivities commemorate the 1862 victory of the Mexican Army over invading French imperial forces in the Battle of Puebla. After this major morale booster, Mexican republicans overthrew Emperor Maximillian I (whom France's Emperor Napoleon III had installed as ruler there) a few years later.

If, like some imbibers, your grasp on 19th-century Mexican history is lacking, Cinco de Drinko is when cheap tequila shots and artificially sweetened Margaritas flow faster from sombrero-clad bartenders than the Rio Grande after a rainstorm. If undiscerning binge-drinking and cringey cultural appropriation aren't your jam, you can celebrate this popular fiesta with plenty of classier libations, namely the Tijuana Lady, crafted by Michael Madrusan at Little Branch in 2008. An artful, nuanced blend of Tequila, lime, and herbal yet semisweet Licor 43, with far more balance than your average taco-stuffed, maraca-shaking happy hour degenerate. You're going to want to savor this party favor.

1½ ounces tequila
1 ounce Licor 43
¾ ounce fresh lime juice

3 dashes Angostura
 bitters
1 lime wedge, for garnish

Combine the tequila, Licor 43, lime juice, and bitters in an ice-filled shaker. Shake vigorously for 25 to 30 seconds and strain into a stemmed cocktail glass. Garnish with the lime wedge.

International No Diet Day

FRENCH KISS

In today's celebrity-focused, influencer-worshipping culture, obsession with body weight poses a very real problem. Instead of improving self-esteem, counting calories too often can lead desperate dieters to develop disorders or pursue dangerous surgeries. The International No Diet Day movement, founded in 1992 by British activist and author Mary Evans Young, has spread around the globe to discourage body shaming and unhealthy behaviors designed to attain unrealistic ideals. It's all about being happy in your own skin!

A big part of maintaining that self-satisfaction is knowing when to treat yourself, and luckily the French Kiss can put your self-love journey into overdrive. Introduced by Attaboy's Parker Marvin in 2017, this creamy, complex, spicy, and sumptuously decadent take on the classic Flip packs more than a few calories but an incalculable amount of much-needed liquid comfort. If the goal of International No Diet Day is to focus on a full-body approach to personal well-being, start with your taste buds and this great drink.

1½ ounces cognac
¾ ounce St. Elizabeth Allspice
    Dram
¾ ounce simple syrup

½ ounce heavy cream
1 egg yolk
Freshly grated nutmeg,
    for garnish

Combine the cognac, allspice dram, simple syrup, heavy cream, and egg yolk in a shaker. Shake without ice (to emulsify the cream and egg yolk) for 10 seconds, then add ice and shake vigorously. Strain into a stemmed cocktail glass. Garnish with freshly grated nutmeg.

DEBUTANTE

"Hi. I'd like a cheeseburger, large fries, and a Cosmopolitan."

For Sex and the City's *Carrie Bradshaw, the soul-soothing power of her favorite neon-pink, vodka-heavy libation was on par with the most delectably greasy fast food. That's no surprise, given that the Cosmo— long considered the poster child for late-20th-century vapid, artificially sweet, chemical-colored monstrosities—proved so popular that someone gave it its own holiday. It's not a terrible drink, per se. But any fashionista knows that even the most iconic brands need a good upgrade now and then. Enter the Debutante, from Little Branch's Lauren Schell. This delightfully effortless trendsetter keeps the Cosmo's crisp tartness and embellishes it with gin's natural botanicals.*

2 ounces gin (or vodka,
    if you insist)
¾ ounce fresh lime juice

¾ ounce pomegranate syrup
2 dashes orange bitters
1 lime wedge, for garnish

 Combine the gin, lime juice, pomegranate syrup, and orange bitters in an ice-filled shaker. Shake vigorously and strain into a coupe. Garnish with the lime wedge.

ANOTHER TIME

A rich, coconut-flavored filling slathered with a liberal layer of real whipped cream and topped with toasted coconut flakes? Say no more! Irresistibly smooth and custardy, the coconut cream pie has satisfied sweet tooths for more than a century. Unlike the many other kinds of cream pies out there, the coconut variety can be made with the freshest ingredients year-round because coconut trees continuously produce new fruit.

Another Time, a Daiquiri-style Piña Colada riff from Riley Perrin at Attaboy Nashville, pays proper respect to this classic dessert. Chockfull of coconut-flavored goodness, it makes good use of a hefty helping of pineapple juice that, when shaken, gives the drink that delightfully frothy, cream-pie texture. You won't want to throw this coconut masterpiece at anyone's face but your own.

1½ ounces Goslings Black Seal rum
1 ounce fresh pineapple juice
½ ounce coconut syrup
½ ounce fresh lime juice
1 thin slice of lime

Combine all ingredients in an ice-filled shaker. Shake vigorously for 25 to 30 seconds and strain into a stemmed cocktail glass.

MIGRATION

Created in 1993 and sponsored by the US Fish & Wildlife Service, International Migratory Bird Day celebrates (on the second Saturday in May) the thousands of species that constantly rove for food, breeding grounds, and better weather, as well as the 86 million American birders who get their kicks watching them.

Theo Lieberman's Migration, which debuted at New York City's Lantern's Keep in 2011, employs rums from Bermuda and the Caribbean as well as sweet vermouth and Cynar from different regions of Italy, a far-flung mixture impressive even by bird standards. What this mud-hued Manhattan riff might lack in bright plumage it more than achieves in complexity and balance. A perfect companion on any voyage, including the one from kitchen to couch.

¾ ounce Goslings Black Seal rum
¾ ounce blackstrap rum

¾ ounce Cynar
¾ ounce sweet vermouth
1 orange twist, for garnish

Combine the rums, Cynar, and sweet vermouth in a double Old-Fashioned glass. Add ice and stir for five or six seconds. Garnish with the orange twist.

CORK COUNTY BUBBLES

Mother's Day founder Anna Jarvis lamented this holiday's increasing commercialism as early as the 1910s. Don't feel obligated to give your mother anything other than unconditional love on the second Sunday of May, but making a nice drink for her wouldn't hurt. Topped with festive champagne to lighten the spirits of any hardworking matriarch, John Coltharp's Cork County Bubbles is an herbal, woodsy thirst quencher that will bring the entire family together. With ample portions of Irish whiskey and overproof Chartreuse, it's boozy enough to make your poor mam forget about the mischievous tribulations you put her through yet delicately well-balanced enough to show her how much you care.

1 ounce Irish whiskey
½ ounce fresh lemon juice
¼ ounce yellow Chartreuse

¼ ounce honey syrup
Champagne, to top
1 lemon twist, for garnish

Combine the whiskey, lemon juice, Chartreuse, and honey syrup in an ice-filled shaker. Shake vigorously and strain into a champagne flute. Top with champagne. Garnish with the lemon twist.

National Eat What You Want Day

RED GRASSHOPPER

Trying to maintain a healthy lifestyle is all well and good until it's dinner-time. Denying yourself the joy of eating comfort favorites such as pizza, pasta, burgers, and ice cream can feel downright brutal, especially if the term "well-balanced" has never entered your vocabulary. Today's holiday suggests taking a much-needed break from restrictions and giving in to carb-loading, sweet-tooth-satisfying bliss.

For many, just the thought of eating insects can ruin an appetite, but many cultures around the world prize these critters as crunchy, protein-rich treats. Michael Madrusan's Red Grasshopper, a spicy-sweet tequila quencher, brims with bright citrus and honey, with a sinus-clearing, slightly savory finish. Its ingredients might not prove as controversial as your culinary choices, but it's perfect for soothing the stomach after the wackiest, most ill-advised gastronomical adventures—and helping you forget about destroying that pesky diet.

2 ounces tequila	**¾ ounce honey syrup**
¾ ounce fresh lime juice	**1 pinch smoked paprika, to top**

Combine the tequila, lime juice, and honey syrup in an ice-filled shaker. Shake vigorously for 25 to 30 seconds and strain into a stemmed cocktail glass. Top with smoked paprika.

PAINKILLER

Managing pain sits near the top of the list of a nurse's many responsibilities. Most alcoholic beverages possess numbing properties, but few do so as deliciously as the Painkiller. This tiki troublemaker emerged in the 1970s as a souped-up Piña Colada spin-off originally popular with sailors for its potency and uncanny knack for reviving the most waterlogged palates. Michael Timmons's decadent tweak features the spicy, exotic interplay of three exemplary Caribbean rums, plenty of pineapple juice, and coconut cream.

1½ ounces fresh pineapple juice
1 ounce Coco Lopez
¾ ounce Jamaican amber rum
¾ ounce spiced rum
½ ounce Smith & Cross Jamaican rum
½ ounce fresh lime juice

4 dashes Angostura bitters
1 thin orange slice
1 orange wheel, for garnish
1 pinch freshly grated cinnamon, for garnish
1 pinch freshly grated nutmeg, for garnish

Combine the juices, rums, Coco Lopez, and the orange slice in a shaker. Muddle gently and dump into a tall glass or mug. Fill the glass two-thirds of the way with crushed ice. Add the bitters and stir briefly with a swizzle stick. Fill the glass to the top with crushed ice. Garnish with the orange wheel, cinnamon, and nutmeg.

OLD-FASHIONED

In 1806, a truly epic year, the kingdom of Bavaria came into being, Sidney's Press published Noah Webster's first American English dictionary, and, most awesomely, the first mention of an alcoholic concoction called a "cocktail" appeared in print. Harry Croswell—editor of The Balance and Columbian Repository, *a Hudson, New York, tabloid—defined it as "a stimulating liquor, composed of spirits of any kind, sugar, water, and bitters." No mixed drink adheres as strictly to the cocktail's humble origins as the Old-Fashioned, which first appeared on menus in the 1860s at the request of patrons already nostalgic for a simpler time. Evolving into its current whiskey-sugar-bitters format around the 1880s, it has had an identity crisis in recent decades, mainly due to heretics who insist that a "real" Old-Fashioned contains gobs of muddled fruit (which defeats the purpose of a spirit-forward cocktail, dummies).*

1 white sugar cube	2 ounces overproof bourbon
4 dashes Angostura bitters	1 lemon twist, for garnish
	1 orange twist, for garnish

Drop the sugar cube in an Old-Fashioned glass. Douse the cube with bitters, muddle, then add the bourbon. Add ice and stir for five or six seconds. Garnish with the lemon and orange twists.

TURN THE PAGE TO
SEE THE ILLUSTRATION
FOR THIS DRINK.

Old-Fashioned
PAGE 167

Underground America Day

COAL MINER

Long before humans lived like hobbits by choice, we headed underground for protection or to make a living by extracting precious resources from the earth. The Coal Miner from Norwegian Mats Lian is a smoke-charred, astringently bitter homage to a gritty livelihood that, like spending lots of time in subterranean darkness, isn't for the fainthearted. That said, peaty Islay scotch enhanced by the poignant coupling of two distinct amari makes for a superb choice at any depth.

1½ ounces Islay scotch
¾ ounce Campari
½ ounce Amaro Averna

¼ ounce honey syrup
2 dashes Peychaud's bitters
1 lemon twist, for garnish

Combine the scotch, Campari, Averna, honey syrup, and bitters in a double Old-Fashioned glass. Add ice and stir for five or six seconds. Garnish with the lemon twist.

National Dinosaur Day

DINO SOUR

We humans and our immediate primate ancestors have dominated the earth's fauna for a couple million years or so, which seems like an impressive achievement. But it's still 163 million fewer than the dinosaurs' unprecedented run of planetary superiority. These thunder lizards have captivated our collective imaginations since the early 1800s, when scientists first realized that their fossils weren't dragon bones but entire classes of extinct animals. Dinosaurs also have left an indelible mark on cocktail history. Eggs from chickens—the descendants of vicious predators like velociraptors—are a vital textural component of drinks such as the Dino Sour, a molasses-rich pleaser wowing palates since prehistoric times (the 1950s). In terms of their flavor profiles, white rum and blackstrap rum are as dissimilar as a pterodactyl and a tyrannosaurus, but when combined, they create a brilliantly multilayered experience with a lusciously foamy finish.

1 ounce white rum

1 ounce blackstrap rum

¾ ounce fresh lemon juice

½ ounce cane syrup

1 egg white

1 lemon wedge, for garnish

1 brandied cherry, for garnish

Combine the rums, lemon juice, cane syrup, and egg white in a shaker. Shake without ice (to emulsify the egg white) for 10 seconds, then add ice and shake vigorously. Strain into a double Old-Fashioned glass over ice. Garnish with the lemon wedge and the brandied cherry.

PICKLED SURFER

In the hierarchy of fermented foods, one fruit rules them all: the pickled cucumber. Vodka-chugging Eastern Europeans have been using pickle juice to cure hangovers for centuries, but not until the 2000s, when Brooklyn bartenders popularized the Pickleback—a shot of whiskey chased by a shot of brine—did pickles transition from folk remedy to star of the party. Around the same time, the NY Food Museum created this essential holiday. If you're looking for an even more immersive boozy-pickle experience, try the Pickled Surfer, originally served at Manhattan's Ditch Plains. It boasts not one but two full ounces of bread-and-butter pickle brine. Deeply savory and surprisingly sippable, with just enough citrus to offset its turmeric-tinged, spicy sweetness and the burn of Irish whiskey, this brackish beauty is nothing to get salty about.

2½ ounces Irish whiskey

2 ounces bread-and-butter pickle juice

¾ ounce fresh lime juice

Old Bay seasoning, to taste

2 bread-and-butter pickle slices, for garnish

1 lime wedge, for garnish

Combine the whiskey, pickle juice, and lime juice in a shaker filled with cracked ice. Shake vigorously four or five times and then dump the entire contents of the shaker into a double Old-Fashioned glass. Lightly sprinkle with Old Bay seasoning. Stab the lime wedge and pickle slices on a toothpick and use as a garnish.

TURN THE PAGE TO
SEE THE ILLUSTRATION
FOR THIS DRINK.

Pickled Surfer

PAGE 171

THE BOARDROOM

If you like your brain food brain-shaped, you're in luck because it's National Walnut Day! These weird-looking seeds have an equally quirky shell, but their hefty health benefits are nothing to gawk at. Native to Asia and North America, walnuts teem with protein and essential fatty acids, promote a healthy gut, lower blood pressure, and help to manage diabetes. Walnut liqueur has been produced in Italy for centuries as a delightful aperitif. It's not nearly as nutritious as its main ingredient, but who cares? It tastes great in cocktails. Perhaps the most elegant of these is the Boardroom, created by New York City bartender Rafa García Febles in 2014. Taking nut love up several notches with walnut liqueur and Amaro Nonino—which possess a similar bittersweet earthiness—this delightful cognac sipper is silky, decadent, and the ideal way to enjoy a full blast of walnut flavor without feeling like you're crunching down on mini petrified brains.

2 ounces cognac

½ ounce walnut liqueur

½ ounce Amaro Nonino

2 dashes Angostura bitters

1 orange twist, to express

1 walnut, for garnish

Combine the cognac, walnut liqueur, Amaro Nonino, and bitters in a mixing glass filled with cracked ice. Stir with a long-handled spoon for 30 seconds and strain into a stemmed cocktail glass. Express the zest of the orange twist along the rim of the glass and discard the twist. Garnish with the walnut.

ARTIST'S SPECIAL

According to Israeli-born American illustrator Maira Kalman, "a visit to a museum is a search for beauty, truth, and meaning in our lives." It's also a great way to convince a date that you care about beauty, truth, and meaning. Whatever your intentions, International Museum Day— coordinated by the International Council of Museums—encourages you to enjoy these vital cultural institutions by raising awareness about the role museums play in the development of society. If you don't have the time or energy to enjoy the many free activities and events held around the world today, take a minute or two to peruse a local museum's online gallery. A little bit of art appreciation goes a long way.

Don't tell the folks at New Orleans's Museum of the American Cock- tail, but alcoholic beverages usually aren't considered artistically signif- icant. A perfectly balanced, carefully crafted, intentionally multilayered potable can stir the senses, though, just like a masterful painting or sculpture. The Artist's Special, a version of which appeared in Harry MacElhone's Barflies and Cocktails *(1927), bears witness to the best kind of whiskey alchemy. Complementary bases of rye and sherry create an intriguing, citrus-embellished harmony that has inspired generations of drinksmiths. This cocktail offers enduring proof that beauty lies in the hand of the drink holder.*

1 ounce rye whiskey

1 ounce Pedro Ximénez sherry

¾ ounce fresh lemon juice

¾ ounce pomegranate syrup

Combine all ingredients in an ice-filled shaker. Shake vigorously for 25 to 30 seconds and strain into a stemmed cocktail glass.

GARDEN GROVE

Whether you live on a large rural property or in a one-window studio apartment, you can make the planet a healthier, happier place with a bit of soil and a few seeds. Plant Something Day raises awareness about the many ways in which plants enrich our lives, from removing carbon emissions from the atmosphere to adding a touch of natural beauty to any environment. One of the best parts of having plants around is being able to turn them into boozy beverages. The Garden Grove pays homage to the most delicious fruits, vegetables, herbs, and spices that you can find sprouting behind any decent cocktail bar. Featuring the agave, lemon, orange, pineapple, almond, ginger, anise, mint, and cacao plants, it's an entire ecosystem in a glass.

1¼ ounces mezcal

¾ ounce fresh lemon juice

¾ ounce ginger syrup

½ ounce curaçao

½ ounce fresh pineapple juice

¼ ounce crème de cacao

¼ ounce yellow Chartreuse

¼ ounce Fernet-Branca

¼ ounce orgeat

2 dashes Peychaud's bitters

1 lemon wedge, for garnish

1 sprig mint, for garnish

Combine the mezcal, juices, ginger syrup, curaçao, crème de cacao, yellow Chartreuse, Fernet-Branca, and orgeat in a shaker. Pour into a tall glass or mug filled two-thirds of the way with crushed ice. Float the bitters and top with more crushed ice. Garnish with the lemon wedge and sprig of mint.

BEEKEEPER'S DAUGHTER

Many people fear bees, but it's even scarier to think about what life would be like if these fuzzy, stinging insects suddenly disappeared. In 2019, international environmental charity Earthwatch Institute declared bees the most important living beings on the planet, essential for 70 percent of all agriculture. In addition to their unparalleled pollination skills, bees also regurgitate the sugary secretions of plants as honey, the most delicious and nutritious vomit-slash-sweetener around! The Beekeeper's Daughter, a creamy riff on Giuseppe Gonzales's Beekeeper, not only features a healthy helping of honey but also corn-based bourbon and herb-based absinthe, which of course benefit from bees' tireless activities. A dessert Old-Fashioned variation is a rare find, but it's got nothing on the incomparably unique ways in which bees impact the earth.

2 ounces bourbon
¼ ounce honey syrup
1 barspoon absinthe

2 dashes Angostura bitters
Hand-whipped cream,
    to top

Combine the bourbon, honey syrup, absinthe, and bitters in an Old-Fashioned glass. Add ice and stir for five or six seconds. Top with a thin layer of cream.

PIMM'S RANGOON

Fruits and veggies are nutritious in any form: fresh, frozen, juiced, or—most delectably—as ingredients in cocktails. Few drinks contain more plant-based goodness than the Pimm's Rangoon, an offshoot of the Pimm's Cup created by London bar owner James Pimm in 1823 that became an instant hit. Bolstered by Pimm's No. 1, a gin-based digestif, and spiced with ginger, this sweet and savory punch contains seven different fruits with distinctly delicious flavors. It might not be the healthiest way to get your daily dose of fruits and vegetables, but it's by far the tastiest.

2 ounces Pimm's No. 1
½ ounce ginger syrup
3 thin cucumber slices
1 lemon wedge
1 lime wedge
1 thin orange slice

1 strawberry
1 blackberry
1 brandied cherry
Sprite, to top
1 piece candied ginger,
    for garnish
1 sprig mint, for garnish

Combine the Pimm's, ginger syrup, cucumber slices, lemon wedge, lime wedge, orange slice, strawberry, blackberry, and brandied cherry in a shaker. Muddle and pour into a tall glass. Add ice and top with Sprite. Garnish with the piece of candied ginger and the mint sprig.

National Maritime Day

DEEP BLUE SEA

*Add this cocktail to your repertoire immediately. Named for its azure hue
and the depth of its flavor profile, this dry yet floral number from Michael
Madrusan makes even the longest voyage to the liquor store worth the
trouble. Like modern freighters that deliver goods faster than their predecessors, it's a marked improvement over the classic Deep Sea, with a
curiously captivating blend of violet, honeyed, zesty, and piney notes that
thankfully you won't have to cross an ocean to enjoy.*

2 ounces gin
¾ ounce Cocchi Americano

¼ ounce crème de violette
2 dashes orange bitters
1 orange twist, for garnish

Combine the gin, Cocchi Americano, crème de violette, and bitters in a
mixing glass filled with cracked ice. Stir with a long-handled spoon for
30 seconds and strain into a stemmed cocktail glass. Garnish with the
orange twist.

TURN THE PAGE TO
SEE THE ILLUSTRATION
FOR THIS DRINK.

Deep Blue Sea
PAGE 179

TORTUGA

Michelangelo, Morla, Bowser, Crush—everyone has a favorite turtle, fictional or otherwise. World Turtle Day, founded in 2000 by American Tortoise Rescue, celebrates the millions of charmingly odd, shell-covered reptiles living around the globe. Turtles don't have teeth, but they still possess dangerous jaw strength. With its 151-proof rum base, the Tortuga—the Spanish word for turtle or tortoise—has an equally impressive bite. Combining enough ingredients to rival the 356 known living species of turtles, it features palate-pleasing elements for cocktail drinkers of all stripes or scales. Drink enough of these tiki classics from Trader Vic's Book of Food & Drink *(1946) and you're guaranteed to come out of your shell, for better or (probably much) worse.*

1 ounce 151 rum	½ ounce pomegranate syrup
1 ounce light rum	½ ounce curaçao
1 ounce orange juice	¼ ounce crème de cacao, light
½ ounce fresh lime juice	1 orange wedge, for garnish
½ ounce sweet vermouth	1 brandied cherry, for garnish

Combine the rums, juices, sweet vermouth, curaçao, pomegranate syrup, and crème de cacao in a shaker. Pour into a tall glass filled two-thirds of the way with crushed ice. Add a straw and top with more crushed ice. Garnish with the orange wedge and brandied cherry.

FULL WINDSOR

"Give my people plenty of beer, good beer, and cheap beer, and you will have no revolution among them," said Queen Victoria. Always one to extoll the virtues of a tipple, the queen's personal preferences veered toward spirits, particularly the whisky she enjoyed on trips to Scotland. The Full Windsor, from Erick Castro at San Diego's Polite Provisions, shares its name with the royal house of Victoria's (renamed) descendants. This stately Bobby Burns riff features plenty of the queen's beloved scotch, as well as fruity notes of apple and Italian vermouth to satisfy a sweet tooth of empire-sized proportions. Rounded out with several herbal components, it's the perfect libation to toast every facet of one of history's most fascinating reigns.

1 ounce blended scotch
1 ounce applejack
¾ ounce sweet vermouth

¼ ounce Bénédictine
2 dashes Angostura bitters
2 dashes Peychaud's bitters
1 orange twist, for garnish

Combine the scotch, applejack, vermouth, Bénédictine, and bitters in a double Old-Fashioned glass. Add ice and stir for five or six seconds. Garnish with the orange twist.

AFRICAN FLOWER

If you think the current political climate looks tumultuous, take a gander at Africa during the middle of the 20th century. As Europe finally began releasing its colonialist grip on the continent, representatives from 30 of its nations—many newly independent and struggling to find their identities on the world stage—met on this date in 1963 to found the Organisation of African Unity. The group, now the African Union, continues to work toward eliminating foreign exploitation and tapping the full potential of all 54 independent African countries. Duke Ellington wrote his 1963 song "Fleurette Africaine" ("African Flower") after visiting the continent. That tune inspired Meeyong McFalls-Schwartz to concoct an equally sultry cocktail of the same name at Little Branch in 2008. A sensational Old-Fashioned riff elevated by stately hints of chocolaty bliss and a bittersweet finish, the African Flower is a prime example of the amazing results possible when seemingly disparate elements come together to achieve a common goal.

2 ounces bourbon

¼ ounce Amaro CioCiaro

¼ ounce crème de cacao

2 dashes orange bitters

1 orange twist, for garnish

Combine the bourbon, Amaro CioCiaro, crème de cacao, and bitters in an Old-Fashioned glass. Add ice and stir for five or six seconds. Garnish with the orange twist.

National Paper Airplane Day

PAPER PLANE

*Originally crafted in ancient China and Japan, paper airplanes have
fascinated brats and fun-loving adults for centuries. Get your nostalgia
on today by designing your own planes or organizing a paper airplane
contest with your coworkers—boss's permission optional. Force your kids
to stop TikToking—good luck—and teach them about the good old days
when most mischief, good-hearted or otherwise, occurred off-screen. Not
just a timeless toy, the Paper Plane is also one of the most iconic modern-
classic cocktails developed by Sam Ross at Milk & Honey in the mid-
2000s and ostensibly named after M.I.A.'s 2007 hit song "Paper Planes."
This summery sipper is as expertly balanced as fliers made by the finest
aeronautical origami masterminds. Its unassuming components of Bourbon, amaro, and citrus are a testament to the notion that the simplest
ideas, when executed properly, can be the most fun.*

¾ ounce bourbon

¾ ounce Amaro Nonino

¾ ounce Aperol

¾ ounce fresh lemon juice

Combine all ingredients in an ice-filled shaker. Shake vigorously for 25 to 30 seconds and strain into a stemmed cocktail glass.

National Grape Popsicle Day

ENZONI

The landscape of summertime snacks changed dramatically in 1905 when 11-year-old Frank Epperson accidentally left some water mixed with flavoring powder on his front porch during one of the coldest nights of the year. The result was the Popsicle, a trademark treat that has enthralled generations of sugar fanatics and is available in a seemingly endless array of flavors. Some of us, however, prefer our fruit-forward concoctions a little stiffer. Thanks to Vincenzo Errico, the Enzoni is more than up to the challenge. Created at Milk & Honey in 2003 as a citrusy, refreshing take on the Negroni, this brisk, bittersweet potation is ideal for grape lovers with a more refined palate. For a sweeter, fuller, juicier taste truer to the undisputed champion of the fruit-on-a-stick world, use Concord grapes. But really—like your Popsicle preferences (no judging, we swear)—it's up to you.

---

1 ounce gin
1 ounce Campari
¾ ounce fresh lemon juice

½ ounce simple syrup
5 seedless grapes
Club soda (optional)

Combine the gin, Campari, lemon juice, simple syrup, and grapes in an ice-filled shaker. Shake vigorously for 25 to 30 seconds and strain into a double Old-Fashioned glass over ice. Top with club soda if desired.

ROSS COLLINS

Beef. It's what's for dinner. When it is, this popular meat often comes in the form of a juicy, succulent burger. It's a bit of a mystery as to who first decided to slap a fistful of ground beef between two slices of bread—with most sources pointing to Connecticut's Louis Lassen in 1900—but there's no question that since then, the burger has become a worldwide favorite and a symbol of American culinary ingenuity and excess. Any pro-level fast-food connoisseur who grew up in the 1980s or '90s will tell you that the finest beverage to wash down a burger was a super-sized cup of Hi-C Orange (later known as Orange Lavaburst). That flavor has been discontinued, but the young at heart can get their citrus fix with Sam Ross's Ross Collins. Concocted at Milk & Honey in 2007, it's a tall, cheerful, effervescent blast of orange and lemon that will take you back to when your metabolism was more forgiving, with plenty of stomach-settling bitters to prepare you for another bite.

2 ounces rye whiskey	3 thin orange slices
¾ ounce fresh lemon juice	4 dashes Angostura bitters
¾ ounce simple syrup	Club soda, to top

Combine the whiskey, lemon juice, simple syrup, bitters, and two orange slices in an ice-filled shaker. Shake vigorously for 25 to 30 seconds and strain into a tall glass filled with ice. Top with club soda and garnish with the other orange slice.

TONY STARK

"I am Iron Man."

A notorious playboy before marrying his former assistant, Pepper Pots, Tony Stark was no stranger to a shindig—or a good drink. His favorite was a whiskey on the rocks, which he sips during Iron Man's *(2008) opening seconds. The infamously impatient genius probably wouldn't want to wait on a conscientiously made cocktail, but the Tony Stark from Brooklyn's Carolyn Gil is worth a few moments of anticipation. Bourbon-based, with an infusion of Chartreuse that's slightly less acerbic than Stark's wit, and rounded with soothing citrus and honey, this might be the closest you'll get to having superpowers. Perfect after a day of thwarting evil or your boss.*

1½ ounce bourbon
¾ ounce yellow Chartreuse
¾ ounce fresh lemon juice

¼ ounce honey syrup
4 dashes Angostura bitters

Combine the bourbon, Chartreuse, lemon juice, and honey syrup in an ice-filled shaker. Shake vigorously for 25 to 30 seconds and strain into a double Old-Fashioned glass over ice. Float the bitters.

MINT JULEP

When it first emerged in Virginia in the late 1700s, the prototype version of this drink— commonly made with gin, brandy, or rum—was used almost exclusively for medicinal purposes. Achieving its final, bourbon-forward form in the first decades of the 19th century, it became less associated with physicians than with having a good time. The cocktail commonly was prescribed by whiskey-loving bartenders—several of whom, including Richmond's Jasper Crouch, received the title "Master of Mint Juleps"—who often recommended one as a pre-breakfast pick-me-up. If you have sampled the official drink of the Kentucky Derby, you know there's never a wrong time for a little muddle-and-sip action.

---

1 handful fresh mint leaves
2½ ounces bourbon

¼ ounce simple syrup
1 white sugar cube
1 sprig mint, for garnish

Gently squeeze mint leaves in your hand (to release fragrance) and drop them in a traditional silver julep cup. Add the bourbon, simple syrup, and sugar cube to the cup. Muddle lightly to break up the sugar cube (but not bruise the mint) and fill the cup two-thirds of the way with crushed ice. Stir with a swizzle stick, then add a straw and top with more crushed ice. Garnish with the mint sprig.

What You Think Upon Grows Day

NINTH WONDER

Created to honor the work of author and positive-thinking pioneer Norman Vincent Peale, What You Think Upon Grows Day compels us not only to increase and harness the positive vibes we create but also to act on them. In the immortal words of The Rocky Horror Picture Show's *Dr. Frank N. Furter, "Don't dream it, be it." If you're going to utilize the power of positive thinking fully, why not go big? Like, Seven Wonders of the World big. After all, even an undertaking as insanely complex and impressive as the Great Pyramid of Giza had to spring from the mind of one optimistic person. Many have debated which, if any, newer human construction—such as the Eiffel Tower—should take the title of Eighth Wonder, but San Diego's Erick Castro already has claimed the next spot in line. His Ninth Wonder is a gorgeous equal-parts blend of sweet, spicy, and chocolaty elements with superior architecture that belies its simple— yet still elegant—presentation.*

¾ ounce tequila blanco

¾ ounce Ancho Reyes

¾ ounce crème de cacao

¾ ounce fresh lime juice

Combine all ingredients in an ice-filled shaker. Shake vigorously for 25 to 30 seconds and strain into a stemmed cocktail glass.

JUNE

				1	2	3
				DARE DAY Electric Current Fizz	INTERNATIONAL SEX WORKERS DAY Adult Film Star	WORLD BICYCLE DAY Bicycle Thief
4	5	6	7	8	9	10
WORLD COGNAC DAY Champs-Élysées	NATIONAL MOONSHINE DAY Heartbreaker	NATIONAL LONG ISLAND ICED TEA DAY Dead Bastard	NATIONAL CHOCOLATE ICE CREAM DAY Silver 19th Century	NATIONAL NAME YOUR POISON DAY Arsenic & Old Lace	DONALD DUCK DAY Fluffy Duck	HERBS AND SPICES DAY The Ancient Mariner
11	12	13	14	15	16	17
CORN ON THE COB DAY High Bridge	INTERNATIONAL CACHAÇA DAY Strawberry Caipirinha	WORLD GIN DAY Gimlet	WORLD CUCUMBER DAY Pepino	GLOBAL WIND DAY Chicago Cocktail	BLOOMSDAY James Joyce	WORLD CROC DAY Killer Croc
18	19	20	21	22	23	24
GO FISHING DAY Offshore Fisherman	WORLD MARTINI DAY Tuxedo No. 2	MIDSUMMER Summer's Day	DAYLIGHT APPRECIATION DAY Sunflower	NATIONAL KISSING DAY Bee's Kiss	PINK FLAMINGO DAY Flamingo #2	NATIONAL FAIRY DAY Death in the Afternoon
25	26	27	28	29	30	
GLOBAL BEATLES DAY Brandy Alexander	FORGIVENESS DAY Shake	NATIONAL ORANGE BLOSSOM DAY Orange Blossom No. 3	PAUL BUNYAN DAY Lumberjack	CAMERA DAY Photo Bomb	ASTEROID DAY Starboy	

ELECTRIC CURRENT FIZZ

Ask a crush out for a drink, finish a project you've been putting off, prank-call an old frenemy. Whatever you choose, keep it (relatively) safe and (mostly) legal. Dares come in all shapes and forms, including the liquid variety. At first glance, the Electric Current Fizz, first recorded in 1895 by George Kappeler as a can't-fail hangover alleviator, seems tame. It's basically a traditional Gin Fizz, except the egg yolk, instead of being discarded, is placed in a separate shot glass and garnished with hot sauce, Worcestershire sauce, salt, and pepper for immediate, raw consumption. To make it slightly more unappetizing, the drink is supposed to be consumed only early in the morning to offset the worst effects of the previous night's revelries. Wake your friends with a round of these to see who among them is a true gastronomic adventurer. Just remember that if you're daring someone to drink something, you'd better be prepared to partake as well!

1 egg
2 ounces gin
¼ ounce fresh lemon juice
¼ ounce simple syrup
Club soda, to top

Tabasco sauce, to taste
Worcestershire sauce, to taste
1 pinch salt
1 pinch cracked black pepper

Separate the egg white and the egg yolk. Place the egg white in a shaker and the egg yolk in a shot glass. Add the gin, lemon juice, and simple syrup to the shaker. Shake without ice (to emulsify the egg white) for 10 seconds, then add ice and shake vigorously. Strain into a fizz glass and top with club soda. Season the shot glass with Tabasco sauce, Worcestershire sauce, salt, and pepper. Shoot the contents of the shot glass as quickly as possible.

International Sex Workers Day

ADULT FILM STAR

International Sex Workers Day, celebrated since 1976, draws attention to the inhumane conditions and violence that too many members of the adult industry suffer on a regular basis, as well as calling out the hypocrisy surrounding a business that many support on some level, even if we don't admit it publicly. Though they often face the same difficulties as their mainstream colleagues, many adult film actors have transcended the negativity surrounding sex work and achieve mainstream acceptance. Created in Los Angeles as a nod to that city's unofficial designation as America's porn capital, the Adult Film Star packs a shocking amount of sexiness into its curvy, wine glass frame. Backed by supple demerara syrup, a splash of sultry Licor 43, and an unabashed blast of cinnamon spice, this titillating Daiquiri spin-off is one indulgence you won't need to keep private.

2 ounces white rum

1 ounce fresh lime juice

¾ ounce demerara syrup

¼ ounce Licor 43

1 pinch freshly grated cinnamon

1 sprig fresh mint, for garnish

Combine the rum, lime juice, and demerara syrup in an ice-filled shaker. Shake vigorously for 25 to 30 seconds and strain into a large wine glass filled with cracked ice. Top with Licor 43 and cinnamon. Garnish with the mint sprig.

BICYCLE THIEF

Bicycle theft is almost as common as bicycles themselves. After you're done traveling for work, sport, or pleasure, remember to lock up your bike. Thankfully, the Bicycle Thief, a delightfully fizzy sipper created by Dutch Kills' Abraham Hawkins and Zachary Gelnaw-Rubin, will steal only your sobriety. This grapefruit-heavy Collins riff is as brisk as a downhill ride with the wind in your face. Its bright, subtly bitter finish feels as satisfying as finishing a stage of the Tour de France.

Though the Bicycle Thief is a relatively low-alcohol tipple, it's still a smart idea (and far more refreshing) to enjoy one or two of these only after a long bike ride.

---

1 ounce gin or mezcal

1 ounce Campari

1½ ounces fresh grapefruit juice

½ ounce fresh lemon juice

½ ounce simple syrup

Club soda, to top

1 thin orange slice,
   for garnish

Combine the spirit, Campari, juices, and simple syrup in a shaker. Whip shake (no ice) and pour into a tall glass filled with ice. Top with club soda and garnish with the orange slice.

CHAMPS-ÉLYSÉES

The only spirit-centric beverage that might be more French than a glass of cognac is the Champs-Élysées, named after the iconic Parisian thoroughfare that runs from the Place de la Concorde to the Arc de Triomphe. First appearing in Nina Toye and Arthur H. Adair's 1925 Drinks—Long & Short *and updated by Joseph Schwartz at Milk & Honey in 2003, this exquisitely herbaceous and refreshing Sidecar riff stands out not only for the eloquence of its cognac base but also for the addition of green Chartreuse, the famously mystical and potent French liqueur. If you're looking to explore cognac's complex tableau in cocktail form, this one's a winner.*

1½ ounces cognac

¾ ounce fresh lemon juice

½ ounce green Chartreuse

½ ounce simple syrup

2 dashes Angostura bitters

1 lemon twist, for garnish

Combine the cognac, lemon juice, Chartreuse, simple syrup, and bitters in an ice-filled shaker. Shake vigorously for 25 to 30 seconds and strain into a stemmed cocktail glass. Garnish with the lemon twist.

National Moonshine Day

HEARTBREAKER

As long as liquor laws have existed, enterprising criminals have ignored them. National Moonshine Day celebrates America's most notorious spirit: an illegally distilled, overproof corn whiskey that reached peak production during the dark years of Prohibition. Back then, a trip to the moonshiner's was often the only way to remedy a thirst—by setting one's throat on fire with the unregulated booze. Unlike the stereotypical gasoline-flavored swill produced by dentally challenged misanthropes in the woods, today's (legal) moonshine usually comes from small-batch distilleries and has a smooth, caramel-forward flavor that lends itself nicely to a variety of classy beverages. Foremost among these is the Heartbreaker from Stillhouse, a bright, bubbly, fruity, quintessentially summery party favor that hardly resembles your great-grandparents' canned hooch. But you'd better believe that, if they could have laid hands on one of these beauties, they would have quaffed it down in a second, legality be damned.

1½ ounces moonshine, such as
    Stillhouse
½ ounce fresh lime juice

½ ounce agave nectar
Prosecco, to top
6 raspberries

Combine the moonshine, lime juice, agave nectar, and five raspberries in an ice-filled shaker. Shake vigorously for 25 to 30 seconds and strain into a champagne flute. Top with prosecco and garnish with another raspberry.

National Long Island Iced Tea Day

DEAD BASTARD

If you're over the age of 25 and can afford to spend more than $5 at happy hour, stop ordering Long Island Iced Teas. Please, we're begging you. These sugary concoctions—traditionally a blend of vodka, gin, tequila, white rum, triple sec, and Coca-Cola—have been ruining livers and human decency since 1972, when New Yorker Robert "Rosebud" Butt unleashed them on unsuspecting citizens of his native island. If you're still dead set on packing the absolute most alcohol into a single beverage, you have much tastier ways to do it. Enter, if you dare, the appropriately named Dead Bastard, a stronger bedmate of the already fiendish Suffering Bastard. Featuring a flavorful combination of four spirits, both brown and white, this potentially hazardous walloper is rendered not only unobtrusive but also shockingly pleasant with the addition of fresh citrus, club soda, and the spicy, digestive properties of ginger, for which you will give thanks. But only if you think you can handle it.

¾ ounce bourbon

¾ ounce cognac

¾ ounce white rum

¾ ounce gin

¾ ounce ginger syrup

½ ounce fresh lime juice

2 dashes Angostura bitters

1 piece candied ginger,
    for garnish

Combine the bourbon, cognac, rum, gin, ginger syrup, lime juice, and bitters in a shaker. Whip shake (no ice) and pour into a tall glass filled with ice. Top with club soda and garnish with the candied ginger.

National Chocolate Ice Cream Day

SILVER 19TH CENTURY

Chocolate and ice cream is a match made in dessert heaven—or, more accurately, Naples, Italy, in 1692, when recipes for chocolate ices first appeared in Antonio Latini's The Modern Steward. *In his 1775 treatise,* De sorbetti, *Italian physician Filippo Baldini touted chocolate ice cream as a cure-all for medical conditions such as gout and scurvy. That's some amazing wishful thinking because the only thing ice cream is guaranteed to improve is a bad mood, just like the Silver 19th Century. A frothy play on a drink from Brian Miller that first graced lips at New York City's Pegu Club in 2006, its effortless mingling of bourbon, crème de cacao, sweet vermouth, and egg white results in a rich mouthfeel and an even more luscious cocoa-flavored finish. As with most kinds of freezing-cold chocolaty magic, this one hits just the right spot.*

1½ ounces bourbon

¾ ounce crème de cacao

¾ ounce sweet vermouth

¾ ounce fresh lemon juice

1 egg white

 Combine all ingredients in a shaker. Shake without ice (to emulsify the egg white) for 10 seconds, then add ice and shake vigorously. Strain into a stemmed cocktail glass.

National Name Your Poison Day

ARSENIC & OLD LACE

Decisions, decisions, decisions. From figuring out what to wear to choosing which direction to swipe on dating apps to determining who to vote for, our days are filled with countless choices. National Name Your Poison Day recognizes these big and small judgments and acknowledges that, while some decisions seem like no-win situations, we eventually must make them, all the same. If you've been wrestling mentally with a seemingly impossible dilemma, today's a perfect time to take a deep breath and make a choice, even if it leaves a bad taste in your mouth. For cocktail enthusiasts, settling on what to drink can result in a truly time-consuming, head-scratching conundrum (as many an impatient bartender will tell you). You could do a lot worse than picking an Arsenic & Old Lace. Named after a play in which two homicidal elderly women poison their guests with tainted elderberry wine, the drink does have a floral component—of the nonlethal variety, of course. With additional hints of juniper, anise, and orange zest, plenty of elements will appease even the most indecisive palate. Just don't plan to make any legitimate decisions before firing up the old mixing glass because this one's boozy.

---

2 ounces gin
¾ ounce dry vermouth

¼ ounce crème de violette
1 barspoon absinthe
1 orange twist, for garnish

Combine the gin, vermouth, crème de violette, and absinthe in a mixing glass filled with cracked ice. Stir with a long-handled spoon for 30 seconds and strain into a stemmed cocktail glass. Garnish with the orange twist.

TURN THE PAGE TO
SEE THE ILLUSTRATION
FOR THIS DRINK.

FLUFFY DUCK

Apologies to Daffy, Count Duckula, and Scrooge McDuck, but in the hierarchy of cartoon birds, The Donald is still top duck. Making his debut on this date in the 1934 short film, The Wise Little Hen, *Donald Fauntleroy Duck has been a mainstay of the Disney animated universe, where his hijinks and irritable moods are just as famous as his nearly unintelligible speech. Donald will forever be the poster bird for curmudgeons everywhere. Modeled after the soft-feathered American Pekin duck, Donald's plumage is most likely quite fuzzy. But his ruffles are no match for the sublime silkiness of the Fluffy Duck, a frothy concoction that first took flight in the Netherlands in the middle of the 20th century. Boasting a rich, custardy texture thanks to the inclusion of advocaat, a traditional Dutch eggnog infused with brandy, this lighthearted sipper is brightened by notes of juniper and orange. Strong enough to inspire a good bit of mischief, a few rounds of these will have you waddling and muttering Donald's trademark phrase: "Oh boy, oh boy, oh boy!"*

1½ ounces dry gin
1½ ounces advocaat
1 ounce orange juice

½ ounce Cointreau
Club soda, to top
1 thin orange slice, for garnish

Combine the gin, advocaat, orange juice, and Cointreau in an ice-filled shaker. Shake and strain over ice into a tall glass. Top with club soda. Garnish with the orange slice.

TURN THE PAGE TO
SEE THE ILLUSTRATION
FOR THIS DRINK.

Herbs and Spices Day

THE ANCIENT MARINER

Embrace the aromatic, flavor freaks, because today's holiday is a zesty one! Herbs and spices are vital components in hundreds of cocktails, especially in the form of St. Elizabeth Allspice Dram, prized by bartenders for intense notes of cinnamon, clove, and nutmeg. A product of Jamaica, the liqueur has been used by tropical-minded drinks pioneers for decades to add depth and dryness to sweet and citrusy drinks, such as Jeff "Beachbum" Berry's Ancient Mariner, which he first concocted at New Orleans's Latitude 29. A rich and complex split-rum sipper, this modern tiki classic has an unusually dry yet oh-so-refreshing finish accentuated by an herbaceous blast of fresh mint. Further proof that there's never a dull moment—or sip—when herbs and spices are involved.

1 ounce aged rum

1 ounce Jamaican amber rum

¾ ounce fresh lime juice

½ ounce fresh grapefruit juice

½ ounce simple syrup

¼ ounce St. Elizabeth Allspice Dram

3 or 4 fresh mint leaves

1 lime wedge, for garnish

1 sprig mint, for garnish

Combine the rums, juices, simple syrup, allspice dram, and mint leaves in a shaker. Muddle gently and pour into a double Old-Fashioned glass filled two-thirds of the way with crushed ice. Add a straw and top with more crushed ice. Garnish with the lime wedge and mint sprig.

HIGH BRIDGE

Lots of festivities can be a little corny, but today's takes the prize—or, more specifically, the cob.

No time for cooking your cobs? No problem! Getting your fix is as easy as picking up a bottle of straight corn whiskey, a barrel-aged cousin of bourbon that contains at least 80 percent corn in its mash bill. With notes of oak, vanilla, and of course corn, it's great for sipping or as the base in a cocktail such as like Lucinda Sterling's High Bridge, which first cropped up at Manhattan's Middle Branch in 2012. Backed by apple brandy, fresh lemon juice, and honey, it's like being able to enjoy an entire farm with every sip. You know, minus the animals, fertilizer, hay, and whatnot.

---

1 ounce Mellow Corn, or comparable straight corn whiskey

1 ounce applejack

¾ ounce fresh lemon juice

¾ ounce honey syrup

Combine all ingredients in an ice-filled shaker. Shake vigorously for 25 to 30 seconds and strain over ice into a double Old-Fashioned glass.

STRAWBERRY CAIPIRINHA

To avoid upsetting all 212 million Brazilians, let's set the record straight: Cachaça is not rum. Both spirits derive from sugarcane, but rum is made mostly from cane byproducts such as molasses, whereas cachaça is produced by fermenting fresh juice. It's also significantly older, dating to the early 1500s, when Portuguese explorers brought sugarcane cuttings to Brazil from the Madeira Islands.

Cachaça's brilliant flavor profile shines best in Brazil's national cocktail, the Caipirinha. Allegedly invented by São Paolo farmers in the 19th century to combat the common cold, this sweetly energizing potable has nothing ordinary about it. Refreshing, funky, and romantic, it's the closest you'll get to an authentic Brazilian experience without going there. Add strawberries to take your glass of fruity perfection to even greater heights.

2 ounces cachaça
5 lime wedges

¾ ounce simple syrup
1 brown sugar cube
2 halved strawberries

Combine all ingredients in a shaker. Muddle thoroughly and fill the shaker with cracked ice. Shake four or five times and pour entire contents of the shaker into a double Old-Fashioned glass.

GIMLET

Soccer (or football, innit) is probably England's most popular cultural export, but gin tastes far better. Emerging in the late 17th century as an often home-distilled version of the Dutch medicinal liquor genever, the juniper-infused spirit quickly became more popular for its ability to get a party going than for its purported health benefits, so much so that gin was identified as one of the main culprits for London's stunted population growth in the 1700s. Unlike their potentially harmful or even deadly predecessors, such as the turpentine-infused "mother's ruin," today's gins—celebrated worldwide on the second Saturday of June—use a wide variety of botanicals for a sipping experience that's delightfully herbaceous and floral and (probably) won't make you go blind! The cocktail world owes the creation of many of its most enduring classics to gin, specifically the illegally manufactured "bathtub" variety made by booze-loving entrepreneurs during Prohibition. Though bartenders developed thousands of creative recipes to mask the notoriously harsh spirit, they more often than not relied on a straightforward blend of lime and sugar, better known as a Gimlet, to get the job done. Instead of hiding the unique properties of the thousands of gin brands available today, the modern Gimlet is ideal for showcasing the most interesting characteristics of each one.

2 ounces gin	¾ ounce simple syrup
1 ounce fresh lime juice	1 lime wedge, for garnish

Combine the gin, lime juice, and simple syrup in an ice-filled shaker. Shake vigorously for 25 to 30 seconds and strain into a stemmed cocktail glass. Garnish with the lime wedge.

World Cucumber Day

PEPINO

It's hard to hate a cucumber. These juicy, crunchy, nutrient-packed fruits (or veggies or gourds, depending on how you're feeling taxonomically) originated in South Asia and are cultivated just about everywhere now due to their seemingly endless versatility. Started by the folks from the famously cucumber-friendly Hendrick's Gin Distillery, World Cucumber Day celebrates the many facets of everyone's favorite cylindrical plant. Bite down on a crunchy pickle, sip on a cucumber-enhanced smoothie or tonic, or put some cooling cucumber over your eyes and enjoy a nice snooze. There's no bad way to get your cuke on. Even though a gin company started World Cucumber Day, it's perfectly acceptable to enjoy the cucumber's bright, inclusive flavor with just about any spirit. Sorry, Hendricks! One of the tastiest of these potations is Michael Madrusan's Pepino—the Spanish word for cucumber—served at Little Branch since 2009. Pleasantly vegetal and frothy with a spicy-sweet finish, this down-to-earth Tequila Sour riff will make you want to plant a garden of your own or simply order another round. If agave isn't your thing or you want to stay true to the holiday's origins, use gin instead.

---

2 ounces tequila
¾ ounce fresh lemon juice
¾ ounce simple syrup

4 thin cucumber slices
1 egg white
1 pinch cayenne pepper

Combine the tequila, lemon juice, simple syrup, three cucumber slices, and egg white in a shaker. Shake without ice (to emulsify the egg white) for 10 seconds, then add ice and shake vigorously. Strain into a stemmed cocktail glass. Top with cayenne pepper and garnish with another cucumber slice.

CHICAGO COCKTAIL

Created by the Global Wind Energy Council, Global Wind Day encourages consumers to learn about the past, present, and, most importantly, future of a technology that—unlike a fictional Spanish buffoon fighting inanimate objects—has the potential to do some real good. Recently, many of America's biggest cities have taken great strides to increase the use of renewable wind energy, with Chicago predictably leading the way. In 2017, the Windy City's top brass pledged that wind would power 100 percent of their municipal government buildings by 2025. An achievement of that magnitude requires an equally impressive toast, and the Chicago Cocktail, a 19th-century favorite of unknown origins, is more than up to the task. A cheerful, boozy whirlwind of rye, vermouth, and curaçao harnessed by a generous dollop of bubbly, this breezy and efficient crowd-pleaser is nothing to get blustery about.

1 ounce rye whiskey
½ ounce sweet vermouth
½ ounce curaçao

1 dash orange bitters
Champagne, to top
1 orange twist, for garnish

Combine the whiskey, vermouth, curaçao, and bitters in a mixing glass filled with cracked ice. Stir with a long-handled spoon for 30 seconds and strain into a stemmed cocktail glass. Top with champagne and garnish with the orange twist.

JAMES JOYCE

It's rare that people honor a fictional character with a celebratory day, especially the protagonist of a novel that many consider one of the most difficult pieces of literature ever written. But Bloomsday, founded to commemorate the exploits of Irish wanderer Leopold Bloom in James Joyce's notorious masterpiece Ulysses, *strangely enough has become a global phenomenon. First held in Dublin 1954 on the 50th anniversary of the book's events, the festivities include cultural activities, readings and theater performances based on the novel and Joyce's other works, early 1900s cosplay, and horse-drawn carriage rides. Which sounds like a lot more fun than slogging through a 750-page tome declared virtually unreadable by more than a few great wordsmiths. An Irish whiskey-based Last Word spin-off, the James Joyce also features green Chartreuse from France, where Joyce wrote many of his most enduring works, including* Ulysses. *Balanced by woodsy, sweet, and sour flavors, it's a potent blend that will have you thinking in stream-of-consciousness (one of Joyce's preferred literary techniques) in no time.*

¾ ounce Irish whiskey

¾ ounce green Chartreuse

¾ ounce maraschino liqueur

¾ ounce fresh lemon juice

1 brandied cherry,
for garnish

 Combine the whiskey, Chartreuse, maraschino liqueur, and lemon juice in an ice-filled shaker. Shake vigorously for 25 to 30 seconds and strain into a stemmed cocktail glass. Garnish with the brandied cherry.

KILLER CROC

When the footwear company Crocs released its first foam clogs in 2002, it seemed like just another fad. But the clunky-shaped, many-hued shoes have defied conventional fashion wisdom for years, with more than 300 million colorful pairs sold to an increasingly rabid customer base. Crocodiles generally aren't known for their cuddliness, which makes them a hilariously ironic mascot for Crocs' lovably squishy products. Likewise, the gin-based Killer Croc, which first appeared on the popular Superhero Cocktails *blog in 2017, gives off ferocious vibes that don't exactly line up with its welcoming flavor profile. Foamy, sweet, and undeniably funky, the highly unusual combination of bitter herbs and muskmelon has converted many skeptical imbibers who, like former Crocs haters, may have been put off by its forebodingly bright appearance. Named for the DC Comics supervillain, this neon-green hero of ingenuity is definitely worth a quaff.*

---

1 ounce gin	¾ ounce fresh lime juice
1 ounce Midori	⅛ ounce green Chartreuse
	1 egg white

Combine all ingredients in a shaker. Shake without ice for 10 seconds (to emulsify the egg white), then add ice and shake vigorously. Strain into a stemmed cocktail glass.

OFFSHORE FISHERMAN

Unless you live in the middle of a desert, there's a good chance you're near a body of water where fish reside. If that's the case, grab a rod and reel today and go catch a few of the slimy little buggers! Fishing is a notoriously challenging activity, but it also can be a great bonding experience and one of the best ways to disconnect from the bustle of daily life. That's what Go Fishing Day is all about.

A day battling the waves in search of an elusive catch requires an extra-hearty potable, such as the Offshore Fisherman from Justin Bazar. This maritime Manhattan riff boasts a hefty helping of Italian digestif Amaro Ramazzotti to settle even the most seasick stomach, with bright notes of scurvy-fighting lemon and a slightly salty finish that's more refreshing than a cold spray of seawater against the face. This impressively balanced sipper is strong enough to have the grouchiest sea dogs singing shanties in no time.

1½ ounces rye whiskey	1 small peel of lemon
1½ ounces Amaro Ramazzotti	1 pinch salt
	1 lemon twist, for garnish

Combine the rye, Amaro Ramazzotti, lemon peel, and salt in a mixing glass. Muddle and strain into a double Old-Fashioned glass. Add ice and stir for five to six seconds. Garnish with the lemon twist.

TUXEDO NO. 2

There's no wrong way to enjoy a Martini: sweet, dry, dirty, perfect, or, according to playwright Noël Coward, "filling a glass with gin then waving it in the general direction of Italy."

No cocktail has inspired more variations, spin-offs, and not-so-subtle homages than the Martini, many of which have become just as legendary. One of the most interesting of these and still faithful to its forebear is the Tuxedo No. 2, which originally appeared as the Turf Cocktail in the 1900 edition of Harry Johnson's Bartender's Manual. *Heavy on the gin and on the drier side, but with just the right amount of floral and herbaceous elements to ramp things up, it's the perfect palate-expanding option for spirit-forward explorers or Martini traditionalists looking to escape their comfort zone.*

2¼ ounces dry gin	2 dashes orange bitters
½ ounce dry vermouth	1 lemon twist, for garnish
¼ ounce maraschino liqueur	1 brandied cherry,
1 dash absinthe	for garnish

Combine the gin, vermouth, maraschino liqueur, absinthe, and bitters in a mixing glass filled with cracked ice. Stir with a long-handled spoon for 30 seconds and strain into a stemmed cocktail glass. Garnish with the lemon twist and brandied cherry.

SUMMER'S DAY

For thousands of years, residents of the Northern Hemisphere have marked the summer solstice, known as Midsummer in many European countries, with all manner of merrymaking, including sun dances, fertility feasts, and flowery rituals. In pre-Christian Scandinavia, pagan priests lit massive bonfires to boost solar energy and to destroy evil spirits. It's probably not the best idea to set gigantic fires, but Midsummer's message is clear: Get out and have some fun (while avoiding the aforementioned demons). Nothing says "summer" like a refreshing, citrusy, frothy, bubbly, and bright cocktail, and no drink exemplifies all of those adjectives quite like the Summer's Day, a slightly fruitier and floral Gin Sour riff created by Michael McIlroy at Milk & Honey in 2010. It'll make you wish it were Midsummer every day, and, once you master this relatively easy-to-mix fountain of flavor, it can be!

2 ounces gin	3 thin orange slices
¼ ounce fresh lemon juice	1 dash Angostura bitters
¼ ounce simple syrup	1 egg white
	Club soda, to top

Combine the gin, lemon juice, simple syrup, two orange slices, bitters, and egg white in a shaker. Shake without ice (to emulsify the egg white) for 10 seconds, then add ice and shake vigorously. Strain into a tall glass filled with ice. Top with club soda and garnish with the other orange slice.

SUNFLOWER

Assuming you aren't a vampire—and if you are: apologies for the lack of blood-based drinks in this book—there's a good chance you're going to feel extra lovely today. On June 21, the sun spends more time in the sky of the Northern Hemisphere than on any other day of the year. Take advantage of the additional daylight by going outside, soaking up a few peak rays, and giving yourself a much-needed blast of vitamin D and the mood-boosting serotonin that comes with it.

Longer daylight also means more time for day drinking! Add some flair to your late lunch or early happy hour (we're not judging) with Sam Ross's spectacular Sunflower. A brighter and, yes, sunnier take on a Corpse Reviver No. 2, this floral and sour gin-based tipple is more summery than a post-8:30 PM sunset. It's important to know your limits when subjecting yourself to the sun's power, and the same goes for this light-hearted yet sneakily potent refresher.

¾ ounce gin

¾ ounce elderflower liqueur

¾ ounce Cointreau

¾ ounce fresh lemon juice

1 dash absinthe

1 lemon twist, for garnish

Combine the gin, elderflower liqueur, Cointreau, and lemon juice in an ice-filled shaker. Shake vigorously for 25 to 30 seconds and strain into a stemmed cocktail glass. Garnish with the lemon twist.

National Kissing Day

BEE'S KISS

Celebrate today by settling in for a nice long smooch session with your partner. If that's not an option, live vicariously through rom-coms or show your classy side by saying hello to acquaintances with a European-style peck on both cheeks. Don't try that last one with your boss, though. Debuting in 1946 in Trader Vic's Book of Food and Drink, *the Bee's Kiss is pure romance in a glass. Smooth and supple, effortlessly sweet and dreamy, this delightful dessert tipple is perfect after a meal or a long kiss with someone special. As a bonus, if you decide to go in for another round of making out after drinking one of these, be prepared for some lovably hilarious cream mustaches.*

---

2 ounces aged rum

¾ ounce heavy cream

¼ ounce honey syrup

1 pinch freshly grated nutmeg, for garnish

Combine the rum, cream, and honey syrup in an ice-filled shaker. Shake vigorously for 25 to 30 seconds and strain into a stemmed cocktail glass. Garnish with the nutmeg.

Pink Flamingo Day

FLAMINGO #2

Flamingos are weird. They eat upside-down, have an unusually low body density, feed their young a super gross mixture of blood and fat cells, and spend their days hopping around on inhospitable alkaline lakes. Despite all that, the awkwardly beautiful birds have been pop-culture fixtures for decades, appearing on preppy clothing, tiki drinkware, and most famously as plastic lawn ornaments dreamed up in 1957 by Don Featherstone, an employee of Union Products in Leominster, Massachusetts. In addition to populating suburban front yards, flamingos have made an impact in bars around the globe. The national bird of the Bahamas has shared its name with dozens of rosy-hued, mostly tropical potations, few as old or as tasty as the Flamingo #2. This puckeringly pink, Prohibition-era soother has a history as mysterious—because no one knows who invented it or if a "#1" preceded it—as the origins of the flamingo's many strange behaviors. A delightfully rich mélange of rum, pineapple, and pomegranate, it might be the yummiest bird standing on one (glass) leg.

2 ounces white rum

1½ ounces fresh pineapple juice

½ ounce fresh lime juice

¼ ounce pomegranate syrup

Combine all ingredients in an ice-filled shaker. Shake vigorously for 25 to 30 seconds and strain into a stemmed cocktail glass.

DEATH IN THE AFTERNOON

Transport yourself to Fairyland today by diving into magic-inspired classics such as Peter Pan *or* A Midsummer Night's Dream. *If you're dead set on seeing a fairy in real life, good luck, but maybe plan a trip to Iceland. Nearly half the population there claims to have interacted with supernatural creatures. Throughout history, those wishing to tap into other realms of consciousness often have relied on alcohol as a spiritual guide. No modern liquor has caused more alleged interactions with supernatural creatures than absinthe, itself often called "the Green Fairy." Though the spirit's shamanistic potential is limited at best, it has replenished the creative juices of countless artists and writers, including Ernest Hemingway, who invented the potent Death in the Afternoon in the 1930s. Simple yet transformative, this bitter and bubbly blast of absinthe and champagne was a favorite of the novelist, who recommended drinking three to five in one sitting. That's easily enough booze to send you on the road to the fairy realm—or a liver transplant.*

1 ounce absinthe	Champagne, chilled

Pour the absinthe into a champagne flute or a stemmed cocktail glass. Top with champagne until sufficiently milky. Sip slowly.

BRANDY ALEXANDER

If you've never heard of the Beatles, let me be the first to welcome you to Earth.

The Beatles marked their later years with the increasing use of hallu-cinogens. ("Lucy in the Sky with Diamonds," anyone?) But the lads still enjoyed a night at the pub. A notorious lightweight, John somewhat surprisingly favored a Brandy Alexander, a pre-Prohibition favorite dating at least to 1916. His fondness for the creamy concoction caused the drink's resurgence in the 1970s, particularly in New York City bars. As an indulgent boozy dessert, it's hard to beat, but opt for something lighter if you're trying to party like a rock and roll legend.

1½ ounces cognac

1 ounce dark crème de cacao

1 ounce heavy cream

1 pinch freshly grated nutmeg,
   for garnish

Combine the cognac, crème de cacao, and heavy cream in an ice-filled cocktail glass. Shake vigorously for 25 to 30 seconds and strain into a stemmed cocktail glass. Garnish with the nutmeg.

Forgiveness Day

SHAKE

Getting done dirty is a fact of life. But unresolved anger toward those who have wronged you can lead to future altercations and tons of unhealthy stress. As Forgiveness Day indicates, the far more liberating course of action is to bury the hatchet (metaphorically, of course). "Kiss and make up" is a nice euphemism, but maybe start with a less invasive gesture when reconciling, like a handshake. If you're feeling extra magnanimous, a bespoke drink also goes a long way toward squashing a beef, which is where the Shake comes in. A style of cocktail first described in W. C. Whitfield's Here's How: Mixed Drinks *(1941), it's basically a combination of any liquor (or liqueur) backed by fresh lime juice and simple syrup. Effortlessly easy to make and able to bring out the best in whatever spirit your former adversary chooses, it makes forgiveness that much easier to swallow.*

---

2 ounces spirit of choice

1 ounce fresh lime juice

¾ ounce simple syrup

1 lime wedge, for garnish

Combine the spirit, lime juice, and simple syrup in an ice-filled shaker. Shake vigorously for 25 to 30 seconds and strain into a stemmed cocktail glass. Garnish with the lime wedge.

National Orange Blossom Day

ORANGE BLOSSOM NO. 3

When people mention oranges, usually they're talking about the fruit or its juices. But take one look or sniff at an orange tree's flowers, and you'll realize quickly that the plant has far more to offer than just vitamin C. Aesthetically pleasing and alluringly fragrant, orange blossoms and their derivatives, such as orange blossom water, are found in numerous dishes and teas. A staple of Middle Eastern cuisine, orange blossom water has been used in a handful of classic cocktails as well, the most infamous being the Ramos Gin Fizz (page 91). But if you're looking for an orange fix of unprecedented proportions, try an Orange Blossom No. 3, the descendant of fruity coolers that have been turning citrus heads onto the joys of gin and juice long before Snoop Dogg hit the scene. Fragrant, sweet, zesty, and featuring ingredients derived from orange juice, orange skin, and, most importantly, orange flowers, it's the closest you'll get to drinking an entire orange tree—minus the bark, leaves, and pollinating insects, of course.

2 ounces orange juice
1½ ounces gin
½ ounce orange liqueur

2 dashes orange blossom water
1 dash orange bitters
1 dash Angostura bitters
1 orange twist, for garnish

 Combine the orange juice, gin, orange liqueur, orange blossom water, and bitters in an ice-filled shaker. Shake vigorously for 25 to 30 seconds and strain over ice into a double Old-Fashioned glass. Garnish with the orange twist.

LUMBERJACK

Only in America can the most famous member of a real profession be a seven-foot-tall fictional behemoth with a massive blue ox for a pet and a mythical backstory created to sell trees. Paul Bunyan's appetite for food and drink was as legendary as his tree-chopping skills. Though it might have taken an entire distillery to satisfy his cravings, one or two rounds of the Lumberjack should soothe any normal-sized imbiber. With origins as murky as Bunyan's, the best versions of this Fix riff call for fortifying cognac, warming apple brandy, and a hearty dollop of maple syrup. Perfect for relaxing the body after a long day of ax work and loosening the tongue around a campfire, it's the stuff of which legends are made.

1½ ounces cognac
¾ ounce fresh lemon juice
½ ounce applejack

½ ounce maple syrup
4 dashes Angostura bitters
1 pinch freshly grated cinnamon,
    for garnish

Combine the cognac, lemon juice, applejack, and maple syrup in a shaker. Pour into a double Old-Fashioned glass filled two-thirds of the way with crushed ice. Add the bitters and stir briefly with a swizzle stick. Add a straw and top with more crushed ice. Garnish with the cinnamon.

PHOTO BOMB

It may seem impossible now, but there once was a time when photography in all its many forms—selfies, cute animal pics, envy-inspiring travel albums, and annoying baby close-ups—didn't exist. The first (non-phone) cameras, dating back 800 years, were simple boxes with holes cut in them that light passed through to create images. If you've spent any time looking up drink recipes online, you know that cocktails can be extremely photogenic. One that's particularly easy on the eyes is the Photo Bomb, which was adapted at Little Branch in 2020. A drier, more botanical-heavy take on the Prohibition-era Depth Bomb, with a not-so-subtle nod to the similarly potent Fish House Punch (page 110), this refreshingly fruity and strikingly colorful cooler looks and tastes good in any filter. Take a picture before you start sipping, though, because this one will be gone before you know it.

1 ounce apricot liqueur
¾ ounce applejack
¾ ounce gin
½ ounce fresh lemon juice

¼ ounce pomegranate
   syrup
2 dashes Angostura bitters
1 lemon wedge, for garnish

Combine the apricot liqueur, applejack, gin, fresh lemon juice, and pomegranate syrup in a shaker. Pour into a tall glass filled two-thirds of the way with crushed ice. Float the bitters and top with more ice. Garnish with the lemon wedge.

STARBOY

With all the nutty stuff happening on our planet, it's easy to forget about the constant chaos raging far above our heads. A group of scientists, astronauts, and artists created Asteroid Day—commemorating the 1908 Tunguska Event, when an asteroid destroyed more than 800 square miles of Siberian forest—to raise awareness about these giant chunks of space rock and to help future generations prepare for a potentially catastrophic event.

You probably can't save the planet from impending asteroid-related doom à la Bruce Willis in Armageddon *unless you work for NASA . . . in which case, get back to work! But you can soothe your asteroid-frazzled nerves with the space-themed Starboy. Created by Zachary Gelnaw-Rubin at Harlem's Lion Lion in 2018, it's a bright, nuanced, slightly fruity riff on the Manhattan but with intergalactic appeal. Down more than a couple of these stiff sippers and you'll find yourself crashing quickly back to earth.*

---

1 ounce rye whiskey
1 ounce applejack
1 ounce Cocchi Americano

2 dashes Angostura bitters
1 lemon twist, for garnish

Combine the rye, applejack, Cocchi Americano, and bitters in in an ice-filled mixing glass. Stir with a long-handled spoon for 30 seconds and strain into a stemmed cocktail glass. Garnish with the lemon twist.

JULY

						1
						CANADA DAY Toronto

2	3	4	5	6	7	8
WORLD UFO DAY Beam Me Up	NATIONAL STAY OUT OF THE SUN DAY Hot in the Shade	INDEPENDENCE DAY Ex-Pat	BIKINI DAY Pink Bikini	NATIONAL FRIED CHICKEN DAY Kentucky Colonel	NATIONAL STRAWBERRY SUNDAE DAY Berrymore	VIDEO GAME DAY Phoenix Down

9	10	11	12	13	14	15
CALL OF THE HORIZON DAY Port of Call	NATIONAL PIÑA COLADA DAY Piña Colada	NATIONAL MOJITO DAY Rich Man's Mojito	SIMPLICITY DAY Stone Fence	GRUNTLED WORKERS DAY Business with Pleasure	BASTILLE DAY Marie Antoinette	INTERNATIONAL SISTER CITIES DAY New York Monte Carlo

16	17	18	19	20	21	22
WORLD SNAKE DAY Rattlesnake	NATIONAL PEACH ICE CREAM DAY Third Date	NATIONAL SOUR CANDY DAY Troublemaker	NATIONAL DAIQUIRI DAY Daiquiri	MOON DAY Moonwalk	LEGAL DRINKING AGE DAY Freshman Daiquiri	NATIONAL HAMMOCK DAY Banana Hammock

23	24	25	26	27	28	29
WORLD MOSQUITO DAY Mosquito	NATIONAL TEQUILA DAY Bravo	NATIONAL DAY OF THE COWBOY Bronco Buster	NETHERLANDS INDEPENDENCE DAY Holland Razor Blade	NATIONAL SCOTCH DAY Athol Brose	NATIONAL WATERPARK DAY Florida Punch	RAIN DAY Age of Aquarius
30 INTERNATIONAL DAY OF FRIENDSHIP Trust Fall	**31** HARRY POTTER BIRTHDAY Butterbeer					

Canada Day

TORONTO

Unlike its neighbor to the south, Canada's journey to self-governance after centuries of direct British rule wasn't as abrupt or—probably because Canadians are so darn friendly—nearly as violent. Originally called Dominion Day, Canada Day celebrates the Constitution Act, 1867, which united the formerly separate colonies of Canada, New Brunswick, and Nova Scotia into a single entity. Many of Canada Day's biggest celebrations happen in Ontario, the country's most populous province and home to its capital, Ottawa, and its largest city, Toronto. The latter serves as inspiration for the Toronto cocktail, a fragrant, bitter Manhattan or Old-Fashioned variation (depending on whom you ask) that originally appeared in Robert Vermeire's 1922 book, Cocktails: How to Mix Them. Still considered the most popular classic cocktail to use the potentially overpowering digestif Fernet-Branca (a nod to Toronto's large Italian community), this smoothly herbal tipple is softened by whisky and sugar for a finish that's bitter but more than polite enough for Canadian sensibilities.

---

2 ounces rye or Canadian whisky   ¼ ounce simple syrup
¾ ounce Fernet-Branca   1 orange twist, for garnish

Combine all ingredients in an ice-filled shaker. Shake vigorously for 25 to 30 seconds and strain into a double Old-Fashioned glass over ice.

BEAM ME UP

The truth is out there. No, really, it is.

Unless you're one of the thousands of people who claim to have been abducted by aliens, you'll have to live vicariously through futuristic media like Star Trek *to get your spacefaring fix. Inspired by that show's method of teleporting travelers onto interstellar craft, including the* USS Enterprise, *the Beam Me Up, a stiff sipper, offers an out-of-this-world experience for whisk(e)y adventurers. Imbued with scotch—the preferred drink of* Enterprise *chief engineer Montgomery Scott—as well as Irish whiskey, sherry, and Amaro Averno, it's the perfect peace offering when confronted by curious visitors from beyond the stars.*

1 ounce Irish whiskey

1 ounce blended scotch

¼ ounce Pedro Ximénez sherry

¼ ounce Amaro Averna

2 dashes chocolate bitters

2 dashes Angostura bitters

1 orange twist, for garnish

Combine the Irish whiskey, scotch, sherry, Amaro Averna, and bitters in an Old-Fashioned glass. Add ice and stir for five or six seconds. Garnish with the orange twist.

HOT IN THE SHADE

Spending a day baking under the sun might sound fantastic—and, in moderation, sunlight is a healthy source of vitamin D—but you have plenty of good reasons to give your skin a break from the sweltering rays once in a while. So put down the beach towel today and recharge indoors with a Netflix marathon or grab a book and find some extra shady foliage to sit under. Release your inner goth and embrace the darkness. Your skin will thank you! Dan Greenbaum's Hot in the Shade, first served at New York City's Diamond Reef in 2017, has all the elements of a tropical paradise without any harmful UV radiation. Vibrantly sweet orgeat, pineapple, and rum take on a darker, more complex hue with the addition of Portuguese fortified wine. A lovely addition to an afternoon spent under an umbrella, haughtily sipping while watching your sun-loving friends wrinkle and fry.

1½ ounces aged rum
1 ounce fresh pineapple juice
½ ounce fresh lime juice
½ ounce orgeat

½ ounce Madeira
1 pinch freshly grated nutmeg,
   for garnish
1 sprig mint, for garnish

Combine the rum, juices, and orgeat in a shaker. Pour into a tall glass filled two-thirds of the way with crushed ice. Float the Madeira, add a straw, and top with more crushed ice. Garnish with the nutmeg and mint sprig.

JULY 4
Independence Day

EX-PAT

In the aftermath of the Revolutionary War, the British Empire lost thousands of square miles of territory and an estimated 2.5 million subjects, all of whom immediately became expatriates of their former country. Summon that same independent spirit with Lauren Schell and Vito Dieterle's Ex-Pat, an all-American modern classic that has been making waves in the cocktail world since it appeared at Little Branch in 2010. Summery, minty, refreshing but not too sweet, with a patriotic bourbon base and a flavor as memorable as the overthrow of a tyrannical regime, this is one taste of freedom you won't take for granted.

2 ounces bourbon
1 ounce fresh lime juice
¾ ounce simple syrup

3 dashes Angostura bitters
3 or 4 mint leaves

Combine all ingredients in an ice-filled shaker. Shake vigorously for 25 to 30 seconds and strain into a stemmed cocktail glass.

TURN THE PAGE TO
SEE THE ILLUSTRATION
FOR THIS DRINK.

Ex-Pat
PAGE 233

PINK BIKINI

Today's swimwear comes in every imaginable shape, color, size, and fabric. But no look is complete without an eye-catching, beach-themed cocktail in hand. The Pink Bikini, adapted from recipes that have been around for almost as long as its namesake, was born to play the role. Made with coconut rum from the Caribbean—where bikinis are a year-round way of life—along with nutty amaretto and colorful raspberries, this fizzy, full-figured, rosy-colored treat is summery sweet and fruity from the first sip to the last. Like most bikinis, it leaves little to the imagination.

1½ ounces coconut rum,
    such as Malibu
1 ounce fresh lemon juice

¾ ounce amaretto liqueur
6 raspberries
Club soda, to top

Combine the rum, lemon juice, amaretto liqueur, and five raspberries in an ice-filled shaker. Shake vigorously for 25 to 30 seconds and strain into a tall glass filled with ice. Top with club soda and garnish with another raspberry.

National Fried Chicken Day

KENTUCKY COLONEL

When it comes to mass-produced fried chicken, there's the Colonel and then there's everyone else. Harland Sanders opened the first Kentucky Fried Chicken restaurant in 1952 with a recipe so beloved that he was given the honorary title of "Kentucky Colonel," the Bluegrass State's highest civilian honor. First served at Los Angeles's Hotel Bel Air, the Kentucky Colonel cocktail is ideal for washing down a hardy plate of southern food or stimulating the appetite just enough to scarf down one last drumstick. Powerful and savory due to Bénédictine's secret blend of botanicals, this Old-Fashioned variation isn't for culinary chickens.

2 ounces bourbon

½ ounce Bénédictine

2 dashes Angostura bitters

1 lemon twist, for garnish

Combine the bourbon, Bénédictine, and bitters in an Old-Fashioned glass. Add ice and stir for five or six seconds. Garnish with the lemon twist.

National Strawberry Sundae Day

BERRYMORE

If you're celebrating today's holiday correctly—with multiple scoops of ice cream doused in strawberry sauce, fresh strawberries, and whipped cream—your only concern should be the next spoonful . . . or the next sip.

The Berrymore, based on a drink that first appeared at Brooklyn's Clover Club, is a refreshingly fruity Sour spin-off that combines all the best components of a strawberry sundae—creamy texture, just the right amount of sweetness, and, um, strawberries—alongside the always-delightful mingling of bourbon and Italian vermouth. It's perfect for those who are lactose intolerant but still want to get down with some berry-infused decadence or for finicky eaters who don't want to approach their daily calorie intake in one sitting. But let's be clear: This isn't a diet drink.

1½ ounces bourbon
¾ ounce sweet vermouth
¾ ounce fresh lemon juice
¾ ounce simple syrup

2 halved strawberries
1 egg white
1 whole strawberry,
   for garnish

Combine the bourbon, vermouth, lemon juice, simple syrup, halved strawberries, and egg white in a shaker. Shake without ice (to emulsify the egg white) for 10 seconds, then add ice and shake vigorously. Strain into a stemmed cocktail glass. Garnish with the whole strawberry.

PHOENIX DOWN

Named after the life-giving feathers of a magical bird that appears in the Final Fantasy *games, this downy-smooth cousin of the Penicillin (page 117) packs enough ginger, lemon, and honey to keep you powered up during even the most intense quests. It even features a blood-red float of Angostura bitters to remind you of all your digitally vanquished enemies or the actual scars you acquired after flipping out on your older brother for running you off the* Mario Kart *track too many times.*

Win or lose, at least your taste buds will feel like you've leveled up.

---

2 ounces bourbon

¾ ounce fresh lemon juice

¾ ounce ginger syrup

¾ ounce honey syrup

Heavy float of Angostura bitters

1 piece candied ginger,
    for garnish

 Combine the bourbon, lemon juice, ginger syrup, and honey syrup in an ice-filled shaker. Shake vigorously and strain into a double Old-Fashioned glass over ice. Float the Angostura bitters on top. Garnish with the candied ginger.

PORT OF CALL

Your third-grade teacher might not agree, but staring off into the distance isn't always a bad thing. Call of the Horizon Day celebrates the feeling you get from concentrating on the convergence of earth and sky and contemplating all its possibilities. What does the future have in store? Travel and adventure? Positive mental and physical growth? Unbridled romance with a yet-undiscovered soul mate? Today is all about dreaming big and, most importantly, forming a concrete plan to make those dreams happen—or just staring aimlessly into space because meditation is perfectly okay, too.

There's nothing like gazing thoughtfully off into the sunset or at a vast expanse of open water. But it's even better with a drink with flavor as big as your aspirations. Sam Ross's Port of Call, served at Attaboy since 2016, is one such inspirational sipper. Named after the term for an intermediate stop on a ship's sailing journey, this imaginative mingling of port's raspberry, caramel, and hazelnut notes with applejack's mellow, slightly charred finish will take you anywhere you want to go.

1½ ounces applejack
¾ ounce port
¾ ounce fresh lemon juice

½ ounce honey syrup
1 pinch freshly grated cinnamon, for garnish

Combine the applejack, port, lemon juice, and honey syrup in an ice-filled shaker. Shake vigorously for 25 to 30 seconds and strain into a double Old-Fashioned glass over ice. Garnish with the cinnamon.

National Piña Colada Day

PIÑA COLADA

Like many iconic drinks, the Piña Colada's origins are a bit murky. Some suggest that 19th-century pirate Roberto Cofresí first served it to boost his crew's morale. Others point to various bartenders in San Juan at the turn of the 20th century. But whatever the case, it's impossible to down-play the deceptively simple drink's impact on Caribbean culture and tiki bars around the world.

If you're not into yoga (a terrible post-beverage activity, trust me) and if you have half a brain, fix yourself a couple of these succulently smooth beauties today and allow yourself to escape to a sunny, sugarcane-tinged paradise. Getting caught in the rain is optional, of course.

---

2 ounces aged rum
2 ounces fresh pineapple juice
1 ounce Coco Lopez

1 lime wedge
1 pinch freshly grated nutmeg,
　for garnish

Combine the rum, pineapple juice, Coco Lopez, and lime wedge in an ice-filled shaker. Shake vigorously for 25 to 30 seconds and strain into a tall glass or mug filled two-thirds of the way with crushed ice. Add a straw and top with more crushed ice. Garnish with the nutmeg.

RICH MAN'S MOJITO

If there was a Mount Rushmore for rum, the Mojito would occupy its most prominent real estate. It's perfectly acceptable and encouraged to use just about any variety of rum for a Mojito, but why stop with just one? Enter the Rich Man's Mojito, first concocted by Toby Maloney at New York City's Milk & Honey in 2004. This savory-sweet, equal-parts combination of black rum and aged rum—two distinctly complex spirits— creates a skillfully multilayered libation that deepens with every sip and will make you feel rich in body and mind. That is, until it's time to pick up the bar tab.

1 ounce aged rum
1 ounce Goslings Black Seal rum
1 ounce fresh lime juice
¾ ounce simple syrup

1 handful fresh mint
1 brown sugar cube
1 sprig fresh mint,
    for garnish

Combine all ingredients in a double Old-Fashioned glass. Gently muddle and fill the glass two-thirds with crushed ice. Add a straw and top with more crushed ice. Garnish with a sprig of fresh mint.

STONE FENCE

We all have had this experience: You're excited to try a new cocktail spot you've heard so much about, but when you get there, the menu is a total disaster. Every drink has at least nine ingredients—many you've never heard of and can't pronounce—with enough questionably baroque bitters and gimmicky infusions to make you want to order a beer and call it a night.

Simplicity Day, founded to celebrate nature lover and modernity hater Henry David Thoreau, gives you a chance to take a step back from your fast-paced life, gadgets, and problematically intricate cocktails to appreciate the peacefulness that comes when things aren't so complicated. Thoreau wasn't a drinker, but he would have appreciated the simplest of tipples, the Stone Fence.

With roots dating back to the Revolutionary War and popularized by acclaimed 19th-century barkeeps such as Jerry Thomas, this utterly uncluttered mixture of bourbon and fresh cider has been called the first truly American cocktail. Featuring straightforward notes of vanilla, oak, and apple, it's an effortless addition to even the most unseasoned novice's repertoire.

2 ounces bourbon   **2.5 ounces fresh apple cider**

Combine both ingredients in an ice-filled shaker. Shake vigorously for 25 to 30 seconds and strain into a double Old-Fashioned glass over ice.

BUSINESS WITH PLEASURE

Whatever your level of workplace satisfaction, the Business with Pleasure is second to none for taking the edge off a long day on the grind. A sweetened riff on Sasha Petraske's The Business, its soothing, citrusy bouquet is perfect for diffusing any interpersonal conflicts that might arise during the workweek. Because who doesn't love fresh pineapple, right? This summery tipple is also slightly lighter, alcoholwise, than other Gimlet variations, meaning there's a greater likelihood that you won't hate your job—and your life—the day after enjoying one (or several).

1½ ounces gin

¾ ounce fresh pineapple juice

¾ ounce fresh lime juice

½ ounce honey syrup

Combine all ingredients in an ice-filled shaker. Shake vigorously for 25 to 30 seconds and strain into a stemmed cocktail glass.

MARIE ANTOINETTE

Overthrowing a corrupt monarchy and ushering in a new era of freedom and democracy definitely call for a party. Which is exactly what the French do every July 14 to commemorate the 1789 storming of the Bastille prison and King Louis XVI renouncing his claim to the throne. Louis and his immediate family members subsequently were beheaded, including his wife, the infamous Marie Antoinette. Remembered as a symbol of the unapologetic excesses of the ruling class, she also lives on in cocktail lore as the alleged inspiration for the coupe glass (purportedly molded from her bosom) and as the namesake of a delightfully opulent Rum Fix riff from Brooklyn's Karin Stanley. It's a little extreme to burn people in effigy, but there's nothing wrong with drinking them, which is why the Marie Antoinette makes an excellent choice for toasting the end of a tyrannical regime. Light, summery, infused with decadent dollops of crème de cacao and fresh raspberries, like the wines that flooded the Parisian streets during the first Bastille Day celebration, it's a perfectly egalitarian sweet-and-sour treat.

2 ounces white rum

¾ ounce fresh lemon juice

⅜ ounce white crème de cacao

⅜ ounce simple syrup

5 raspberries

Combine the rum, lemon juice, crème de cacao, and simple syrup in a shaker. In a double Old-Fashioned glass, muddle four raspberries and top with crushed ice. Pour the mixture from the shaker into the glass. Add a straw, then top with more ice. Garnish with a raspberry.

International Sister Cities Day

NEW YORK MONTE CARLO

No, a "sister city" doesn't refer to a place where a sibling makes her home, though it's entirely possible that she or you might live in one. Monte Carlo, a district of Monaco, isn't one of Manhattan's 12 sister cities, but the two globally significant locales are both centers of commerce, banking, tourism, and recreation for some of the world's wealthiest people. They're also joint namesakes of one of the most wonderfully opulent Old-Fashioned variations. The New York Monte Carlo, *an offshoot of a potable from David A. Embury's* The Fine Art of Mixing Drinks, *features American whiskey, French cognac, Bénédictine, and Angostura bitters, which have roots in both the Old and New World. This revelatory sipper tastes just as delightful regardless of which side of the Atlantic you find yourself.*

1 ounce cognac	2 dashes Angostura bitters
1 ounce rye whiskey	1 dash orange bitters
½ ounce Bénédictine	1 lemon twist, for garnish

Combine the cognac, whiskey, Bénédictine, and bitters in an Old-Fashioned glass. Add ice and stir for five or six seconds. Garnish with the lemon twist.

RATTLESNAKE

Slytherins and Cobra Kai *devotees, your time to hiss has arrived! World Snake Day honors this fascinatingly diverse group of reptiles often treated unfairly for thousands of years (you know, that whole Garden of Eden thing). Many ancient cultures worshipped serpents as powerful deities, however. Generally speaking, alcohol is useless as snake antivenom, but a potent quaff of elixir from your favorite bartender certainly can settle the nerves if you're planning on spending time in an area where snakes are plentiful. One of the most popular and enduring concoctions in Harry Craddock's* Savoy Cocktail Book, *the Rattlesnake, is a Rye Sour riff as smooth as a snake's underbelly (we're assuming). You may be tempted to down one of these citrusy, foamy sippers faster than the 20 minutes it takes for a Black Mamba's poison to run its lethal course, but this formidable creature's absinthe-backed bite will slither up on you if you aren't careful.*

---

2 ounces overproof rye
whiskey

¾ ounce fresh lemon juice

¾ ounce simple syrup

1 barspoon absinthe

1 egg white

 Combine all ingredients in a shaker. Shake without ice (to emulsify the egg white) for 10 seconds, then add ice and shake vigorously. Strain into a stemmed cocktail glass.

National Peach Ice Cream Day

THIRD DATE

You're probably thinking, Wow, there's a lot of ice cream–related holidays! *And what exactly is the problem with that? It might not get as much press as its strawberry, chocolate, and vanilla cousins, but frozen food zealots adore peach ice cream for its mellow, slightly tart, and sweet taste, not to mention its irresistible golden chunks of fuzzy fruit.*

The delectable combination of peaches and dairy long has been considered a symbol of romance (okay, sex), nowhere more blatantly than in R&B group 112's scandalous 2001 hit track, "Peaches and Cream." For an equally suggestive and positively peachy tipple, try the Third Date from Zachary Gelnaw-Rubin. First mixed at Harlem's Lion Lion in 2018, this layered, silky, juicy delight pairs bourbon's finest floral elements with a generous serving of peach liqueur and just enough crème de cacao to set the mood. Have a couple of these on a night out with that special someone and you'll be asking for the check long before dessert.

1½ ounces bourbon
¾ ounce peach liqueur

½ ounce crème de cacao
1 barspoon honey syrup
Hand-whipped cream float

Combine the bourbon, peach liqueur, crème de cacao, and honey syrup in a mixing glass filled with cracked ice. Stir with a long-handled spoon for 30 seconds and then strain into a stemmed cocktail glass. Float the cream.

TROUBLEMAKER

For generations, the young and young at heart have enjoyed great lip-smacking alternatives to overly sweet treats, from relatively tame Lemonheads and Laffy Taffy to more extreme (and possibly tear-jerking) Sour Patch Kids and Warheads. Prized for the energizing taste sensations they create, sour candies also trigger the release of serotonin, a mood-regulating compound that aids in everything from sleep and digestion to healthy functioning in the bedroom. That should be reason enough to hit up the local candy shop now and then. Danny Gil's Troublemaker, a brighter, more citrusy take on a Pimm's Cup, has a signature tang instantly recognizable to anyone who has scarfed down handfuls of Now and Laters or Jolly Ranchers. While it does exude a fair bit of sweetness, it's far from cloying due to the invigoratingly dry properties of lemon juice, cucumber, and Muscat grapes.

1 ounce pisco
1 ounce sweet vermouth
¾ ounce fresh lemon juice
½ ounce simple syrup

2 halved strawberries
3 thin cucumber slices
Club soda, to top
1 whole strawberry, for garnish

Combine the pisco, vermouth, lemon juice, simple syrup, the halved strawberries, and two cucumber slices in an ice-filled shaker. Shake vigorously for 25 to 30 seconds and strain into a tall glass filled with ice. Top with club soda. Garnish with the whole strawberry and the remaining cucumber slice.

DAIQUIRI

Rum, lime, and sugar—these three simple ingredients, when combined properly, form a libation that Ernest Hemingway described as looking "like the sea where the wave falls away from the bow of a ship," a tipple so sublime that Golden Age Hollywood actress Tallulah Bankhead professed it "makes living more tolerable."

But it's not easy to pull off properly, as mixologists worth their jiggers will tell you. Finding the right rum, adjusting for the acidity of a particular batch of lime juice, and using just the right amount of simple syrup can take years to perfect, which makes the Daiquiri the perfect barometer of a bartender's attention to detail. The next time you visit a cocktail establishment for the first time, order one before asking for anything more complicated. If it's not up to snuff, you're better off sticking to beer or wine.

2 ounces rum of choice
1 ounce fresh lime juice

¼ ounce simple syrup
1 lime wedge, for garnish

Combine the rum, lime juice, and simple syrup in an ice-filled shaker. Shake vigorously for 25 to 30 seconds and strain into a stemmed cocktail glass. Garnish with the lime wedge.

MOONWALK

The first men to make footprints on the lunar surface were NASA astronauts Neil Armstrong and Buzz Aldrin, who successfully completed the Apollo 11 mission's goal on this date in 1969. One small step for a man, one giant leap for . . . cocktail kind? Entrepreneurial types have created thousands of gifts, collectibles, and other commemorative items to mark our foray to Earth's closest neighbor, but none taste nearly as good as the Moonwalk. Dreamed up in early 1969 by Joe Gilmore, head bartender at the Savoy Hotel's American Bar in London, the effervescent sipper was the first drink Armstrong and Aldrin enjoyed after returning to earth. An invigorating and fragrant blend of citrus, orange liqueur, rose water, and champagne, it's a perfect pick-me-up after a stressful return trip from a celestial body or just an annoyingly long commute.

1 ounce Grand Marnier

1 ounce fresh grapefruit juice

1 barspoon cane syrup

3 drops rose water

Champagne, to top

1 thin orange slice, for garnish

Combine the Grand Marnier, grapefruit juice, cane syrup, and rose water in an ice-filled shaker. Shake vigorously for 25 to 30 seconds and strain into a stemmed cocktail glass or a champagne flute. Top with champagne and garnish with the orange slice.

Legal Drinking Age Day

FRESHMAN DAIQUIRI

You (hopefully) remember the glorious day when you turned 21, finally able to enjoy a sip of alcohol legally for the very first time. One of the unfortunate effects of the American drinking age situation is that college kids who have swigged any swill they can get their hands on generally take a long time to develop their palates properly. Be a champ and get your newly legal friends and family members on the right track by acquainting them with the Freshman Daiquiri from New York City's Theo Lieberman. This lovely, unobtrusive introduction to well-balanced rum sippers and tiki-style potations tastes sweet but not syrupy, complex yet refreshing. A transcendent treat for newbies who still consider a Malibu and Coke a luxury.

2 ounces white rum

1 ounce fresh lime juice

¼ ounce John D. Taylor's Velvet Falernum

¼ ounce orgeat

1 thin orange slice

1 lime wedge, for garnish

Combine the rum, lime juice, velvet falernum, orgeat, and orange slice in an ice-filled shaker. Shake vigorously for 25 to 30 seconds and strain into a stemmed cocktail glass. Garnish with the lime wedge.

BANANA HAMMOCK

Placement is everything. On its own, a piece of fabric or netting is just a piece of fabric or netting. But when stretched and suspended between two posts or trees, it becomes a hammock, a gently swaying bed and an instantly recognizable symbol of relaxation. Want to make an evening in a hammock even more restful? All you need is a tropically appropriate, ice-cold beverage such as the Banana Hammock, a charmingly exotic cooler created by Dan Greenbaum at Attaboy in 2016. Its name might suggest a risqué men's undergarment—and doubling up in the close confines of a hammock certainly can inspire all sorts of romantic activities— but this bodacious blend of fresh juices, banana liqueur, and two highly compatible yet very different rums is still pure enough for the most innocent of drinkers. In other words, don't sleep on this tried-and-true tiki relaxer, regardless of your intentions.

1½ ounces white rum
1 ounce fresh lime juice
½ ounce banana liqueur
½ ounce orgeat

½ ounce Smith & Cross
   Jamaican rum
1 sprig mint, for garnish
1 pinch freshly grated nutmeg,
   for garnish

Combine the white rum, lime juice, banana liqueur, and orgeat in a shaker. Pour into a tall glass filled two-thirds of the way with crushed ice. Float the Smith & Cross, add a straw, and top with more crushed ice. Garnish with the mint sprig and nutmeg.

MOSQUITO

Of all the billions of creatures that exist alongside us humans, we hate few as universally as mosquitoes. Not all mosquitoes should be avoided, however. First served at Attaboy in 2017, the Mosquito cocktail is a bitter, smoky, spicy zinger with a bite that, instead of making you want to itch, will have the mezcal-inclined coming back for more. It also features healthy doses of fresh lime juice and ginger, which, coincidentally (or not) are two of the most popular home remedies for combating malaria. Sip this one slowly because, even though it won't drain your blood, the Mosquito will give you a buzz worthy of its namesake if you aren't careful.

¾ ounce mezcal
¾ ounce Campari
¾ ounce fresh lime juice

¾ ounce ginger syrup
1 piece candied ginger,
for garnish

Combine the mezcal, Campari, lime juice, and ginger syrup in an ice-filled shaker. Shake vigorously for 25 to 30 seconds and strain into a stemmed cocktail glass. Garnish with the candied ginger.

TURN THE PAGE TO
SEE THE ILLUSTRATION
FOR THIS DRINK.

Mosquito
PAGE 253

BRAVO

Sure, Margaritas, Palomas, and even Tequila and Sodas are perfectly acceptable drinks to make with "Mexican Champagne," but if you've got your hands on a great bottle of aged tequila and want to appreciate its wood-enhanced flavors and aromas fully, mix yourself a Bravo. This simple take on a south-of-the-border Old-Fashioned originally appeared on the menu at Dallas's Alma Restaurant and features a double dose of bitters and succulent agave nectar. Oaky, herbal, chocolaty, or smoky, depending on which tequila you choose, it's the best way to immerse yourself fully in agave-based bliss without going straight for the bottle.

2 ounces tequila, preferably añejo or reposado

¼ ounce agave nectar

2 dashes Angostura bitters

1 dash orange bitters

1 grapefruit twist, for garnish

Combine the tequila, agave nectar, and bitters in an Old-Fashioned glass. Add ice and stir for five or six seconds. Garnish with the grapefruit twist.

National Day of the Cowboy

BRONCO BUSTER

Ready your trustiest steed and let out your best "Yeehaw!" because today we're all cowboys. National Day of the Cowboy honors the stoic, hard-working, Stetson-hat-wearing cattle herders who have been the most recognizable symbol of the American West since the late 1800s. Cattle-herding requires numerous skills, one of the most important being bronco busting, or breaking a wild horse to ride it. The dangerous practice serves as inspiration for the Bronco Buster, a formidable, distinctly American classic found in 1951's Bottoms Up *by Ted Saucier. With a pleasantly peppery and fruity bouquet of rye, applejack, and curaçao, this bone-dry Whiskey Sour spin-off goes down easier than a calf expertly lassoed by a veteran cowboy, but its high alcohol content still packs a wallop for cock-tail novices still learning the ropes. Don't plan on more than one of these before a long journey, or you may fall asleep in the saddle.*

1 ounce rye whiskey
1 ounce applejack

¾ ounce curaçao
¾ ounce fresh lemon juice
1 orange twist, for garnish

Combine the whiskey, applejack, curaçao, and lemon juice in an ice-filled shaker. Shake vigorously for 25 to 30 seconds and strain into a double Old-Fashioned glass over ice. Garnish with the orange twist.

HOLLAND RAZOR BLADE

No spirit is as distinctly Dutch as genever (or jenever), a gin precursor made with malt wine and juniper berries and distilled since the earliest days of the republic. But you don't need to be a history nerd to appreciate the uniquely complex flavors and aromas of this woody and smoky liquor, especially when it's used as the base in a Holland Razor Blade. Appearing in Charles H. Baker Jr.'s The Gentleman's Companion *(1939), the refreshing, sporty, and spicy Sour riff effortlessly mingles citrus, botanicals, malt, and pepper. If you can't get your hands on a bottle of genever, use gin, but know that it might get you "in Dutch" with cocktail purists.*

2 ounces genever

¼ ounce fresh lemon juice

¼ ounce simple syrup

Cayenne pepper, to taste

Combine the genever, lemon juice, and simple syrup in an ice-filled shaker. Shake vigorously for 25 to 30 seconds and strain into a stemmed cocktail glass. Top with the cayenne pepper.

National Scotch Day

ATHOL BROSE

Commonly considered a solo sipper (or opened with a wee bit of water or ice, if you must), scotch has been a mainstay of cocktail culture long before the word "cocktail" even existed. In fact, it's the base spirit in perhaps the earliest mixed drink, the Athol Brose. Invented in 1475 by the Earl of Atholl, who allegedly trapped one of his enemies by filling a well with it, the drink has become Scotland's unofficial holiday tipple. In The Gentleman's Companion, Charles H. Baker Jr. first described the definitive modern version, a decadently sweet and creamy introduction to a spirit that really doesn't need one.

2¼ ounces scotch
½ ounce honey syrup

Hand-whipped cream,
to top

Combine the scotch and honey syrup in a mixing glass filled with cracked ice. Stir with a long-handled spoon for 30 seconds and strain into a stemmed cocktail glass. Float the cream.

FLORIDA PUNCH

The town of Wisconsin Dells bills itself as the "Waterpark Capital of the World," and, weirdly enough, South Dakota has the most waterparks per capita. But for sheer volume and variety, there's nowhere quite like Florida, which boasts 103 parks, including Disney's iconic Blizzard Beach and Typhoon Lagoon and Tampa's Adventure Island. After a long day of hitting the Sunshine State's thousands of slides—or those at your local park—treat yourself to a Florida Punch. A quasi-tiki cooler served since at least the middle of the 19th century, it's chock-full of Floridian citrus, two kinds of rum, and refreshing notes of vanilla, almond, and pomegranate. Slide one or two of these fruity crowd-pleasers down your gullet today!

¾ ounce aged rum
¾ ounce spiced rum
½ ounce fresh grapefruit juice
½ ounce orange juice
½ ounce fresh lime juice

¼ ounce John D. Taylor's Velvet Falernum
¼ ounce Licor 43
¼ ounce pomegranate syrup
4 dashes Angostura bitters
1 thin orange slice, for garnish
1 brandied cherry, for garnish

Combine the rums, juices, velvet falernum, Licor 43, and pomegranate syrup in a shaker. Pour into a tall glass or mug filled two-thirds of the way with crushed ice. Float the bitters and top with more crushed ice. Garnish with the orange slice and the brandied cherry.

AGE OF AQUARIUS

The only thing better than sitting by a window and watching the pitter-patter of a life-giving rainstorm is experiencing it with a cocktail in hand. If you're feeling particularly precipitation-minded, try an Age of Aquarius, created by bartender Devojka at Montreal's Pink Panther in 2018. Inspired by the water-themed constellation of the same name, this smoky, fruity, bittersweet blend of mezcal, Campari, and passion fruit tastes great in any weather. But sipping one of these icy beauties during a storm allows all its complex characteristics to shine.

1½ ounces mezcal

¾ ounce fresh lime juice

¾ ounce passion fruit syrup

¼ ounce honey syrup

½ ounce Campari

1 sprig mint, for garnish

Combine the mezcal, lime juice, passion fruit syrup, and honey syrup in a shaker. Pour into a double Old-Fashioned glass filled two-thirds of the way with crushed ice. Float the Campari, add a straw, and top with more crushed ice. Garnish with the mint sprig.

International Day of Friendship

TRUST FALL

No matter what hardships you may face in life, they're always easier when you've got friends. But one of the most nerve-racking portions of any mandatory team-building exercise is a trust fall, where a person deliberately falls backward, trusting the other members of the group to catch him or her. In such an event, you want true mates behind you (unless you have the type of friends who'd think it was hilarious to watch you drop). You want people for whom you gladly would mix a Trust Fall, an extraordinarily amiable concoction from Rene Hidalgo. Whatever curveballs the world throws at you, this boozy, bittersweet, vanilla- and spice-infused Old-Fashioned spin-off has got your back.

1 ounce bourbon

1 ounce cognac

⅛ ounce Licor 43

¼ ounce St. Elizabeth Allspice Dram

2 dashes Peychaud's bitters

1 orange twist, for garnish

Combine the bourbon, cognac, Licor 43, allspice dram, and bitters in an Old-Fashioned glass. Add ice and stir for five or six seconds. Garnish with the orange twist.

BUTTERBEER

It might seem odd to celebrate the birthday of a fictional wizard as a holiday. But few characters, living or created, have reached the same insane heights of global popularity as Harry James Potter. After a rough day of classes or vanquishing hordes of demonic creatures, Harry and his pals like nothing more than to head to a local pub for a tall, foamy mug of thick and rich butterbeer. The jovial dessert beverage described by J. K. Rowling as "a little bit like less-sickly butterscotch" contains no alcohol, but this variation features a decadent combination of vanilla vodka and butterscotch schnapps to satisfy the cravings of any booze-loving muggle or magician of legal drinking age. Topped with a special blend of marshmallow fluff, whipping cream, and amaretto, this powerful potion will send you into an instant state of sugary bliss without even having to learn a spell first.

6 ounces cream soda

1 ounce vanilla vodka

1 ounce butterscotch schnapps

Homemade Cream Topping (recipe follows)

Combine the cream soda, vanilla vodka, and butterscotch schnapps in a frosty mug. Garnish with the homemade cream topping.

HOMEMADE CREAM TOPPING

¼ cup heavy whipping cream

½ ounce amaretto

1 tablespoon marshmallow fluff

In a mixing bowl, add the whipping cream and whip with a hand mixer until soft peaks form. Add the amaretto and marshmallow fluff. Continue beating the mixture until hard peaks form.

		1	2	3	4	5
		NATIONAL GIRLFRIENDS DAY Better Half	**AMERICAN FAMILY DAY** American Trilogy	**GRAB SOME NUTS DAY** Kitchen Nuts	**COAST GUARD DAY** Narragansett Cooler	**NATIONAL OYSTER DAY** Archangel
6	7	8	9	10	11	12
NATIONAL FRESH BREATH DAY Chinatown Rickey	**PROFESSIONAL SPEAKERS DAY** La Otra Palabra	**INTERNATIONAL CAT DAY** Jaguar	**NATIONAL WOMEN'S DAY** Perfect Lady	**NATIONAL LION DAY** Leo Season	**WORLD KUNG FU DAY** Five Point Palm Exploding Heart Technique	**INTERNATIONAL DIAMOND DAY** Diamond Fizz
13	14	15	16	17	18	19
INTERNATIONAL LEFTHANDERS DAY Left Hand	**NATIONAL CREAMSICLE DAY** Golden Cadillac	**NATIONAL RELAXATION DAY** Lazy Man Flip	**NATIONAL RUM DAY** Zombie	**NATIONAL VANILLA CUSTARD DAY** Silver Lining	**SERENDIPITY DAY** Negroni Sbagliato	**NATIONAL AVIATION DAY** Aviation No. 1
20	21	22	23	24	25	26
NATIONAL LEMONADE DAY Easy Street	**HAWAIIAN STATEHOOD DAY** Blue Hawaii	**NATIONAL EAT A PEACH DAY** Georgia Julep	**VALENTINO DAY** Blood and Sand	**KNIFE DAY** Cloak & Dagger	**NATIONAL WHISKEY SOUR DAY** Whiskey Sour	**NATIONAL DOG DAY** Asta Collins
27	28	29	30	31		
BANANA LOVERS DAY Calypso Dynamite	**NATIONAL BOW TIE DAY** Bow Tie	**LEMON JUICE DAY** Lemon Smack	**NATIONAL MAI TAI DAY** Mai Tai	**NATIONAL MATCHMAKERS DAY** Cupid Deluxe		

BETTER HALF

*One of new wave band Talking Heads' biggest hits was a funky little ditty
from 1984 called "Girlfriend Is Better." As anyone with a girlfriend or
a girl as a friend will tell you, voicing that sentiment, emphatically and
often, is one of the keys to a happy and successful partnership. Take the
positive vibes to even greater heights by serving your number-one gal
a Better Half from Juyoung Kang, head bartender at Las Vegas's The
Dorsey. Dry, nutty, light-bodied, buttery, yet impeccably well rounded,
this low-ABV tipple is perfect for imbibers of all persuasions and rela-
tionship statuses. But make no mistake, it's still nicest when shared with
someone special.*

1½ ounces amontillado sherry
1 ounce vodka

½ ounce Chablis
1 barspoon Grand Marnier
1 orange twist, for garnish

Combine the sherry, vodka, Chablis, and Grand Marnier in
an ice-filled mixing glass. Stir with a long-handled spoon
for 30 seconds and strain into a stemmed cocktail glass.
Garnish with the orange twist.

AUGUST 2
American Family Day

AMERICAN TRILOGY

Holidays like Mother's Day and Father's Day honor specific, conventional roles, but today's families rarely conform to tradition. First proposed in 1977 by Arizona resident John Makkai, American Family Day encourages you to spend time with and cherish those you hold dearest, regardless of relation—and even if you're technically not related. Like people, cocktails come in families of all shapes and sizes. One of the most diverse started with the Old-Fashioned and has branched out to include modern classics such as the American Trilogy, brought to life by Michael McIlroy and Richard Boccato at Milk & Honey in 2006. Slightly drier than many of its spirit-forward, whiskey-based "relatives," this delightfully straight-forward sipper has a sophisticated, calming nose that becomes even more charming as it evolves in the glass. You will want to adopt this beacon of potent positivity into your inner circle immediately.

1 ounce rye whiskey

1 ounce applejack

1 brown sugar cube

2 dashes orange bitters

1 orange twist, for garnish

Combine the whiskey, applejack, sugar cube, and bitters in an Old-Fashioned glass. Muddle to break up the sugar cube, then add ice and stir for five or six seconds. Garnish with the orange twist.

KITCHEN NUTS

Get your head out of the gutter! Grab Some Nuts Day celebrates the little nuggets of goodness found in a mixed-nuts jar, even the ones that technically aren't nuts (peanuts, walnuts, cashews). Nuts frequently add a flavorful crunch to desserts and salads, but their unique gastronomic properties make them a great addition to a vast array of dishes and, of course, beverages. Kitchen Nuts, created in collaboration with Michael Timmons at Little Branch in 2020, is just such a versatile concoction. Brimming with notes of almond, pistachio, agave, chili, anise, cinnamon, and citrus, it's like a deranged chef taking the entire contents of a kitchen cabinet and dumping it together in the hopes of producing some sinister (albeit well-balanced) culinary magic. The surprisingly delicious result is a spicy, savory, bittersweet, and, yes, extremely nutty blend of tiki goodness.

1½ ounces tequila

½ ounce Ancho Reyes

½ ounce fresh lime juice

½ ounce pistachio syrup

¼ ounce John D. Taylor's Velvet Falernum

1 barspoon absinthe

2 dashes Angostura bitters

2 dashes Peychaud's bitters

1 pinch freshly grated cinnamon, for garnish

Combine the tequila, Ancho Reyes, lime juice, pistachio syrup, velvet falernum, and absinthe in a shaker. Pour into a tall glass filled two-thirds of the way with crushed ice. Add bitters and stir briefly with a swizzle stick. Add a straw, then top with more crushed ice. Garnish with the cinnamon.

NARRAGANSETT COOLER

To patrol the nation's shorelines more efficiently, the US Coast Guard erected hundreds of lifesaving stations throughout the 19th century, including a magnificent building made of solid granite that still overlooks Rhode Island's Narragansett Bay. Though it has become a restaurant, you still can become intimately acquainted with the drink it inspired, the Narragansett Cooler. This pre-Prohibition Highball variation benefits from the addition of orange juice and oil, making for a fruity, gingery, fizzy refresher as energizing as the blast of an ocean breeze, with a quenchingly crisp finish that even landlubbers can get behind.

2 ounces bourbon
¾ ounce ginger syrup
½ ounce fresh lime juice

2 thin orange slices
Club soda, to top
1 piece candied ginger,
   for garnish

Combine the bourbon, ginger syrup, lime juice, and orange slices in an ice-filled shaker. Shake vigorously for 25 to 30 seconds and strain into a tall glass filled with ice. Top with club soda and garnish with the piece of candied ginger.

ARCHANGEL

When enjoying a delicacy such as oysters, you want something equally posh to wash it down. Champagne traditionally has done the trick, but for a brighter and brisker drink with a boozier kick, you're better off with a great Martini variation, namely the Archangel, created by Michael McIlroy and Richard Boccato at Milk & Honey in 2006. Featuring a delightfully balanced blend of summery and refreshing cucumber and stomach-settling, slightly bitter Aperol swimming in a veritable sea of gin, this appetite enhancer will help you rampage through a couple dozen of your favorite mollusks.

2¼ ounces gin

¾ ounce Aperol

2 thin cucumber slices

1 lemon twist, for garnish

Combine the gin, Aperol, and cucumber slices in a mixing glass. Gently muddle and fill with cracked ice. Stir with a long-handled spoon for 30 seconds and strain into a stemmed cocktail glass. Garnish with the lemon twist.

National Fresh Breath Day

CHINATOWN RICKEY

What good is a winning smile if no one wants to get near it? Break out the mints or mouthwash for National Fresh Breath Day (and hopefully most other days), a celebration of good oral hygiene founded by concerned dental professionals to remind you of the importance of keeping your gob clean and kissable. Before the invention of modern toothpaste, humans used a variety of methods for maintaining a healthy mouth. American Indians often cleaned debris from their teeth with pine needles and chewed pleasant-smelling plants like mint for an extra boost of crispness. That utilitarian herb also plays a key role in the Chinatown Rickey, a brisk, bodacious refresher created by Sam Ross at Attaboy in 2017. Named as an homage to that bar's neighborhood, this tipple's herbaceous, woodsy, nutty aromatics will have your mouth feeling like a million bucks. Trust us, no one's going to shame you for having cocktail breath this good.

1½ ounces gin
1 ounce fresh lime juice
½ ounce fino sherry
¾ ounce simple syrup

3 or 4 mint leaves
Club soda, to top
1 sprig mint, for garnish
1 lime wedge, for garnish

Combine the gin, lime juice, sherry, simple syrup, and mint leaves in an ice-filled shaker. Shake vigorously for 25 to 30 seconds and strain into a tall glass filled with ice. Top with club soda. Garnish with the mint sprig and lime wedge.

LA OTRA PALABRA

The rhetorically inclined like to finish their speeches on a meaningful and memorable note. Few things are more gratifying than hammering home one final point, a sense of satisfaction shared with those who have tried Los Angeles bartender Eric Alperin's La Otra Palabra ("the other word" in Spanish). A mezcal-based sequel to the pre-Prohibition Last Word cocktail, this sultry lip-loosener pairs herbaceous Chartreuse and citrus with notes of cherry and agave for a taste that turns inarticulate loners into blabbermouths. We could belt out entire soliloquies about this increasingly popular modern classic, but you're better off trying one for yourself.

2 ounces mezcal	¼ agave nectar
1 ounce fresh lime juice	1 barspoon maraschino liqueur
¼ ounce yellow Chartreuse	1 brandied cherry, for garnish

 Combine the mezcal, lime juice, Chartreuse, agave nectar, and maraschino liqueur in an ice-filled shaker. Shake vigorously for 25 to 30 seconds and strain into a stemmed cocktail glass. Garnish with the brandied cherry.

International Cat Day

JAGUAR

Ancient Egyptians worshipped the first domesticated cats as deities. If today's pampered purr-balls could talk, they'd tell you that they expect the same treatment. With all the joy that these quirky, cuddly, and occasionally bitey and scratchy creatures bring to our lives and social media feeds, that seems like a fair deal. International Cat Day encourages you to show love to the nearly 40 species of wild felines, many endangered and in need of our help as much as the millions of their smaller cousins stuck in shelters around the world. One of the most recognizable big cats, the jaguar is a stealthy predator with a beautiful spotted coat that has inspired countless breeders to try to replicate its patterns in their domestic litters. A product of highly unusual—some would say unnatural—genetics, the Jaguar cocktail is both an aged rum Daiquiri variation and a slightly sweet, agave-forward mash-up with a tiki twist (a nod to the jaguar's lushly tropical habitat) that works surprisingly well. Regardless of how you want to classify it, it's liquid catnip for drinkers of all stripes or spots.

1¾ ounces tequila

¾ ounce fresh lime juice

½ ounce aged rum

½ ounce honey syrup

¼ ounce velvet falernum

1 lime twist, for garnish

Combine the tequila, lime juice, rum, honey syrup, and velvet falernum in an ice-filled shaker. Shake vigorously for 25 to 30 seconds and strain into a stemmed cocktail glass. Garnish with the lime twist.

PERFECT LADY

This is ladies' night—and ladies' morning, afternoon, and . . . you get the idea. No one of any gender is flawless, but some women and cocktails come delightfully close. Created by Sidney Cox at London's Grosvenor House and winner of the 1936 British Empire Cocktail Competition, the Perfect Lady is a vibrant ode to feminine grace and charisma in liquid form. Smooth, strong, multilayered, and endlessly compelling, it makes an ideal toast to the women in your life who exemplify all those positive attributes and so many more. While most cocktails are considered gender-neutral, save this juniper-forward, peachy, crisp, no-nonsense beauty for the special women in your life.

1½ ounces gin
1 ounce peach liqueur

½ ounce fresh lemon juice
1 egg white

Combine all ingredients in an ice-filled shaker. Shake without ice (to emulsify the egg white) for 10 seconds, then add ice and shake vigorously. Strain into a stemmed cocktail glass.

National Lion Day

LEO SEASON

You might be thinking, since we recently celebrated International Cat Day, that it's redundant to highlight another feline-centric holiday. But have you ever seen a lion?

Highlighting the lion's dwindling numbers, mostly due to poaching and habitat loss, is a vital part of today's festivities, and one of the best ways to do that is with a memorable lion-themed cocktail. Lauren Schell's Leo Season is just the ticket: a spicy Margarita riff with some serious cayenne-powered fangs. An homage to the zodiac sign inspired by the king of the savannah, this smoky, citrusy, agave-forward heavyweight will have you dominating any conversation like a stereotypical Leo in no time.

1 ounce tequila reposado	½ ounce simple syrup
1 ounce mezcal	3 thin orange slices
1 ounce fresh lime juice	Cayenne pepper, to taste

Combine the tequila, mezcal, lime juice, simple syrup, two orange slices, and cayenne pepper in an ice-filled shaker. Shake vigorously for 25 to 30 seconds and strain into a stemmed cocktail glass. Garnish with another orange slice and a dash of cayenne pepper.

FIVE POINT PALM EXPLODING HEART TECHNIQUE

Star of the seminal 1970s TV series Kung Fu, *David Carradine is perhaps best recognizable to younger martial arts fans as the titular character in Quentin Tarantino's* Kill Bill *films, in which he plays an aging kung fu master whose downfall (spoiler alert!) is the Five Point Palm Exploding Heart Technique. Inspired by that always-lethal series of jabs, this cocktail, developed by Erick Castro at New York City's Boilermaker, is a supremely choreographed, slightly less bitter Mezcal Negroni variation. With coffee liqueur to get you hyped before a* Karate Kid–*style tournament and a soothing herbal component if you're simply looking to center your chi, this modern classic deserves a cocktail black belt.*

1½ ounces mezcal

¾ ounce Punt e Mes

½ ounce **Caffé Lolita**

1 dash **chocolate bitters**

Combine all ingredients in an Old-Fashioned glass. Add ice and stir for five or six seconds.

DIAMOND FIZZ

"I never worry about diets," quipped classic Hollywood sex symbol Mae West. *"The only carrots that interest me are the number you get in a diamond."*

One of the perks of shopping—or pretending to shop—at a high-end diamond emporium like Tiffany's is scoring a complimentary glass of champagne. The Diamond Fizz, which first appeared in David A. Embury's The Fine Art of Mixing Drinks, *takes the decadence up a notch by topping an already sumptuous Sour with a generous helping of bubbly. Just as diamonds come in a wide variety of sizes and colors, the Diamond Fizz works well with almost any spirit, whatever your well-heeled heart desires. If you can't give your significant other a diamond ring or necklace, one of these classy concoctions is the next best thing. (Okay, maybe not, but it's the thought that counts!)*

---

2 ounces spirit of choice	¼ ounce simple syrup
¾ ounce fresh lemon juice	1 egg white
	Champagne, to top

Combine the spirit, lemon juice, simple syrup, and egg white in a shaker. Shake without ice (to emulsify the egg white) for 10 seconds, then add ice and shake vigorously. Strain into a fizz glass and top with champagne.

International Lefthanders Day

LEFT HAND

Left-handers have it rough. Struggling with scissors, can openers, and tape measures; constantly getting smudgy from writing; and frequently bumping elbows with neighbors at crowded dinner parties, it's not easy living in a world that sometimes seems designed exclusively for righties. First observed in 1976 by Dean R. Campbell, founder of International Lefthanders, Inc., International Lefthanders Day sheds light on the many tribulations faced by the approximately 708 million left-handed individuals around the world.

Cocktail glassware is suited perfectly for either hand—and sometimes both simultaneously! One libation that you might be tempted to double-fist is the Left Hand, one of several "Hand" cocktails created at Milk & Honey in the early 2000s. It's a supple, more cocoa-heavy take on a Boulevardier, or a cross between a Negroni and a Manhattan, depending on whom you ask. The simple yet masterful addition of chocolate bitters gives the drink its striking texture. Even a slight shift outside the box, like putting yourself in the shoes of a long-suffering lefty, can offer a world of perspective.

1½ ounces bourbon

¼ ounce Campari

¼ ounce sweet vermouth

2 dashes chocolate bitters

1 brandied cherry,
for garnish

Combine the bourbon, Campari, vermouth, and bitters in a mixing glass filled with cracked ice. Stir with a long-handled spoon for 30 seconds and strain into a stemmed cocktail glass. Garnish with the brandied cherry.

National Creamsicle Day

GOLDEN CADILLAC

When it comes to creamy, citrusy desserts, the Creamsicle is the orange standard. That winning one-two punch of orange and cream has improved everything from cupcakes and candies to sodas and even vodkas over the years, so it shouldn't surprise you to find a cocktail or two influenced by the same combination. The most famous of these, the Golden Cadillac, was created in 1952 at Poor Red's, a roadside restaurant in El Dorado, California. Inspired by the flavor requests of a visiting couple and named after their shiny new car, this easy sipper is the dessert drink by which to measure all others. Its low alcohol content makes it tempting to put down several of these in one sitting, but you'd best take it easy or prepare to suffer a Cadillac-sized tummy ache.

1½ ounces orange juice	¾ ounce heavy cream
¾ ounce crème de cacao	¼ ounce Galliano

Combine all ingredients in an ice-filled shaker. Shake vigorously for 25 to 30 seconds and strain into a stemmed cocktail glass.

LAZY MAN FLIP

Feel like doing absolutely nothing and lying around? That's great! You're already in the spirit of today's holiday. National Relaxation Day encourages you to slow down and unwind. You're reading this book, so you're probably quite familiar with alcohol's soothing effects on mind and body. For those in the know, there's no easier or tastier method of achieving a Zen-like state than by downing Harry Craddock's ultracalming Lazy Man Flip, one of the many highlights of his Savoy Cocktail Book *(1930). The cocktail features applejack and port wine, two fruity favorites famous for their anti-agitation properties, and the easygoing additions of cream and egg yolk dial down the tension even further. It's not the easiest drink to make, but it definitely will make you feel like taking a load off.*

1 ounce applejack

¾ ounce port

¾ ounce heavy cream

½ ounce simple syrup

1 egg yolk

1 pinch freshly grated nutmeg, for garnish

Combine the applejack, port, cream, simple syrup, and egg yolk in a shaker. Shake without ice (to emulsify the egg yolk) for 10 seconds, then add ice and shake vigorously. Strain into a stemmed cocktail glass. Garnish with the nutmeg.

AUGUST 16
National Rum Day

ZOMBIE

Beyond the classics, it doesn't get much more rum-centric than a Zombie. One of Donn Beach's most legendary and diabolical creations, this tiki masterpiece—or horror show, depending on your alcohol tolerance—features three distinctly flavorful rums balanced with just enough fresh juices and pleasantly herbal notes to lure its victims into a false sense of security. Many bars impose a strict two-drink limit on these sugarcane-fueled monsters, due to the impressively high amount of booze packed into each one. Follow that rule unless your idea of a good time is stumbling brainless into the night like the walking dead.

1½ ounces aged rum
1½ ounces Jamaican amber rum
1 ounce 151-proof rum
¾ ounce fresh lime juice
¼ ounce velvet falernum
¼ ounce fresh grapefruit juice

¼ ounce pomegranate syrup
¼ ounce cinnamon syrup
1 barspoon absinthe
1 dash Angostura bitters
1 sprig mint, for garnish

Combine the rums, juices, velvet falernum, pomegranate syrup, cinnamon syrup, absinthe, and bitters in a shaker. Whip shake (no ice) and pour into a tall glass or mug filled two-thirds of the way with crushed ice. Add a straw and top with more crushed ice. Garnish with the mint sprig.

TURN THE PAGE TO
SEE THE ILLUSTRATION
FOR THIS DRINK.

Zombie
PAGE 281

National Vanilla Custard Day

SILVER LINING

Texturally rich, undeniably light and creamy, and bursting with delicious flavor—there's nothing like vanilla custard. What's not as simple is trying to mimic custard's flavor and texture in cocktail form. Luckily, Joseph Schwartz has done just that with his magnificent Silver Lining, a silky Rye Fizz riff that found its way onto the bar and into the mouths of count- less satisfied patrons during Milk & Honey's earliest days. Substituting Licor 43, which counts vanilla as one of its primary components, for the traditional simple syrup, this tall glass of egg-frothed smoothness checks all the right boxes for a proper dessert beverage, minus any hint of a cloy- ing, sugary aftertaste. Who knew you could drink your custard, too?

1½ ounces rye whiskey

¾ ounce Licor 43

¾ ounce fresh lemon juice

1 barspoon cane syrup

1 egg white

Club soda, to top

Combine the whiskey, Licor 43, lemon juice, cane syrup, and egg white in a shaker. Shake without ice (to emulsify the egg white) for 10 sec- onds, then strain into a fizz glass. Top with club soda.

NEGRONI SBAGLIATO

Serendipity Day, created by author Madeleine Kay, rejoices in the unknown and embraces whatever chaos life throws at you. Stop worrying about what might happen and lose yourself in the moment, in the joy of simply being alive. One of the most serendipitous events in cocktail history allegedly occurred at Bar Basso in Milan, Italy, in 1972. When asked by a pushy customer to make a Negroni, overworked bartender Mirko Stocchetto inadvertently substituted champagne for gin. But instead of tossing the drink back in Mirko's face, the customer loved it, and who wouldn't? This bright, playful variation is perfect for anyone looking for a bubbly, less boozy experience that still retains the Negroni's signature Campari-forward sharpness. Sbagliato usually has a negative connotation in Italian, meaning "messed up" or "mistaken." This accident has been making cocktail lovers happy for decades.

---

1 ounce sweet vermouth

1 ounce Campari

1 ounce champagne, to top

1 orange twist, for garnish

Combine the vermouth and Campari in a double Old-Fashioned glass. Add ice and stir for five or six seconds. Top with the champagne. Garnish with the orange twist.

AVIATION NO. 1

In any discussion of major aviation achievements, the Wright brothers' famous flight inevitably arises, but people were taking to the skies long before 1903. The Mongolfier brothers successfully completed a hot air balloon trip near Versailles, France, in 1783, and British polymath George Cayley built the world's first practical glider in 1853. National Aviation Day honors the inventors whose creations have sent humanity's aspirations into the stratosphere and beyond and those who continue to push those boundaries ever higher. Don't believe us? Just look up. When it comes to flight-themed cocktails, the Aviation No. 1 usually receives top billing, and it's no surprise why. Created in 1916 by Hugo Ensslin, a bartender at New York City's Hotel Wallick, the dry, floral classic thrived for much of aviation's golden age until the 1960s, when its signature ingredient, crème de violette, became scarce in America. Recently, it has enjoyed a resurgence thanks to its exceptional bouquet and distinctly sour, slightly botanical finish. These go down a little too easily, so clear your morning-after schedule in the event of an unintended crash landing.

2 ounces gin
¼ ounce fresh lemon juice
⅜ ounce crème de violette

¾ ounce maraschino liqueur
1 brandied cherry,
   for garnish

Combine the gin, lemon juice, crème de violette, and maraschino liqueur in an ice-filled shaker. Shake vigorously for 25 to 30 seconds and strain into a stemmed cocktail glass. Garnish with the brandied cherry.

TURN THE PAGE TO
SEE THE ILLUSTRATION
FOR THIS DRINK.

Aviation No. 1
PAGE 285

EASY STREET

Few activities feel more like summer than coming home after a long day in the sun and gulping down a freezing-cold glass of fresh lemonade. The consumption of sweetened lemon juice has existed in places such as Egypt since at least the 13th century, and a carbonated version of the drink first appeared in England in the 1830s. Anthony Schmidt took it to another level at San Diego's Noble Experiment in 2010, when he debuted the Easy Street. A fizzy, rejuvenating Collins riff made even more delightful with elderflower and cucumbers, it has all the liquid sunshine you'll ever need. The only problem with this crowd-pleasing, boozy balm is that it's so popular with guests, you might need to start a lemonade stand as a side hustle to pay for more bar supplies this summer.

1½ ounces gin (or vodka, if preferred)
¾ ounce elderflower liqueur

¾ ounce fresh lemon juice
4 thin cucumber slices
Club soda, to top
1 lemon wedge, for garnish

Combine the gin, elderflower liqueur, lemon juice, and three cucumber slices in an ice-filled shaker. Shake vigorously for 25 to 30 seconds and strain into a tall glass filled with ice. Top with club soda. Garnish with another cucumber slice and the lemon wedge.

BLUE HAWAII

Hawaiian beauty comes in every conceivable hue, from the midnight black of its volcanic beaches to the bright sapphire of its sparkling waters. That shade of blue perfectly describes the Blue Hawaii, the state's most famous beverage. Created in 1957 at Honolulu's Kaiser Hawaiian Village by bartender Harry Yee, this eminently sweet and sip-worthy, classic tiki marriage of pineapple, coconut rum, and blue curaçao is cooler than the Pacific trade winds and even more refreshing. Even if a trip to Hawaii isn't in the cards, you can experience an epic taste of the island lifestyle that goes down easier than a ukulele solo by the late, great Hawaiian musician Israel Kamakawiwoʻole.

2 ounces fresh pineapple juice
1½ ounces coconut rum
¾ ounce blue curaçao

½ ounce fresh lime juice
1 pineapple wedge, for garnish
1 brandied cherry, for garnish

Combine the juices, rum, and blue curaçao in a shaker. Pour into a tall glass or mug filled two-thirds of the way with crushed ice. Add a straw and top with more crushed ice. Garnish with the pineapple wedge and brandied cherry. Cocktail umbrella optional.

National Eat a Peach Day

GEORGIA JULEP

Wondering why you're feeling so peachy today? Because it's National Eat a Peach Day, duh! If you're a kitchen novice whose cobbler-making skills might be lacking or nonexistent, you have plenty of less time-consuming ways to enjoy the peach's uniquely concentrated zest. The best of these, for those of us who prefer to drink our fruits, is the Georgia Julep. It's a little-known fact that many of the first julep recipes in the mid-19th century called for peach brandy instead of bourbon or rye, and it's easy to taste why. Savory-sweet, rich, and pleasantly cooling, this mellow delight certainly deserves the right to be named after the Peach State.

1 handful fresh mint leaves	1 white sugar cube
1¼ ounces cognac	1 sprig mint, for garnish
¾ ounce peach liqueur	1 thin peach slice, for garnish

Gently squeeze mint leaves in your hand (to release fragrance) and drop them in a traditional silver julep cup. Add the cognac, peach liqueur, and sugar cube to the cup. Muddle lightly to break up the sugar cube (but don't bruise the mint) and fill the cup two-thirds of the way with crushed ice. Stir with a swizzle stick, then add a straw and top with more crushed ice. Garnish with the mint sprig and the peach slice.

BLOOD AND SAND

If you're wondering why we're celebrating Valentine's Day a second time, please read again. Valentino *Day honors the life and work of early Hollywood icon Rudolph Valentino, who appeared in renowned silent films including* The Four Horsemen of the Apocalypse, The Sheik, *and* The Eagle. *Valentino also famously appeared in the 1922 Paramount Pictures drama* Blood and Sand, *in which he portrayed Spanish bullfighter Juan Gallardo, a brash young man whose sudden rise and tragic downfall cemented the actor's place on the A-list. That film also inspired a popular Prohibition-era cocktail of the same name. With a hue that recalls the film's dusty, gore-streaked milieu, the Blood and Sand has an unusually robust tang that, like silent films, doesn't always translate well with today's drinkers. But the select few enjoy it with the exuberance of a thespian giving his all to make audiences swoon.*

¾ ounce blended scotch

¾ ounce sweet vermouth

¾ ounce Cherry Heering

¾ ounce fresh orange juice

Combine all ingredients in an ice-filled shaker. Shake vigorously for 25 to 30 seconds and strain into a stemmed cocktail glass.

CLOAK & DAGGER

Whether made of metal, stone, flint, or bone, knives are essential for cooking, eating, hunting, fishing, construction, and—after the invention of the Swiss Army knife—pretty much any task you can imagine. If you're feeling especially punny, tell everyone you encounter today to "have a knife day!" On second thought, maybe don't. A sharp pocketknife is an indispensable implement in any drink-slinger's toolkit, whether you need to peel an orange slice for a garnish, open a wine bottle, or halve a lime to extract the juice for a Cloak & Dagger. This knife-inspired Daiquiri riff from Ted Saucier's Bottoms Up *(1951) features black and aged rums for a deceptively multilayered potable. Tart and mellow with an effortlessly quaffable finish, this is one double-edged blade you won't mind sinking your teeth into.*

1 ounce aged rum
1 ounce Goslings Black Seal rum

1 ounce fresh lime juice
¼ ounce simple syrup
1 lime wedge, for garnish

Combine the rums, lime juice, and simple syrup in an ice-filled shaker. Shake vigorously for 25 to 30 seconds and strain into a stemmed cocktail glass. Garnish with the lime wedge.

WHISKEY SOUR

If you dig the classics, it doesn't get much more old-school than the Whiskey Sour, and by "old-school," we're talking about a time before most people even went to school. The key to whipping up an excellent version of this all-time refresher—besides using fresh ingredients and not a chemical-filled mix—is, like most things in life, all about balance. Using equal parts lemon juice and simple syrup ensures that the cocktail won't taste too sweet or tangy and that the bourbon's woodsy, floral notes will shine to succulent perfection. We highly recommend including the egg white, faithful to the drink's 19th-century description, for a fun texture and shinier appearance. Whether you prefer your Sours served up or on the rocks, follow an even-keeled recipe and you'll keep coming back for more.

2 ounces bourbon
¾ ounce fresh lemon juice
¾ ounce simple syrup

1 egg white
2 dashes Angostura bitters,
   for garnish

Combine the bourbon, lemon juice, simple syrup, and egg white in a shaker. Shake without ice (to emulsify the egg white) for 10 seconds, then add ice and shake vigorously. Strain into a Sour glass. Garnish with the bitters.

ASTA COLLINS

Of all the dog days of summer, this one barks the loudest. National Dog Day, founded by animal rescue activist, dog trainer, and author Colleen Paige in 2004, urges you to shower your furry buddies with unconditional love (as if you needed any extra encouragement), to recognize the large number of dogs in shelters that need rescuing, and to honor family and working dogs for their countless contributions to society. From Toto and Lassie to Beethoven and Air Buddy, thousands of iconic canine characters have graced screens big and small for generations. One of the earliest doggie superstars was a wire fox terrier named Skippy, who famously played the role of Asta in the 1934 detective comedy The Thin Man, *starring William Powell and Myrna Loy. If you're looking for a liquid companion for this notoriously boozy film or any other work of dog-related cinema, shake up an Asta Collins. A scintillating mixture of vodka, Campari, and fresh juices, this crisp energizer will have you bouncing around like a puppy in no time.*

1¼ ounces vodka
1 ounce fresh grapefruit juice
½ ounce fresh lime juice

½ ounce simple syrup
¼ ounce Campari
Club soda, to top
1 lime wedge, for garnish

Combine the vodka, juices, simple syrup, and Campari in a shaker. Whip shake (no ice) and pour into a tall glass filled with ice. Top with club soda. Garnish with the lime wedge.

CALYPSO DYNAMITE

Not obsessed with bananas? Well, you should be. That's the message from the folks who started Banana Lovers Day (whoever they might be) and for good reason. Ain't no party like a banana party—which might not make sense until you try Matthew Linzmeier's Calypso Dynamite. Created while he was working in New Orleans and listening to Caribbean music, this scotch-based tiki showstopper tastes smoky, sweet, funky, and citrusy, with each of its components elevating a generous helping of banana liqueur. A flashier version requires hollowing out half a lime, flipping it inside out, pouring in the overproof rum, and lighting it on fire, but leave that to the professionals. This super-boozy cooler might impair your judgment, so probably just stick to dancing.

¾ ounce blended scotch
¾ ounce Islay scotch
¾ ounce banana liqueur
½ ounce orgeat

½ ounce fresh lemon juice
½ ounce fresh lime juice
3 dashes Angostura bitters
1 pinch freshly grated cinnamon,
　for garnish

Combine the scotches, banana liqueur, orgeat, juices, and bitters in a shaker. Pour into a tall mug filled two-thirds of the way with crushed ice. Top with more crushed ice and garnish with the cinnamon.

OPTIONAL GARNISH: *Halve a lime, remove the pith, and flip it inside out. Crown drink with the lime, fill it with ½ ounce of overproof Jamaican rum, and set alight. Grate cinnamon above the flame.*

BOW TIE

The bow tie has strong associations with formal weddings, intellectuals, and people who use "summer" as a verb. Author Warren St. John once wrote that the bow tie suggests "a fusty adherence to a contrarian point of view," which certainly describes the Bow Tie cocktail, a recipe for which first appeared on Liquor.com. You'd be hard-pressed to find a drink with three more opposing ingredients, but the eccentric combination of cognac, dry vermouth, and pineapple juice tastes surprisingly balanced and fruity, yet still dry and boozy enough for the spirit-forward set. The best part is that it's infinitely easier to mix than tying a bow tie.

2 ounces cognac

1 ounce dry vermouth

¾ ounce fresh pineapple juice

1 pineapple frond, for garnish

Combine the cognac, dry vermouth, and pineapple juice in an ice-filled shaker. Shake vigorously for 25 to 30 seconds and strain over ice into a double Old-Fashioned glass. Garnish with the pineapple frond.

Lemon Juice Day

LEMON SMACK

Yes, lemons are certainly nice to behold, and the oil expelled from their skins makes for quite an aromatic treat. But today is specifically about the globally popular fruit's mouth-puckering inner beauty—the juice! When life hands you lemons, make lemonade. When it also hands you vodka (thanks, life!), mix yourself a Lemon Smack. The irresistibly tangy brainchild of Naren Young of New York City's Dante, this Mount Rushmore of lemon worship includes not only lemon juice but also limoncello, lemon soda, lemon curd, and zest from its lemon peel garnish. A citrus powerhouse that honors every component of everyone's favorite edible yellow orb, it's summery lemonade for the slightly grizzled adult soul, and that's nothing to be sour about.

1 ounce vodka

1 ounce limoncello

¾ ounce fresh lemon
   juice

¾ ounce simple syrup

1 barspoon of lemon curd

Lemon soda, to top

1 lemon twist, for garnish

Combine the vodka, limoncello, lemon juice, simple syrup, and lemon curd in an ice-filled shaker. Shake vigorously for 25 to 30 seconds and strain into a double Old-Fashioned glass over ice. Top with the lemon soda. Garnish with the lemon twist.

MAI TAI

Victor "Trader Vic" Bergeron claimed to have invented the Mai Tai—a delightful mixture of rum, lime juice, curaçao, and orgeat—at the Oakland location of his popular restaurant chain in 1944. However, his longtime rival, Donn "The Beachcomber" Beach, alleged that Bergeron stole the idea from the similar-tasting Q.B. Cooler that he'd been serving since 1933, leading to an uncharacteristically heated feud between the two laid-back beach bros. That's because the Mai Tai, named after the Tahitian word for "excellence" or "the best," is worth fighting over. Fresh, balanced, and highlighting the top qualities of each of its ingredients (to say nothing of its ingenious garnish that's looks like an island with a palm tree), it's one of the purest ways to escape to tropical paradise without leaving the comfort of your local bar. Fruity, spicy, and molasses-forward, it's a rich one-two peacemaking punch that even Trader Vic and The Beachcomber would agree upon.

1½ ounces Jamaican amber rum
½ ounce fresh lime juice
½ ounce curaçao
½ ounce orgeat

½ ounce Goslings Black
   Seal rum
1 lime wedge, for garnish
1 sprig mint, for garnish

Combine the Jamaican rum, lime juice, curaçao, and orgeat in a shaker. Pour into a double Old-Fashioned glass filled two-thirds of the way with crushed ice. Float the Goslings, add a straw, and top with more crushed ice. Garnish with the lime wedge and mint sprig.

CUPID DELUXE

Being a good matchmaker requires savvy, timing, and understanding your friends' personalities and motivations. Mythologically speaking, no one better exemplifies those qualities than Cupid, the childlike Roman god of erotic love, attraction, and affection, whose arrows fill their targets with uncontrollable yearning. The notoriously mischievous cherub also serves as the main inspiration for the Cupid Deluxe, created by José Cardenas at Dutch Kills in 2019. Exercise caution if you decide to mix up this aphrodisiacal blend of scotch, banana, pineapple, and ginger because even one sip can produce instant feelings of Cupid-level desire.

1½ ounces blended scotch

¼ ounce banana liqueur

¼ ounce fresh pineapple juice

¼ ounce fresh lemon juice

½ ounce ginger syrup

2 dashes chocolate bitters

Club soda, to top

1 piece candied ginger, for garnish

Combine the scotch, banana liqueur, juices, ginger syrup, and bitters in a shaker. Whip shake (no ice) and pour into a tall glass filled with ice. Top with club soda. Garnish with the piece of candied ginger.

SEPTEMBER

					1	2
					NATIONAL BOURBON HERITAGE MONTH Kentucky Maid	V-J DAY None but the Brave
3	4	5	6	7	8	9
NATIONAL SKY-SCRAPER DAY Imperial Fizz	NATIONAL WILDLIFE DAY Wild-Eyed Rose	LABOR DAY Manhattan	NATIONAL COFFEE ICE CREAM DAY Café con Leche Flip	THREATENED SPECIES DAY Red-Eyed Tree Frog	NATIONAL GRAND-PARENTS DAY Dirty Grand-mother	WONDERFUL WEIRDOS DAY La Sardina
10	11	12	13	14	15	16
TV DINNER DAY Bullshot	PATRIOT DAY Improved New York Cocktail	NATIONAL DAY OF ENCOURAGE-MENT Gloom Chaser	NATIONAL HOT CHOCOLATE DAY Mexican Hot Chocolate	NATIONAL LIVE CREATIVE DAY Waldorf	NATIONAL CRÈME DE MENTHE DAY Apotheke	MEXICAN INDE-PENDENCE DAY Paloma
17	18	19	20	21	22	23
INTERNATIONAL COUNTRY MUSIC DAY Country Life	US AIR FORCE BIRTHDAY Sky Pilot	INTERNATIONAL TALK LIKE A PIRATE DAY Pirate's Julep	NATIONAL RUM PUNCH DAY Puka Puka Punch	INTERNATIONAL DAY OF PEACE Los Amigos	FALL EQUINOX Autumn in Jersey	NATIONAL DOGS IN POLITICS DAY Rob Roy
24	25	26	27	28	29	30
NATIONAL FAMILY HEALTH & FITNESS DAY Chin Up	BETTER BREAK-FAST DAY Turn of the Screw	SHAMU THE WHALE DAY Salty Whale	WORLD TOURISM DAY Suitcase	NATIONAL GOOD NEIGHBOR DAY Trader Vic's Tiki Punch	NATIONAL BISCOTTI DAY Tuscan Night	NATIONAL HOT MULLED CIDER DAY Mulled Cider

National Bourbon Heritage Month

KENTUCKY MAID

For a quintessentially American spirit, and one with an entire month dedicated to its heritage, bourbon's origins still remain rather murky. Historians think that Scotch-Irish immigrants in and around Bourbon County, Kentucky, first distilled the barrel-aged whiskey, made primarily from corn, in the late 18th century. We could spend weeks investigating bourbon's birth, but that would defeat the purpose of this month's festivities—drinking the stuff! Most frequently associated with spirit-forward classics such as the Old-Fashioned and Manhattan, bourbon's woodsy, flowery, piquant qualities lend themselves just as nicely to citrusy sippers, as any Whiskey Sour (page 292) aficionado will let you know. The Kentucky Maid, first served at New York City's East Side Company Bar in 2005, takes its cue from that drink, as well as the Daiquiri and Mint Julep, for a mellow, tart, and exceptionally refreshing pick-me-up. This boldly vegetal excursion is a hell of a lot more fun than arguing about historical minutiae.

---

2 ounces bourbon

1 ounce fresh lime juice

¾ ounce simple syrup

4 thin cucumber slices

3 or 4 fresh mint leaves

1 sprig mint, for garnish

Combine the bourbon, lime juice, simple syrup, three cucumber slices, and mint leaves in a shaker. Shake vigorously for 25 to 30 seconds and strain into a double Old-Fashioned glass over ice. Garnish with another cucumber slice and the mint sprig.

NONE BUT THE BRAVE

Most students of 20th-century history know the iconic Life *magazine cover featuring a sailor and woman passionately kissing in Times Square during the conclusion of World War II. That photo, taken on V-J Day, specifically commemorates America's victory over Imperial Japan. Months before the Allied forces' triumph over the Axis powers, creatives had begun touting the impending victory with songs, art, the occasional saucy photo, and cocktails, including Crosby Gaige's None but the Brave, an aromatic Buck variation that first appeared in the 1945 edition of his seminal* Cocktail Guide. *An ode to the people who served in the US military during the deadliest years in human history, this potent cognac sipper is fortified with allspice and a heaping helping of ginger for a tantalizingly brisk yet smooth finish. Despite the name's allusion to wartime, it's far more likely to end a conflict than start one.*

2 ounces cognac

¾ ounce ginger syrup

½ ounce fresh lime juice

¼ ounce St. Elizabeth Allspice Dram

Club soda, to top

1 piece candied ginger, for garnish

Combine the cognac, ginger syrup, lime juice, and allspice in a shaker. Whip shake (no ice) and pour into a tall glass filled with ice. Top with club soda. Garnish with the piece of candied ginger.

IMPERIAL FIZZ

It would seem odd today for a major city not to have any skyscrapers, but these feats of engineering have been around only for about a century, starting with Chicago's 10-story Home Insurance Building in 1885. Before later marvels such as the World Trade Center and Dubai's 2,722-foot Burj Khalifa, one structure was synonymous with architectural supremacy: the Empire State Building, the crown jewel of Midtown Manhattan, constructed in 1930 and still the sixth-tallest freestanding structure in the Western Hemisphere. A similarly bright, lofty, and innovative work of cocktail design, the Imperial Fizz from Brandon Wise of Portland, Oregon, uses the highly unusual combination of rye and Jamaican rum to frothy perfection. Each complex sip is like discovering another fascinating aspect of a building you thought you knew. If you're prone to vertigo, down one of these after checking out the Empire State Building's famed 102nd-floor observation deck.

1 ounce Jamaican amber rum

1 ounce rye whiskey

¾ ounce fresh lemon juice

¼ ounce simple syrup

1 egg white

Club soda, to top

Combine the rum, whiskey, lemon juice, simple syrup, and egg white in a shaker. Shake without ice (to emulsify the egg white) for 10 seconds, then add ice and shake vigorously. Strain into a tall glass filled with ice. Top with club soda.

TURN THE PAGE TO
SEE THE ILLUSTRATION
FOR THIS DRINK.

Imperial Fizz
PAGE 303

WILD-EYED ROSE

National Wildlife Day implores you to open your eyes and heart to all the scaly, slimy, furry, and feathery critters with whom you share the planet. Efforts to preserve and improve the world's natural habitats and their billions of residents have reached an all-time high, but the threats to wildlife have never been greater. Spending quality time getting up close to earth's fauna can put the most human-centric observers in touch with their wild side. Channel that inner beast with the Wild-Eyed Rose, a naturally simple sipper from Victor "Trader Vic" Bergeron that first graced the pages of his classic collection Bartender's Guide by Trader Vic, *in 1947. Light, citrusy, and just sweet enough to pique every part of your palate, it's a shockingly simple, quick-to-fix recipe from a man known for complicated tiki time-drainers—and that's a good thing if you don't want to miss any of the animal action going on outside your window.*

2 ounces Irish whiskey

¼ ounce fresh lime juice

¼ ounce grenadine

Combine all ingredients in an ice-filled shaker. Shake vigorously for 25 to 30 seconds and strain over ice into a double Old-Fashioned glass.

MANHATTAN

The first group to suggest a day to celebrate contributions of workers to our economy by, um, not working was the Central Labor Union of New York, Brooklyn, and Jersey City, which organized the first Labor Day parade in Manhattan on this date in 1882. A staple of bar and restaurant menus since the 1860s, when a bartender named George Black most likely invented it at a pub near Broadway and Houston Street, this American masterpiece has enthralled generations of booze lovers with its simple yet timeless one-two punch of bold American whiskey (originally rye) and a distinctive blend of herbal and bitter undertones. It's hard to think of a better way to salute the people who keep America running than with the drink that helped create an entire industry and raised drink-making to the status it enjoys today.

2 ounces rye whiskey or bourbon
1 ounce sweet vermouth

4 dashes Angostura bitters
1 brandied cherry, for garnish

Combine the rye, vermouth, and bitters in a mixing glass filled with cracked ice. Stir with a long-handled spoon for 30 seconds, then strain into a stemmed cocktail glass. Garnish with the brandied cherry.

CAFÉ CON LECHE FLIP

When it's a toss-up between coffee and ice cream, the decision is obvious: Choose both! High-energy mixologists have been combining coffee, cream, and liquor since producers created the first coffee liqueurs in Spain in the 1600s. None of these creations tastes as indulgent as the Café con Leche Flip, though, an eggnog-like masterpiece that originated at hallowed New York City drinking den Pegu Club in the mid-2000s. Goslings Black Seal rum deepens and sweetens the coffee liqueur's naturally nutty, herby, smoky qualities, while the egg yolk provides a uniquely pleasant texture and mouthfeel. Graciously topped with fragrant nutmeg, this dandy might just become your new cheat day go-to—and by cheat day we mean every day.

1 ounce Goslings Black Seal rum	¾ ounce simple syrup
1 ounce Caffé Lolita	1 egg yolk
¾ ounce heavy cream	1 pinch freshly grated nutmeg, for garnish

 Combine the rum, Caffé Lolita, cream, simple syrup, and egg yolk in a shaker. Shake without ice (to emulsify the egg yolk) for 10 seconds, then add ice and shake vigorously. Strain into a stemmed cocktail glass. Garnish with the nutmeg.

Threatened Species Day

RED-EYED TREE FROG

*Sorry to harsh your vibe, but a lot of wildlife is in real danger. Accord-
ing to the International Union for Conservation of Nature, more than
40,000 species of animals and plants face immense pressure to survive
from loss of habitat, hunting, disease, pollution, and invasive species.
It's not all doom and gloom, however. The red-eyed tree frog, a native of
Central America famed for its brilliant neon skin and bulbous peepers,
has made a comeback in recent years. Inspired by this gorgeous creature,
the Red-Eyed Tree Frog cocktail is a tropical relaxer every bit as colorful
as its name suggests. Made with Cacique Guaro, Costa Rica's mellow,
sugarcane-distilled national spirit (or white rum or vodka, in a pinch)
and rounded out with cheerful citrus, nutty pistachio syrup, and a hint
of anise, its flavor profile is as unique as a glimpse of its notoriously
elusive namesake.*

---

2 ounces Cacique Guaro

1 ounce fresh lime juice

¾ ounce pistachio syrup

1 barspoon absinthe

2 dashes Angostura bitters

2 dashes Peychaud's bitters

2 brandied cherries, for garnish

1 lime wedge, for garnish

Combine the Cacique Guaro, lime juice, pistachio syrup, and absinthe
in a shaker. Pour into a tall glass filled two-thirds of the way with
crushed ice. Add the bitters and stir briefly with a swizzle stick. Add a
straw and top with more crushed ice. Garnish with the brandied cherries and lime wedge to form a frog face.

TURN THE PAGE TO
SEE THE ILLUSTRATION
FOR THIS DRINK.

Red-Eyed Tree Frog
PAGE 309

DIRTY GRANDMOTHER

Whatever you call them—Grandma and Grandpa, Meemaw and Peepaw, Nana and Poppop—your parents' parents are something special. It may seem preposterous, but your grandparents were young once. Chances are, they let it all hang out at a swinging shindig or two, and who knows? Maybe they still like to get funky every now and then. If they do, mix them up a Dirty Grandmother. This rum-based White Russian riff has been delighting drinkers of all (legal) ages since the middle of the 20th century, when your grandparents probably were doing their hardest partying. As sweetly satisfying as the chocolates your grandparents used to sneak you when your parents weren't looking, this ancestral cocktail ages as wonderfully as memories of times spent with them.

1½ ounces aged rum
1 ounce Kahlúa

Heavy cream or whole milk, to taste

Combine the rum and Kahlúa in a double Old-Fashioned glass. Add ice and stir for five or six seconds. Top with the cream or milk.

LA SARDINA

Get wild today, try some unusual food, watch an odd movie, or listen to some crazy tunes. What seems weird to some strikes others as perfectly natural, so there's no wrong way to celebrate today's holiday—as long as it makes you feel wonderful! Countless booze-loving mad scientists have attempted to imbue a sense of weirdness into their beverages, but few drinks hit that mark as perfectly and deliciously as La Sardina. Appearing on the drinks-themed website Supercall in 2017, this totally bonkers take on a Dirty Martini takes its name from a gin base infused with fatty sardine oil. Coupled with olive brine and garnished with sardine-stuffed olives for extra eccentricity, this silky, buttery, oh-so-salty oddity will make you the talk of any cocktail party. If fish-flavored brine doesn't do it for you, you can sit this one out, but where's the fun in that?

2 ounces sardine oil–washed gin
(recipe follows)

¼ ounce dry vermouth

¼ ounce olive brine

2 sardine-stuffed olives,
for garnish

Combine the gin, vermouth, and olive brine in a mixing glass filled with cracked ice. Stir with a long-handled spoon for 30 seconds, then strain into a stemmed cocktail glass. Garnish with the olives.

SARDINE OIL–WASHED GIN

1½ cups gin

1 ounce sardine oil

Pour the gin and oil into a sealable jar and shake well. Place the jar in a freezer and freeze until the fat solidifies at the top of the jar. Scrape off the fat layer and discard or save for cooking. Strain the gin through a cheesecloth-lined funnel into a clean jar.

For a vegan substitution for the sardine oil, use 1 ounce avocado oil and sea salt to taste.

BULLSHOT

Few foods scream "20th century" quite like TV dinners. Introduced by C.A. Swanson and Sons on this date in 1953, the original, Thanksgiving-themed frozen meal consisted of turkey, peas, cornbread dressing, and sweet potatoes, all neatly compartmentalized on an aluminum tray for quick oven heating. If you're chowing down on a classic TV dinner tonight, you'll want an equally retro, delightfully kitschy cocktail to accompany it, namely the Bullshot. This savory Bloody Mary alternative originally found fame in 1950s Detroit at the Caucus Club and remained a hit well into the 1970s, even making a brief cameo in the film A Clockwork Orange *before fading into obscurity. The aggressive and spicy blend of vodka, beef bouillon, citrus, and hot sauce isn't for everyone—much like a TV dinner—but this smudge-colored slice of lost Americana might have you craving seconds.*

---

3 ounces beef bouillon (or consommé)

2 ounces vodka

½ ounce fresh lemon juice

4 dashes Cholula hot sauce

2 dashes Worcestershire sauce

Salt, to taste

Cracked black pepper, to taste

1 lemon wedge, for garnish

Combine the bouillon, vodka, lemon juice, hot sauce, and Worcestershire sauce in a shaker. Whip shake (no ice) and pour into a tall glass filled with cracked ice. Sprinkle salt and pepper. Garnish with the lemon wedge.

IMPROVED NEW YORK COCKTAIL

As with the greatest calamities, it's impossible to forget, if you were old enough to remember, where you were on the morning of September 11, 2001. In the aftermath of the tragedy, the US Congress proclaimed today Patriot Day to honor those who perished in the attacks, the first responders who sacrificed their lives and health to save others, and the thousands of soldiers who fought to make sure that something like 9/11 never happens on American soil again. So far, it hasn't, thanks to increased safety measures at airports and other high-traffic areas, including Manhattan, where One World Trade Center—formerly the Freedom Tower and currently the tallest building in the Western Hemisphere—now stands on the site of the original World Trade Center. A symbol of perseverance in the face of devastation, it stands as a source of pride for New Yorkers, whose spirits sorely bent in 2001 but thankfully never broke. There's no more appropriate sipper for Patriot Day than the Improved New York Cocktail, Dan Greenbaum's riff on the classic Improved Whiskey Cocktail. Stiff, multifaceted, slightly sweet, and blissfully herbaceous, it offers a powerful reminder that, as dark as things may get, better times always lie on the horizon.

1 ounce rye whiskey	3 dashes Peychaud's bitters
1 ounce cognac	1 dash absinthe
½ ounce maraschino liqueur	1 lemon twist, for garnish

 Combine the rye, cognac, maraschino liqueur, bitters, and absinthe in an Old-Fashioned glass. Add ice and stir for five or six seconds. Garnish with the lemon twist.

GLOOM CHASER

Feeling dejected? Uninspired? Hopeless? Most of us fall into a bit of a funk every now and then, but a little reassurance from others can go a long way toward getting us back on track. Proposed in 2007 by a group of students at Arkansas's Harding University and later made official by President George W. Bush, the National Day of Encouragement urges you to make a helpful impact on those around you. If you want to congratulate people for hard work done well (and make buddies for life), give them the unbeatable gift of this bright cocktail dedicated to happiness. Harry Craddock's Gloom Chaser made its first appearance in his Savoy Cocktail Book. *With a double dose of delightfully dry orange liqueur in the form of Grand Marnier and curaçao, this glass of motivational energy tastes brisk, fresh, and light enough to keep you focused on any ambition you might have, even if that's just to mix up another round.*

---

1 ounce Grand Marnier

1 ounce curaçao

1 ounce fresh lemon juice

½ ounce pomegranate syrup

1 orange twist, for garnish

Combine the Grand Marnier, curaçao, lemon juice, and pomegranate syrup in an ice-filled shaker. Shake vigorously for 25 to 30 seconds and strain into a stemmed cocktail glass. Garnish with the orange twist.

MEXICAN HOT CHOCOLATE

Chocolate is a rare food in that you can enjoy it freezing cold, at room temperature, or delightfully warm and gooey. National Hot Chocolate Day celebrates a rich liquid consumed in Central and South America for more than 2,000 years before Spanish explorers brought it to Europe in the 1500s. Booze-lovers of all centuries have found ways to embellish practically every kind of drink with alcohol, and hot chocolate is no exception. Named for its sweet and spicy, south-of-the-border ingredients, namely agave nectar and chipotle chili powder, the Mexican Hot Chocolate is a deliciously complex dessert beverage that both calms the nerves and startles the senses with its peppery finish. Even with a healthy dose of spirit, this one goes down exceptionally smoothly, but make no mistake: This isn't your grandmother's cocoa—unless she happens to be supercool.

6 ounces milk

2 ounces dark chocolate, chopped

1½ ounces brown spirit of choice

¼ ounce agave nectar

1 pinch cinnamon

1 pinch ground chipotle chili powder

2 dashes chocolate bitters

Hand-whipped cream, to top

 In a saucepan over medium heat, add the milk and chopped chocolate. Heat slowly, stirring often, until the chocolate melts and the mixture is smooth. Add the agave nectar, cinnamon, chili powder, and bitters while continuing to stir. Add the spirit and continue to heat until steaming. Pour into a mug and float the cream.

National Live Creative Day

WALDORF

The aptly named Creative, an Illinois-based promotional products company, founded National Live Creative Day in 2016. Invent, dream, explore, discover. Do whatever it takes to get those innovative juices flowing today! Being creative doesn't mean you have to reinvent the wheel, though. Sometimes a simple tweak to an established style of art, meal, or cocktail can produce truly groundbreaking results. That's what happened in the early 20th century, when bartenders at New York City's Waldorf Hotel added absinthe to their Bourbon Manhattans. Customers enjoyed the variation so much that these enterprising drink-slingers eventually named it after their place of business. The modern Waldorf, adapted by Dale DeGroff, tastes bold, complex, and aromatic, a totally different experience than its predecessor, thanks to one small spark of creativity.

2 ounces bourbon
1 ounce sweet vermouth

2 dashes Angostura bitters
1 barspoon absinthe
1 lemon twist, for garnish

Combine the bourbon, vermouth, bitters, and absinthe in an ice-filled mixing glass. Stir with a long-handled spoon for 30 seconds and strain into a stemmed cocktail glass. Garnish with the lemon twist.

APOTHEKE

We usually think of doctors as know-it-all killjoys who shame us for drinking, but that wasn't always the case. Highly respected (or slightly shady) medical professionals created many of the tastiest and most interesting liqueurs as tonics or cure-alls, and crème de menthe is no exception. Designed by French pharmacist Emile Giffard to cool the stomach and aid in digestion, this sweet, peppermint-flavored favorite is prized as a solo after-dinner tipple or as a crisp addition to creamy desserts.

The Grasshopper is the most well-known cocktail to feature crème de menthe, but Harry MacElhone's Apotheke, which first appeared in the 1919 edition of Harry's ABC of Mixing Cocktails, is a better option to combat the effects of a gluttonous meal. Named after the German word for drugstore, it has exceptionally minty properties amplified by Fernet-Branca—a barrel-aged, highly herbal amaro and a powerful digestif in its own right—as well as the calming notes of chamomile, cardamom, and coriander found in sweet vermouth. Your doctor won't prescribe one for you, but sipping an Apotheke sure beats chewing an antacid any day of the week!

1 ounce Fernet-Branca

1 ounce crème de menthe
1 ounce sweet vermouth

Combine all ingredients in a mixing glass filled with cracked ice. Stir with a long-handled spoon for 30 seconds, then strain into a stemmed cocktail glass.

PALOMA

By this date in 1810, Miguel Hidalgo y Costillo had had enough of colonialism. Understandably irked by three centuries of oppressive Spanish rule, the Catholic priest in the town of Dolores, Mexico, rang his church's bell and publicly demanded freedom for his country. Known as the Grito de Dolores *(Cry of Dolores), his speech jump-started the Mexican War of Independence that ended in 1821, when Spain withdrew its troops and recognized its former colony as an independent nation. If you want to toast that rebellious spirit today, do it with Mexico's national drink. Named after the popular 1860s folk song "La Paloma" ("The Dove") and allegedly created by bartender Don Javier Delgado y Corona at La Capilla cantina in Tequila, Mexico, the Paloma cocktail is fizzy, citrus-forward, and refreshing, a perfectly delicious ode to the unique flavors of its country of origin.*

¡Viva México!

2 ounces tequila

1 ounce fresh grapefruit juice

½ ounce fresh lime juice

½ ounce simple syrup

1 pinch salt

Club soda, to top

1 thin orange slice, for garnish

Combine the tequila, juices, simple syrup, and salt in a shaker. Whip shake (no ice) and pour into a tall glass filled with ice. Top with club soda. Garnish with the orange slice.

COUNTRY LIFE

If you find yourself spontaneously singing about cheap whiskey, pickup trucks, failed romances, football, nostalgia for simpler times, or friends in low places, you may have an addiction to country music. A far cry from the days of good ole boys such as Hank Williams, Merle Haggard, and Johnny Cash, modern country stars, including Canadian Shania Twain and Australian Keith Urban, come from every corner of the globe—which is why the name and ingredients of the Country Life make it a perfect fit for today's festivities. A fascinating spirit-forward bracer from Crosby Gaige's 1945 Cocktail Guide, it's got a bourbon base, straight from country music's traditional heartland, balanced by port from Europe and rum from the Caribbean. This drink assembles a gorgeous melting pot of flavors guaranteed to fire up your taste buds, regardless of your musical preferences.

1½ ounces bourbon
¼ ounce Jamaican amber rum

¾ ounce port
2 dashes orange bitters
1 orange twist, for garnish

Combine the bourbon, rum, port, and bitters in a double Old-Fashioned glass. Add ice and stir for five or six seconds. Garnish with the orange twist.

SKY PILOT

*Starting in 1907, the US Air Force operated as a part of the Army. By
the late 1930s, it was a given in military circles that the Army's rapidly
expanding Aeronautical Division soon would go independent. Around
this time, perhaps anticipating this impending development, the first
recipes for the Sky Pilot appeared in cocktail literature, most notably
William Tarling's* Café Royal Cocktail Book *(1937). (The USAF became
autonomous a decade later, thanks to a cow—specifically the* Sacred Cow,
*the presidential aircraft aboard which President Harry Truman signed
the National Security Act of 1947, which paved the way for the USAF to
become a full-service branch of the military.) A rum-infused Jack Rose
riff that's smoother than a turbulence-free flight, this fruity, no-frills
tipple will have you soaring higher than a Lockheed SR-71 Blackbird,
a notoriously stealthy, high-altitude spy plane. If you decide to go hard
on this easily sipped jet fuel tonight, make sure you have a safe landing
zone prepared.*

1½ ounces applejack

½ ounce aged rum

¾ ounce fresh lime juice

¾ ounce pomegranate syrup

Combine all ingredients in an ice-filled shaker. Shake vigorously
for 25 to 30 seconds and strain into a stemmed cocktail glass.

TURN THE PAGE TO
SEE THE ILLUSTRATION
FOR THIS DRINK.

Sky Pilot
PAGE 321

Pirate's Julep
PAGE 324

PIRATE'S JULEP

Ahoy, me hearties! Are ye ready to weigh anchor and hoist the mizzen? Hornswoggle some landlubbers out of their booty? Send a scallywag or two to Davy Jones's Locker? If not, you'd better start working on your yo-ho-hos and shiver-me-timbers because it's International Talk Like a Pirate Day!

You can prepare for today's holiday in plenty of ways: by bingeing all the Pirates of the Caribbean *movies, memorizing Pirate Steve's lines in* Dodgeball, *or downing a hefty dose of your favorite rum. Better yet, put that spirit to good use by fixing yourself and your closest seadogs a Pirate's Julep or two. Originally appearing in the German manual* Cocktailian: Das Handbuch der Bar, *this powerfully minty, nutty, and fruity grog is more refreshing than an unexpected ocean breeze. But with 3 ounces of booze per serving, swill these in moderation or you'll soon be feeling like you just walked the plank.*

---

1 handful fresh mint leaves
3 ounces gold rum
¼ ounce curaçao
¼ ounce orgeat
1 sprig mint,
   for garnish

Gently squeeze mint leaves in your hand (to release fragrance) and drop them in a traditional silver julep cup. Add the rum, curaçao, and orgeat to the cup. Muddle lightly and fill the cup two-thirds of the way with crushed ice. Stir with a swizzle stick, then add a straw and top with more crushed ice. Garnish with the mint sprig.

TURN THE PAGE TO
SEE THE ILLUSTRATION
FOR THIS DRINK.

PUKA PUKA PUNCH

Sometimes a disgusting situation can create something beautiful. Originally served by colonial-era sailors to prevent scurvy—a disease that had horror-movie symptoms including spontaneous bleeding, unhealing wounds, ulceration of the gums, and tooth loss (lovely)—the first rum punches were simply multi-serving bowls of the spirit mixed with a bit of lime or lemon juice. Rum-obsessed tiki bartenders elevated rum punches in the 20th century, often adapting their concoctions to a single yet still abundantly boozy serving. A staple of Los Angeles's Hawaii-themed Tiki-Ti bar since the 1960s, the Puka Puka Punch marries smooth and pure rhum agricole and deeply complex Jamaican rum with passion fruit and fragrant notes of citrus, almond, and cinnamon for a tropical taste explosion guaranteed to knock your socks (or sandals) off. Punches are meant to be enjoyed as a group beverage, so double or triple the ingredients for this summery cooler and share!

---

1 ounce aged rhum agricole
1 ounce Jamaican amber rum
¾ ounce fresh lime juice
¾ ounce passion fruit syrup

½ ounce velvet falernum
1 pinch freshly grated cinnamon, for garnish
1 sprig mint, for garnish

Combine the rums, lime juice, passion fruit syrup, and velvet falernum in a shaker. Whip shake (no ice) and pour into a tall glass or mug filled two-thirds of the way with crushed ice. Add a straw and top with more crushed ice. Garnish with the cinnamon and mint.

LOS AMIGOS

Peace: It does a body and the entire world a whole lot of good. Established in 1981 by the United Nations General Assembly, the International Day of Peace aims to end discrimination and hatred and build a "more equal, more just, equitable, inclusive, sustainable, and healthier" world.

Most spiritual traditions advocate for peace, but few are as explicit as the Religious Society of Friends, commonly known as the Quakers. Members of this Christian sect actively promote nonviolence and take the additional step of refusing to bear arms in any conflict. They also serve as the inspiration for the Quaker cocktail, a nifty, berry-infused Whiskey Sour riff from Harry Craddock's Savoy Cocktail Book. *Los Amigos, named after the Spanish term for Quakers, switches the rye and cognac for tequila and mezcal, creating a bright, smoky kick amplified by agave nectar and smoothed by a healthy handful of raspberries. You won't want to object, conscientiously or otherwise, to this delightful peace offering.*

1½ ounces tequila
½ ounce mezcal

¾ ounce fresh lemon juice
½ ounce agave nectar
6 raspberries

Combine the tequila, mezcal, lemon juice, agave nectar, and five raspberries in an ice-filled shaker. Shake vigorously for 25 to 30 seconds and strain into a stemmed cocktail glass. Garnish with the remaining raspberry.

Fall Equinox

AUTUMN IN JERSEY

Fall is in the air, which means enjoying the brisk days by wrapping your-self in warmer clothing, peeping the changing foliage, going apple picking, drinking hot cider, and pretending that you haven't been fiending over pumpkin spice when your coffee shop receipts suggest otherwise. It's also the time of the fall equinox, when the North Pole begins to tilt away from the sun. Facing that encroaching gloom requires a positive attitude and an even better drink. Anthony Schmidt's Autumn in Jersey, first served at San Diego's Noble Experiment in 2010, will keep the good vibes flowing in any weather. Combining crisp, bright, nutty flavors and fortified by the seasonally fruity bliss of applejack—New Jersey's signature spirit and the oldest continuously distilled brandy in America—this fresh yet sneakily potent fall favorite will cool your nerves and warm your heart.

2 ounces applejack
¾ ounce fresh lemon juice
¾ ounce orgeat

2 dashes Angostura bitters
1 sprig mint, for garnish

Combine the applejack, lemon juice, orgeat, and bitters in a shaker. Pour into a double Old-Fashioned glass filled two-thirds of the way with crushed ice. Top with more ice. Garnish with the mint sprig.

National Dogs in Politics Day

ROB ROY

When it comes to showering man's best friend with affection, presidents are no exception. Since the earliest days of the White House, almost every commander-in-chief has counted at least one dog as a member of the First Family. One popular First Dog was Rob Roy, a white collie who owner Calvin Coolidge described as "a stately gentleman of great courage and fidelity" and who also loved riding in fishing boats and chasing on-screen animals during White House film screenings. Such a good boy deserves an equally excellent drink, and the Rob Roy cocktail is more than up to the task. Originally named for a Scottish folk hero (who wasn't loveably furry, so whatever), this 1894 Waldorf Astoria classic has enough elegance to match the most regal of presidential pets. Initially smoky and slightly bitter, it has an underlying sweetness at its heart, which, like the best dogs, makes for an always irresistible and loyal companion.

2 ounces blended scotch
1 ounce sweet vermouth

2 dashes Angostura bitters
1 brandied cherry, for garnish

Combine the scotch, vermouth, and bitters in a mixing glass filled with cracked ice. Stir with a long-handled spoon for 30 seconds and strain into a stemmed cocktail glass. Garnish with the brandied cherry.

National Family Health & Fitness Day

CHIN UP

Arnold Schwarzenegger knows a thing or two about fitness and once said, "If you don't find the time, if you don't do the work, you don't get the results." No one's saying you need to replicate the Austrian Adonis' old workout routines, but National Family Health & Fitness Day offers a good reminder of why you should put down the video game controller and get some exercise with your familiars. But you know what they say about all work and no play. When you're done lifting or spinning, reward yourself—in moderation—with Sam Ross's Chin Up, originally assembled at Milk & Honey in 2005. Sharing a name with the strength-training exercise and the once-ubiquitous bars on children's playgrounds, this vegetal, gin-based Martini variation is a top-notch exercise for the taste buds. With the artichoke-infused Cynar and fresh cucumber slices, it's easier to convince yourself that you're drinking healthy, even after down-ing a few of these herbal workhorses.

---

2 ounces gin
½ ounce dry vermouth

½ ounce Cynar
3 thin cucumber slices
1 lemon twist, for garnish

Combine the gin, vermouth, Cynar, and cucumber slices in a mixing glass. Gently muddle the cucumber slices and fill the glass with cracked ice. Stir with a long-handled spoon for 30 seconds and strain into a stemmed cocktail glass. Garnish with the lemon twist.

TURN OF THE SCREW

We all have been reminded annoyingly at some point that breakfast is the most important meal of the day, usually when we're late, trying to stuff half a Pop-Tart and an energy drink down our gullets, and madly searching for keys. When time isn't an issue, there's no better way to enjoy a leisurely first meal—and even out some of those weekday health gains—than with a refreshing and boozy breakfast potation. The Turn of the Screw (no relation to the 1898 Henry James novella) takes its inspiration from two of the most popular orange juice–based sippers, the Screwdriver and the Mimosa. Packing a vodka and prosecco punch made pleasantly drier and more herbaceous with the addition of Grand Marnier and Licor 43, it's the sexiest way to ease into the day—or end it extremely quickly, depending on how hard you decide to go.

4 ounces orange juice	¼ ounce Licor 43
½ ounce vodka	Prosecco, to top
½ ounce Grand Marnier	1 thin orange slice, for garnish

Combine the orange juice, vodka, Grand Marnier, and Licor 43 in a large wine glass filled with cracked ice. Top with prosecco. Garnish with the orange slice.

SALTY WHALE

If these incredibly social cetaceans enjoyed cocktails, they'd favor a drink as complex and rich as their fascinating inner lives. The Salty Whale, a mezcal- and rum-based riff on Sasha Petraske's Dominicana, beautifully mimics the orca's distinctive black and white coloring and its briny environment. Smoky, creamy, and elevated by herbaceous Amaro Averna and coffee liqueur, it's an ideal finisher after a big meal of fish, birds, or meat—the orca's main diet—or whatever food satisfies a whale-sized appetite. Like the graceful creatures for which it's named, this recipe should never stay locked up.

¾ ounce mezcal
¾ ounce blackstrap rum
¾ ounce Amaro Averna
¾ ounce coffee liqueur

1 pinch salt
Hand-whipped cream, to top
1 pinch freshly grated cinnamon,
   for garnish

Combine the mezcal, rum, Amaro Averna, coffee liqueur, and salt in an ice-filled mixing glass. Stir for 30 seconds and strain into a stemmed cocktail glass. Float the cream. Garnish with the cinnamon.

TURN THE PAGE TO
SEE THE ILLUSTRATION
FOR THIS DRINK.

Salty Whale
PAGE 331

SUITCASE

Amazing as traveling is, it can become a logistical nightmare without proper preparation. Once you have bought the plane tickets, settled the itinerary, and packed the bags, celebrate your impending journey with a Suitcase from Chris Covey. Featuring bicoastal ingredients, including rye (historically made in Pennsylvania), Seattle-based Scrappy's bitters, and Amaro Ramazzotti from Italy, this rich, chocolaty, salty sipper's ingredients have come from far and wide to produce its distinctive blend of spirit-forward magic. Transport yourself to whiskey-based bliss today.

2 ounces rye whiskey
¼ ounce Amaro Ramazzotti
¼ ounce honey syrup

2 dashes Scrappy's chocolate bitters
1 pinch salt
1 lemon twist, for garnish

Combine the whiskey, Ramazzotti, honey syrup, bitters, and salt in an Old-Fashioned glass. Add ice and stir for five or six seconds. Garnish with the lemon twist.

National Good Neighbor Day

TRADER VIC'S TIKI PUNCH

It's not hard to be a good neighbor. You just have to be kind, helpful, and, like Wilson from the 1990s sitcom Home Improvement, *ready to dispense worldly wisdom and relevant quotes for any situation while conspicuously hiding behind a fence. Okay, maybe you don't have to go full Wilson, but listening to problems and giving honest advice are never a bad idea. With face-to-face communication becoming increasingly rare, especially among younger generations, it's all the more important to create a sense of trust and community with those whom we live beside, above, or below. Few gestures encourage neighborly relations quite like the gift of a giant bowl filled with delectable booze. Bartending legend Victor "Trader Vic" Bergeron had hospitality on his mind when he created his famous Tiki Punch. More closely related to a souped-up Sidecar, this gin- and champagne-soaked behemoth doesn't contain any tiki-specific ingredients, but we'll let the misnomer slide because it's so darn delicious! After one sip of dry, bubbly, orange- and citrus-tinged, botanical-laden bliss, your neighbors will agree—that is, unless you "accidentally" finish most of this multi-serving treat yourself.*

8 ounces gin

8 ounces Cointreau or triple sec

3 ounces fresh lime juice

1½ bottles (750 ml each) champagne

Combine the gin, Cointreau, and lime juice in a large bowl filled with ice. Stir briefly with a long-handled spoon and top with champagne. Serves 8 to 10 of your closest friends.

National Biscotti Day

TUSCAN NIGHT

We normally don't associate the Roman Empire with cookies, but we have it to thank for biscotti. Imperial soldiers loved the twice-baked almond biscuits, munching them on long wartime journeys and while relaxing at home. Infused with flavors of chocolate, hazelnut, pistachio, lemon, and cherry, modern versions of these crunchy, well-preserved treats go better with a relaxing cup of coffee or glass of wine than bloody battles with Germanic tribes, but that doesn't make them any less scrumptious. If ancient Italians loved one thing more than military campaigns, it was turning their favorite flavors into spirits, and biscotti are no exception. Confectionary-minded bartenders recently have been infusing concoctions with biscotti liqueur, northern Italy's Faretti in particular, and none tastes as luscious as the Tuscan Night from Anthony Schmidt at San Francisco's Noble Experiment. Peppery, hard-nosed rye whiskey perfectly complements Faretti's delicately nutty, calming aromatics for a layered Old-Fashioned-style sipper with a finish that's pure cookie-flavored bliss.

2¼ ounces rye whiskey
½ ounce biscotti liqueur, such as Faretti

3 dashes Angostura bitters
1 orange twist, for garnish

Combine the whiskey, biscotti liqueur, and bitters in an Old-Fashioned glass. Add ice and stir for five or six seconds. Garnish with the orange twist.

MULLED CIDER

What's better than fresh apple cider on a gorgeous fall day? Steaming hot spiced cider, duh! The tradition of adding mulling spices—mixtures that usually include cinnamon, cloves, allspice, and nutmeg—to heated wines dates to second-century CE Italy, where the ancient Romans needed an extra kick to get through the frigid winter nights.

Mulled Cider works amazingly with virtually any brown spirit, from soft and supple brandy and aged rum to sharper cold-weather darlings such as bourbon or scotch. Try red wine if you're feeling particularly faithful to cider's antiquated origins. Whatever your alcohol preference, your taste buds will love the pungent notes of peppercorn and juniper paired with apple cider's unbeatably sweet and tart bouquet. So grab a thermos, fill it with hot liquid cheer, and head outside to take advantage of (objectively) the best season of the year.

3 ounces fresh apple cider
2 ounces brown spirit of choice
½ ounce St. Elizabeth Allspice Dram

3 dashes Angostura bitters
1 pinch freshly grated cinnamon, for garnish
1 pinch freshly grated nutmeg, for garnish

Combine the cider, spirit, allspice dram, and bitters in a small saucepan and heat over medium-low heat until steaming. Serve in a mug, garnished with the cinnamon and nutmeg.

OCTOBER

1	2	3	4	5	6	7
INTERNATIONAL COFFEE DAY Frenchman's Cove	PEANUTS DAY Charlie Brown	UK NATIONAL POETRY DAY Poet's Dream	NATIONAL VODKA DAY Caipiroska	NATIONAL GET FUNKY DAY Better & Better	NATIONAL MAD HATTER DAY Mad Hatter	NATIONAL INNER BEAUTY DAY Imperial Buck

8	9	10	11	12	13	14
NATIONAL CHILDREN'S DAY Infante	LEIF ERIKSON DAY Tender Viking	MOTORSPORTS MEMORIAL DAY Rolls-Royce	SOUTH-ERN FOOD HERITAGE DAY A La Louisiane	NATIONAL GUMBO DAY Battle of New Orleans	NATIONAL CHESS DAY Sir Knight	NATIONAL CHOCOLATE-COVERED INSECTS DAY Noisy Cricket

15	16	17	18	19	20	21
NATIONAL GROUCH DAY El Diablo	NATIONAL LIQUEUR DAY Americano	NATIONAL PASTA DAY Little Italy	NATIONAL COMIC STRIP APPRECIATION DAY Port Flip	INTERNATIONAL GIN AND TONIC DAY Jadoo	NATIONAL BRANDIED FRUIT DAY Cherry Smash	NATIONAL MEZCAL DAY White Old-Fashioned

22	23	24	25	26	27	28
NATIONAL COLOR DAY Rum Swizzle	SCORPIO DAY Scorpion Kick	NATIONAL CRAZY DAY Cock 'n' Bull Special	INTERNATIONAL ARTISTS DAY September Morn	NATIONAL MULE DAY Gin Gin Mule	CRANKY COWORKERS DAY Debbie, Don't	NATIONAL IMMIGRANTS DAY Arawak

29	30	31				
NATIONAL HERMIT DAY Monk Buck	DEVIL'S NIGHT Satan's Whiskers	HALLOWEEN Nightmare				

FRENCHMAN'S COVE

Of the numerous coffee-related holidays scattered throughout the calendar, this one takes the cream and two sugars. However you prefer your java, the International Coffee Organization (yes, a real group) wants you to celebrate the more than 100 varieties of beans growing around the globe. Once you've powered through the day with a caffeinated boost or six, keep the festivities rolling with a coffee cocktail. You could be #basic and go with an Espresso Martini, but your taste buds will thank you for trying something a little more exotic, such as the Frenchman's Cove, a rich, tropically inclined sensation from Attaboy's Zac Pease. Not exactly "tiki" and not strictly an after-dinner affair, it's unquestionably bright, creamy, nutty, and slightly smoky with enough booze to soothe the most frazzled of nerves. Which is just the ticket after hours spent downing more liquid rocket fuel than you'd like to admit.

1½ ounces Jamaican amber rum

¾ ounce coffee liqueur

½ ounce fresh lemon juice

½ ounce simple syrup

½ ounce heavy cream

1 thin orange slice, for garnish

1 pinch freshly grated nutmeg,
   for garnish

 Combine the rum, coffee liqueur, lemon juice, simple syrup, and cream in a shaker. Whip shake (no ice) and pour into a tall glass or mug filled two-thirds of the way with crushed ice. Add a straw and top with more crushed ice. Garnish with the orange slice and nutmeg.

OCTOBER 2
Peanuts Day

CHARLIE BROWN

Peanuts remains so endearing, in part, because of Charlie Brown's complex, realistic outlook. The archetypal lovable loser, he could be anxious, pessimistic, and riddled with self-doubt but also incredibly perceptive and able to see the big picture, regularly spouting gems such as "All you need is love, but a little chocolate now and then doesn't hurt." The Charlie Brown cocktail, created at Little Branch in 2021, fulfills both obligations with plenty of bourbon and cognac affection and a healthy dollop of crème de cacao. If good ol' Chuck, as Peppermint Patty liked to call him, were old enough to drink, he'd sip one of these to soothe his worries—and to numb himself to whatever racket Snoopy was creating in his doghouse.

1 ounce bourbon
1 ounce cognac
¼ ounce crème de cacao (dark)
¼ ounce honey syrup

2 dashes chocolate bitters
1 dash Angostura bitters
1 pinch salt
1 lemon twist, for garnish

Combine the bourbon, cognac, crème de cacao, honey syrup, bitters, and salt in an Old-Fashioned glass. Add ice and stir for five or six seconds. Garnish with the lemon twist.

POET'S DREAM

Seminal English poet George Byron once remarked, "If I do not write to empty my mind, I go mad." Mind alteration can be an important part of the writing process, whether through drugs, romance, traveling, or a few sips of an exceptionally potent concoction. The Poet's Dream is one such fount of inspiration, a fragrant Martini riff that first appeared in William Tarling's Café Royal Cocktail Book *and possibly took inspiration from this line in John Milton's poetic work* Comus: *"One sip of this will bathe the drooping spirits in delight, beyond the bliss of dreams." Though this lulling, ambrosial sipper warrants a refill, stop after two because, as Oscar Wilde suggests, during the third drink, "you see things as they really are, and that is the worst thing in the world."*

2 ounces gin
¾ ounce dry vermouth

¼ ounce Bénédictine
2 dashes orange bitters
1 lemon twist, for garnish

Combine the gin, vermouth, Bénédictine, and bitters in a mixing glass filled with cracked ice. Stir with a long-handled spoon for 30 seconds and strain into a stemmed cocktail glass. Garnish with the lemon twist.

CAIPIROSKA

At the beginning of the craft cocktail renaissance, if you asked a Very Serious Bartender for a drink with vodka, you would get a grudging eye roll, an attempt to sway you away from the neutral spirit (gin, perhaps?), or a flat-out refusal. Flavorless by law (unless you consider "burn" a flavor), today's vodka features countless cloying and—if you've ever stepped foot in a fraternity house—party- rage-, and tear-inducing artificial elements. For a blessedly natural but still fruity vodka-based potable that won't leave you trying to scrape yourself off a random acquaintance's floor in the morning, try a Caipiroska. This fresh and delicious take on the equally yummy Caipirinha tastes just sweet and citrusy enough to wean you off boring Vodka and Sodas yet light enough to make you feel like you're still being relatively health-conscious. It's so effortlessly drinkable that you may wind up on the floor anyway.

2 ounces vodka
¾ ounce simple syrup

5 lime wedges
1 thin orange slice
1 brown sugar cube

Combine all ingredients in a shaker. Muddle and fill the shaker with cracked ice. Shake three to four times. Pour the entire contents of the shaker into a double Old-Fashioned glass.

BETTER & BETTER

Until fairly recently, you probably wouldn't want to be described as funky. Originally defined as musty, unpleasant, peculiar, or depressing, the word received a major upgrade in the mid-1960s, when African-American artists such as James Brown, Jimi Hendrix, and Parliament Funkadelic fused R&B, jazz, and soul into a danceable, rhythmic, and all-around hip new genre of music they dubbed funk. In cocktail parlance, "funk" might not conjure a Bootsy Collins bass solo, but it still powerfully describes earthy, acrid, rancid-in-a-good-way flavors found in some of the dankest Caribbean rums. Jazziest among these spirits is Smith & Cross, a wildly aromatic amber beauty that always brings the noise, especially when featured in the Better & Better, a mezcal-based Old-Fashioned riff created by Jan Warren at Dutch Kills. Nutty, smoky, and not for the faint of palate, it's a one-of-a-kind powerhouse that's guaranteed to turn up the volume and get you in the groove.

1½ ounces mezcal
½ ounce Smith & Cross
    Jamaican rum

¼ ounce velvet falernum
1 lemon twist,
    for garnish

Combine the mezcal, Smith & Cross, and velvet falernum in an Old-Fashioned glass. Add ice and stir for five or six seconds. Garnish with the lemon twist.

MAD HATTER

Held on this day as a nod to the "10/6" tag that appears in Alice in
Wonderland *on the Hatter's iconic top hat (which represents its cost:
10 shillings and sixpence), Mad Hatter Day celebrates the antics of fic-
tion's weirdest haberdasher. To wrap your head around the Hatter's
absurd persona, you're going to need something stronger than tea. Making
its first splash in Ted Saucier's 1951* Bottoms Up, *the Mad Hatter cocktail is a rye-based dandy that contains lime and lemon juices and a mischievous dollop of absinthe for a flavor as bold and bright as the Hatter's
wardrobe, with plenty of potency to send you down a delightfully booze-
fueled rabbit hole. Knock back a few of these at your next dinner party and
you'll be spewing nonsense in no time.*

2 ounces rye whiskey
¾ ounce simple syrup
⅜ ounce fresh lime juice

⅜ ounce fresh lemon juice
1 barspoon absinthe
1 lemon twist, for garnish

Combine the whiskey, simple syrup, juices, and absinthe in
an ice-filled shaker. Shake vigorously for 25 to 30 seconds
and strain into a stemmed cocktail glass. Garnish with the
lemon twist.

National Inner Beauty Day

IMPERIAL BUCK

Never judge a book—or anything else, for that matter—by its cover. On National Inner Beauty Day, created by businesswoman and activist Roma Newton, forget about the mirror and focus on being your best, total self. Embrace the qualities and passions that make you a uniquely beautiful human and strive to create a better world by allowing them to shine. Just as importantly, today's holiday raises awareness of human trafficking and helps survivors of this shockingly common practice to remember how beautiful they are, inside and out. Never evaluate people or cocktails entirely by physical appearance. A great example is the Imperial Buck, a Cruzan take on a Dark 'n' Stormy from Milk & Honey. Blackstrap rum, heavy with molasses, gives the drink a slightly sludgy consistency, with a hue that some have described not-so-generously as "septic." What it lacks in ambiance the drink more than makes up in flavor, with a soul-satiating blast of ginger, pineapple, and that tropical tang unique to the darkest of Caribbean rums. Remember: Always sip before you judge.

---

2 ounces blackstrap rum

1 ounce fresh pineapple juice

¼ ounce ginger syrup

½ ounce fresh lime juice

Club soda, to top

1 piece candied ginger, for garnish

1 thin orange slice, for garnish

Combine the rum, juices, and ginger syrup in a shaker. Whip shake (no ice) and pour into a tall glass filled with ice. Top with club soda. Garnish with the candied ginger and the orange slice.

National Children's Day

INFANTE

For most parents and teachers, kids are adorable blessings who give life meaning. For others, they're diabolical little monsters whose every petulant wail is a nuisance to be endured. Dealing with even moderately well-behaved children for a significant amount of time can become a major source of stress, which is why, once those little bundles of energetic terror are tucked safely into bed, you're need a drink like the Infante to ease the tension. With a name that means "prince" in Spanish and that pays homage to Mexican actor and singer Pedro Infante, Giuseppe González's popular spin on a Tequila Sour is sweet, nutty, and aromatic, with an innate ability to soothe the most child-frazzled nerves. Let this modern classic lull you into a false sense of peace until the pitter-patter of little feet wakes you before the crack of dawn.

---

2 ounces tequila

¾ ounce fresh lime juice

¾ ounce orgeat

3 drops orange blossom water

1 pinch freshly grated nutmeg, for garnish

Combine the tequila, lime juice, orgeat, and orange blossom water in an ice-filled shaker. Shake vigorously for 25 to 30 seconds and strain into a double Old-Fashioned glass over ice. Garnish with the nutmeg.

TENDER VIKING

Think you have a serious case of wanderlust? It's got nothing on the all-consuming desire for travel that fueled 10th-century Viking explorers. Bored after raiding the coasts of western Europe, these notorious warriors from Norway sailed into the vastness of the North Atlantic in boats that make economy class seem like a luxury jet, landing in the Faroe Islands, Iceland, and Greenland by 985 CE. Discovery-crazed chieftain Leif Erikson eventually established the first European settlement in mainland North America at L'Anse aux Meadows, Newfoundland, in the year 1000. Unlike their stereotypically gentle-natured descendants, the Vikings are remembered as ferocious glory seekers for whom plunder, battle, and a stiff drink were life's greatest pleasures. Today's Norwegians still love a tipple, and no drink is more Scandinavian than aquavit, a locally distilled spirit flavored by anise, cardamom, dill, fennel, and other spices. Michael Timmons's Tender Viking harnesses this potent liqueur's adventurous bouquet and combines it with ingredients from countries influenced (and often exploited) by the ancient Norse, creating a wonderfully lithe, floral potation that would be a hit in any era. Pre-batch a few of these for your next voyage of discovery.

2 ounces aquavit
½ ounce dry vermouth
½ ounce manzanilla sherry

¼ ounce St-Germain
3 dashes peach bitters
1 dash absinthe
1 lemon twist, for garnish

Combine the aquavit, vermouth, sherry, St-Germain, bitters, and absinthe in an ice-filled mixing glass. Stir with a long-handled spoon for 30 seconds and strain into a stemmed cocktail glass. Garnish with the lemon twist.

ROLLS-ROYCE

Ladies and gentlemen, start your engines! For the past century or so, auto racing has been one of America's most popular and dangerous activities. Participants routinely flirt with disaster at speeds that mere mortal drivers (or Grand Theft Auto players) can't fathom. Today, Rolls-Royce has a reputation associated with luxury and being chauffeured while disdainfully glancing at peasants who must drive themselves. But the British automobile maker led the pack in the early motorsports game in the 1900s and 1910s. Its models routinely won races and hit speeds of 80 miles per hour when most cars of the day couldn't crack 40. It also serves as inspiration for one of the oldest Martini variations, a savory classic from 1930's Savoy Cocktail Book by Harry Craddock. Smooth, simple, and elegant, this is one post-race victory trophy you'll want to hoist again and again.

2 ounces gin
½ ounce dry vermouth
½ ounce sweet vermouth

1 barspoon Bénédictine
1 dash orange bitters
1 lemon twist, for garnish

Combine the gin, vermouths, Bénédictine, and bitters in a mixing glass filled with cracked ice. Stir with a long-handled spoon for 30 seconds and strain into a stemmed cocktail glass. Garnish with the lemon twist.

A LA LOUISIANE

Snobby French gourmands and Italian buongustaios tend to scoff at American cuisine, which in their eyes consists solely of cheeseburgers, hot dogs, and apple pies. Contrary to this dreadfully misinformed perspective, the various regions of the United States offer mouthwatering gastronomic delights as tasty as they are innovative.

Louisiana's European, indigenous, and African-influenced food scene represents one of the most fertile subregions in the American culinary landscape. Not surprisingly, it's also a cocktail hotbed, where innovative classics like the A La Louisiane provide a perfect accompaniment to all manner of southern feasts. Rich, savory, and unapologetically boozy, this signature sipper from New Orleans's Restaurant de la Louisiane is the best way to experience the eye-popping flavors of an entire region without going there (which you should).

1½ ounces rye whiskey

¾ ounce sweet vermouth

¾ ounce Bénédictine

2 dashes Peychaud's bitters

1 dash absinthe

1 lemon twist, for garnish

Combine the rye, vermouth, Bénédictine, bitters, and absinthe in a double Old-Fashioned glass. Add ice and stir for five or six seconds. Garnish with the lemon twist.

National Gumbo Day

BATTLE OF NEW ORLEANS

Yesterday's festivities paid homage to the cuisine of an entire region, and today focuses on one of the American South's signature delicacies. Born in the bayous of Louisiana in the early 1800s, gumbo is the state's official dish and a favorite of Cajun food lovers everywhere.

If a hard-core culinary battle is right up your alley, some potent liquid encouragement might be just what it takes to put you over the top. If armed combat isn't your thing, try a Battle of New Orleans anyway. Named for a decisive encounter between American and British forces in the War of 1812, it first appeared in Crosby Gaige's Cocktail Guide and Ladies' Companion. *As integral to its city's cocktail history as its older cousin, the Sazerac, this brooding, anise-imbued, Old-Fashioned-esque delight is a great complement to any Cajun feast and, like an expertly constructed gumbo, just as unforgettable.*

2½ ounces bourbon
¼ ounce simple syrup
2 dashes Peychaud's bitters

1 dash orange bitters
1 dash absinthe
1 lemon twist, for garnish

Combine the bourbon, simple syrup, bitters, and absinthe in an Old-Fashioned glass. Add ice and stir for five or six seconds. Garnish with the lemon twist.

National Chess Day

SIR KNIGHT

Bobby Fischer, an eccentric and controversial 20th-century chess genius, never minced words when it came to his chosen game. "Chess is war over a board," the prodigy once explained in an interview. "The object is to crush the opponent's mind." One of the most flexible pieces on the chess board is a knight, represented by a horse's head and uniquely able to move in an L shape. It's unknown whether the Sir Knight, a popular cognac-based sipper dating to the early 1900s, took inspiration from the game or, you know, dudes in armor, but it's just as versatile as the piece. Dryly fruity from its orange liqueur modifier, with an equal dose of herbaceous yellow Chartreuse, this grape-forward Manhattan riff is perfect as a post-checkmate celebration or a pick-me-up after a hard-fought loss. Just be sure to save this potent potable for the postgame.

---

2 ounces cognac

½ ounce Cointreau

½ ounce yellow Chartreuse

2 dashes Angostura bitters

1 lemon twist, for garnish

Combine the cognac, Cointreau, Chartreuse, and bitters in an ice-filled mixing glass. Stir with a long-handled spoon for 30 seconds and strain into a stemmed cocktail glass. Garnish with the lemon twist.

National Chocolate-Covered Insects Day

NOISY CRICKET

*Looking for the ultimate protein source? It's probably crawling near your
feet or buzzing above your head right now. Gram for gram, bugs such as
caterpillars, crickets, and mealworms are more nutritious than chicken
or beef. Your first introduction to insect cuisine—besides the ones you
accidentally swallow— probably requires some liquid courage. The Noisy
Cricket is ready and willing to settle your nerves. No, this richer, more
medicinal Grasshopper riff from Seattle bartender Jim Romdall doesn't
contain any bug-related ingredients, but it has more than enough chocolaty and minty flavor to zap any offending taste-bud trespassers. This
drink is perfect for soothing the senses and cleansing the palate between
rounds of healthy yet terrifying insect treats.*

1½ ounces Branca Menta	¾ ounce heavy cream
¾ ounce crème de cacao (dark)	1 mint leaf, for garnish

Combine the Branca Menta, crème de cacao, and heavy cream
in an ice-filled shaker. Shake vigorously for 25 to 30 seconds
and strain into a stemmed cocktail glass. Garnish with the
mint leaf.

EL DIABLO

No one's happy all the time. Even the peppiest optimist has a dour moment every now and then. But we all know one or two professional curmudgeons who can turn wallowing in misery into a piece of performance art. If we're talking mythological grumps, it doesn't get much crankier than demons. But hey, you'd be pissed off too if you were banished from paradise and had to spend eternity in a smelly, fiery underworld surrounded by other evil jerks. If you're feeling equally black-hearted today, shake yourself up a Diablo, a peppery, gingery number from Trader Vic's Bartender's Guide. *Pleasantly tart and topped with a murky cassis drizzle representing demonic blood, this one will raise the grouchiest spirits, at least temporarily. Then you can go back to being the hater everyone loves to loathe.*

2 ounces tequila

¾ ounce ginger syrup

½ ounce fresh lime juice

¼ ounce crème de cassis

Club soda, to top

1 piece candied ginger,
    for garnish

Combine the tequila, ginger syrup, and lime juice in a shaker. Whip shake (no ice) and pour into a tall glass filled with ice. Top with club soda and drizzle the cassis. Garnish with the piece of candied ginger.

AMERICANO

Liqueurs are so individually complex that they usually take a back seat in cocktails as modifiers. But a few classic drinks, including the Americano, buck that trend quite deliciously. Bittersweet, herbaceous, and utterly refreshing, this fizzy, digestion-aiding blend of sweet vermouth and Campari arose in the 1860s in Milan, Italy, and allegedly received its name for its popularity among American tourists. It's also one of the many drinks ordered by James Bond, a character with impeccable, well documented taste in booze.

Liqueur or liquor? When it tastes this good, does it even matter?

1½ ounces sweet vermouth

1 ounce Campari

Club soda, to top

1 long orange twist, for garnish

Combine the sweet vermouth and Campari in a tall glass filled with ice. Top with club soda. Garnish with the orange twist.

National Pasta Day

LITTLE ITALY

Don't let anyone tell you that all carbs are the same. Pasta is just built different. You can find it in one form or another wherever food is sold, but if you want the most authentic experience outside Italy, you have to go to New York City's Little Italy neighborhood. The now-tiny slice of downtown Manhattan is the epicenter of the Italian-immigrant diaspora and the inspiration for a formidable cocktail of the same name, created by Audrey Saunders at Pegu Club in 2006. This wonderfully savory Manhattan variation features a double dose of Italian ingredients in the form of sweet vermouth and Cynar. Their many blessed digestive benefits will come in handy after you inevitably overindulge today.

2ounces rye whiskey

¾ ounce Cynar

½ ounce sweet vermouth

1 orange twist, for garnish

Combine the rye, Cynar, and vermouth in a mixing glass filled with cracked ice. Stir with a long-handled spoon for 30 seconds and strain into a stemmed cocktail glass. Garnish with the orange twist.

PORT FLIP

Shockingly, not long ago, if you wanted to know what was going on in the world, you had to stumble into your yard and find the newspaper that some preteen punk threw into your bushes at 5 AM. If current events weren't your thing, you at least checked out the latest antics of your favorite characters in the comics section. Comics rarely portray alcohol use—probably due to some nonsense about appealing to all ages—but Andy Capp *is a notable exception. Red Smythe's raucous strip, starring an English lowlife of the same name, debuted in 1957 and takes place mostly in pubs, portraying countless acts of debauchery. By the 1970s, the face of the charismatic Mr. Capp advertised everything from hot chips to his own brand of port, which is also the main ingredient (duh) of the Port Flip. A version of this nutty, nog-like dessert beverage appeared in Jerry Thomas's 1862* Bartender's Guide: How to Mix Drinks: A Bon Vivant's Companion. *Like a good comic strip, this thick and rich refresher will have you chuckling in no time.*

1½ ounces port
1 ounce cognac
¼ ounce simple syrup

1 egg yolk
1 pinch freshly grated nutmeg, for garnish

 Combine the port, cognac, simple syrup, and egg yolk in a shaker. Shake without ice (to emulsify the egg yolk) for 10 seconds, then add ice and shake vigorously. Strain into a stemmed cocktail glass. Garnish with the nutmeg.

International Gin and Tonic Day

JADOO

Peanut butter and jelly, Simon and Garfunkel, Netflix and chill. Some things just go together. International Gin and Tonic Day shows much-deserved love to the booziest of bedfellows, a combination associated with aristocratic indulgence (and two-for-one happy hour specials) since the 1700s. That's when British doctors realized that the quinine in tonic water could treat malaria and that patients would quaff the bitter liquid when combined with the most English of spirits. The Gin and Tonic is a nearly flawless concoction on its own, but there's nothing wrong with adding a little zest to an all-time classic. In the case of the Jadoo, that zest comes specifically from tastefully tart chunks of muddled lime. This early G&T variation, known in some circles as a British Mojito, also employs a generous dose of fresh mint for an herbal, bittersweet blast of flavor that will wow the most modifier-averse gin purists. It's a can't-fail twist that's easy to make and even easier to love.

---

2 ounces gin
¼ ounce simple syrup
5 lime wedges

1 small handful mint leaves
Tonic water, to top
1 sprig mint, for garnish

Combine the gin, simple syrup, lime wedges, and mint leaves in a shaker. Muddle and fill the shaker with cracked ice. Shake lightly for 10 seconds and dump the entire contents of the shaker into a double Old-Fashioned glass. Top with tonic water. Garnish with the mint sprig.

CHERRY SMASH

Brandied cherries have become the preferred garnishes for hundreds of cocktails, including all-time heavy hitters such as the Manhattan (page 306), Aviation No. 1 (page 285), and Tuxedo No. 2 (page 215). But these burgundy beauties aren't just for decoration. As its name suggests, the Cherry Smash depends on them for its eminently fruity, slightly sweet flavor profile. It works well with just about any brown spirit, such as American whiskey, scotch, or aged rum, but it's probably most compatible with cognac for a grape-forward finish that's refreshingly citrusy and smashingly complex.

2 ounces brown spirit of choice
5 lemon wedges
¾ ounce simple syrup

7 brandied cherries
3 or 4 fresh mint leaves
1 sprig mint, for garnish

Combine the spirit, lemon wedges, simple syrup, six brandied cherries, and mint leaves in a shaker. Thoroughly muddle, add ice, and shake vigorously for 25 to 30 seconds. Strain into a double Old-Fashioned glass filled with cracked ice. Garnish with the mint sprig and another brandied cherry.

National Mezcal Day

WHITE OLD-FASHIONED

If you've asked your local know-it-all barkeep about the difference between mezcal and tequila, you may have heard a nifty-sounding response like, "All tequilas are mezcals, but not all mezcals are tequilas." To put it more clearly, mezcal is any liquor made from agave, whereas tequila comes from a specific type of agave and from around Tequila, Mexico. National Mezcal Day celebrates both!

Traditionally mezcal is sipped straight, but it has become an uber-popular base in hundreds of modern cocktails, including the White Old-Fashioned, crafted at Melrose Umbrella Co. in Los Angeles. Featuring two opposing yet beautifully balanced modifiers in crème de cacao and yellow Chartreuse, this spirit-forward tipple leaves plenty of room for your mezcal of choice to take center stage. Salud!

2 ounces mezcal

⅜ ounce crème de cacao

¼ ounce yellow Chartreuse

2 dashes orange bitters

1 lemon twist, for garnish

Combine the mezcal, crème de cacao, Chartreuse, and bitters in an Old-Fashioned glass. Add ice and stir for five or six seconds. Garnish with the lemon twist.

RUM SWIZZLE

Some holidays are for the dogs, but this one certainly isn't. Our canine friends can see blues, yellows, and grays, but most of us humans can see a broader range of colors, from the darkest reds to the palest violets. These colors powerfully impact every aspect of our lives. They affect our moods, allow us to appreciate natural phenomena such as fall foliage or the aurora borealis, feed our creativity and self-expression, and serve as symbols of welcome and warning. Observe National Color Day by decking yourself out in your favorite shades, checking out or creating your own eye-pleasing art, or just relaxing with a vibrantly hued drink, and observing all the wonderful colors constantly swirling around you.

Many of the most intensely colored beverages owe their striking appearances to artificial food coloring and syrups. (That neon-blue raspberry Margarita isn't what we'd call "natural.") That's not the case with the Rum Swizzle, a vibrant part of island culture for hundreds of years. Beautifully layered with shades of deep purple, red, orange, green, and yellow, it offers a feast for the eyes and—thanks to its luscious combination of rum, curaçao, and fresh fruit—the mouth.

1½ ounces rum	3 blackberries
¼ ounce curaçao	2 lemon wedges
½ ounce fresh lime juice	3 dashes Angostura bitters
	1 sprig fresh mint, for garnish

 Combine the rum, curaçao, and lime juice in a shaker. Muddle two blackberries and one lemon wedge in a tall glass. Fill the glass two-thirds of the way with crushed ice. Add the contents of the shaker and float the bitters. Top the glass with more crushed ice. Garnish with the mint sprig, as well as the additional blackberry and lemon wedge.

SCORPION KICK

Even if astrology isn't your thing, avoid getting on a Scorpio's bad side. Those born under this notoriously volatile sign, which begins today, are—according to people who put stock in such matters—prone to sudden and forceful mood swings, episodes of rage and jealousy, and an obsessive desire to avenge any perceived slight. Mixing a succulent cocktail is a surefire method for curing an ill temper, regardless of your sign. Dan Greenbaum first served the Scorpion Kick, a particularly soothing potation for today's celebration, at Brooklyn's Diamond Reef in 2017. This sweet and herbaceous play on that all-time soother, the Daiquiri, has a bit more bite, thanks to the addition of crème de cacao and mint. Best of all, for any impatient Scorpios reading this, you easily can whip up one of these verdant beauties "in a pinch."

2 ounces white rum
1 ounce fresh lime juice

½ ounce crème de cacao
¼ ounce cane syrup
3 or 4 mint leaves

Combine all ingredients in an ice-filled shaker. Shake vigorously for 25 to 30 seconds and strain into a stemmed cocktail glass.

COCK 'N' BULL SPECIAL

"Some may never live, but the crazy never die." Few people allow them-selves to stray far enough from rationality and social norms to determine whether that Hunter S. Thompson quote has merit, but it can't hurt to go nuts occasionally. National Crazy Day encourages you to get a little unhinged while breaking away from rules and routines.

The Cock 'n' Bull Special, an achievement in 1950s drink-making, still seems ludicrous to cocktail traditionalists. Introduced at Los Angeles's famed Sunset Strip pub, this floral, leathery, herbaceous sipper defies conventional logic by breaking with the template that virtually all other Old-Fashioned variations follow, meaning 2 ounces of spirit backed by bitter and sweet modifiers in smaller proportions. Is bourbon the base here or Bénédictine? What about the cognac? Does it matter? Maybe to semantics nerds, but the most important take away from this slightly sweet yet ludicrously complex libation is that it's just crazy enough to taste absolutely delicious.

¾ ounce bourbon

¾ ounce Bénédictine

½ ounce cognac

¼ ounce Cointreau

1 orange twist, for garnish

Combine the bourbon, Bénédictine, cognac, and Cointreau in an Old-Fashioned glass. Add ice and stir for five or six seconds. Garnish with the orange twist.

SEPTEMBER MORN

Pablo Picasso, born on this date in 1881, once quipped, "Every child is an artist. The only problem is how to remain an artist once he grows up." International Artists Day encourages you to channel that youthful exuberance by immersing yourself in the work of painters, sculptors, photographers, musicians, digital artists, writers, and other creative badasses like Picasso, whose imaginations add immeasurable beauty to the world. Art often challenges convention and pushes the boundaries of social acceptability, as did September Morn, a controversial oil painting by French artist Paul Chabas in 1912. Critics considered the image of a young woman bathing nude, relatively tame by modern standards, as scandalous for its "fetishization of innocence." It went on to inspire songs, stage shows, films, and, most tastefully, a wonderfully sumptuous Rum Sour variation. A fruity, citrusy classic from Harry Craddock's Savoy Cocktail Book, the September Morn is frothy, decadent, and a delight for all manner of palates and palettes. This easily quaffed tipple is a bona fide masterpiece.

---

2 ounces white rum

¾ ounce fresh lemon juice

¾ ounce pomegranate syrup

1 egg white

Combine all ingredients in an ice-filled shaker. Shake without ice (to emulsify the egg white) for 10 seconds, then add ice and shake vigorously. Strain into a stemmed cocktail glass.

TURN THE PAGE TO
SEE THE ILLUSTRATION
FOR THIS DRINK.

September Morn
PAGE 363

GIN GIN MULE

Among the noblest of beasts, the Mule is also the name of a highly
regarded family of cocktails, the most famous being the Moscow Mule,
a fizzy potable made with vodka, ginger, and lime and created in New
York City in 1941. More than 60 years later, in the same city, Pegu Club's
Audrey Saunders unleashed the Gin Gin Mule, a brighter, minty version
of the drink that substitutes gin for vodka. An immediate sensation, the
spicy sipper has become synonymous with the 21st-century craft cocktail
renaissance and a can't-miss favorite of seasoned bartenders and gin
newbies. This mule was bred from truly exceptional stock.

2 ounces gin
1 ounce fresh lime juice
½ ounce ginger syrup
½ ounce simple syrup

6 mint leaves
Club soda, to top
1 piece candied ginger,
    for garnish
1 sprig fresh mint, for garnish

Combine the gin, lime juice, ginger syrup, simple syrup, and mint
leaves in an ice-filled shaker. Shake vigorously for 25 to 30 seconds and
strain into a tall glass filled with ice. Top with club soda. Garnish with
the piece of ginger candy and the mint sprig.

Cranky Coworkers Day

DEBBIE, DON'T

Created by Thomas and Ruth Roy, Cranky Coworkers Day gives you a chance to snap back at your colleagues by dispensing with the pleasantries and telling them how you really feel. As glorious as the freedom to clap back can feel, don't get carried away with the grumbling, or you might develop a reputation as the new office crank. Annoying workmates come in all shapes and sizes, and some aren't even living! Zachary Gelnaw-Rubin's Debbie, Don't takes its name from a particularly irritating ghost that allegedly haunts the bar at Long Island City's Dutch Kills, spooking her non-supernatural colleagues and patrons. Originally appearing in Sasha Petraske's Regarding Cocktails, *this dour-looking Tequila Sour spin-off is a good-natured, spirits-lifting treat that's bold, playful, herbaceous, and always on its best behavior. Instead of lashing out at cranky coworkers today, fix them a few of these agave-based refreshers. If their moods don't immediately improve, they really are the worst.*

1 ounce tequila reposado
1 ounce Amaro Averna
¾ ounce fresh lemon juice

½ ounce maple syrup
2 dashes orange bitters
1 lemon wedge, for garnish

Combine the tequila, Amaro Averna, lemon juice, maple syrup, and bitters in an ice-filled shaker. Shake vigorously for 25 to 30 seconds and strain into a stemmed cocktail glass. Garnish with the lemon wedge.

National Immigrants Day

ARAWAK

If you live in America, you descend from immigrants. Known as the "world's melting pot," the United States saw its greatest influx of foreigners during the late 19th and early 20th centuries, when millions of Europeans fled their homelands and passed through Ellis Island in New York Harbor.

We think of large-scale immigration to North America as a relatively recent phenomenon, but enterprising travelers had been journeying to the New World thousands of years before Europeans knew it existed. One of the last areas of the continent to be settled, the Caribbean was originally home to a group of peoples called the Arawaks, who had immigrated from South America. Made with rum produced in their new homeland, the Arawak, which first appeared in the 1945 edition of Trader Vic's Bartender's Guide, is rich, potent, and nutty, a spirit-forward sipper as complex as our ancestors' migration routes. Thankfully, like all timeless drinks, it's immune to border restrictions.

2¼ ounces Jamaican rum	3 dashes Angostura bitters
½ ounce Pedro Ximénez sherry	1 orange twist, for garnish

Combine the rum, sherry, and bitters in an Old-Fashioned glass. Add ice and stir for five or six seconds. Garnish with the orange twist.

MONK BUCK

No matter how extroverted you think they are, you need an occasional break from other people to recharge your social battery. Hermits take self-imposed seclusion to extreme levels, usually for religious reasons. Like hermits, monks spend most of their time cloistered from common society in quiet contemplation, either alone or alongside similarly non-chatty brethren. When they aren't praying, many of them partake in secular pursuits, such as the distilling of spirits, including Chartreuse, made in French monasteries since the 18th century. The yellow variety of this herbaceous liqueur helps define the Monk Buck, a gingery, rejuvenating ode to isolation satisfying drinkers both gregarious and reclusive since Charles H. Baker introduced it in his 1939 Jigger, Beaker, and Glass: Drinking around the World. *Frequently used by Baker as "something to cause nerves to join and coordinate" after a long night, it's worth breaking a vow of silence to order one.*

---

2 ounces cognac
¼ ounce ginger syrup
½ ounce fresh lime juice
¼ ounce yellow Chartreuse

1 dash Angostura bitters
Club soda, to top
1 piece ginger candy,
    for garnish

Combine the cognac, ginger syrup, lime juice, Chartreuse, and bitters in a shaker. Whip shake (no ice) and pour into a tall glass filled with ice. Top with club soda. Garnish with the piece of candied ginger.

SATAN'S WHISKERS

Costumed creeps and ghouls run amok on Halloween, but on Devil's Night the real troublemakers rule the darkness. Also known as Mischief Night or Cabbage Night in parts of northeastern and Midwestern America, this date long has been known as a time for children and teenagers to take to the streets for occasionally good-natured but usually rascally pranks.

If you're a (somewhat) functioning adult and running amok isn't your thing (anymore), you can reminisce about the naughty adventures of your youth over a diabolically themed cocktail. Creatures of the night have been enjoying Satan's Whiskers since at least 1930, when it appeared in Harry Craddock's Savoy Cocktail Book. *Heavy on the orange notes, this easy-to-quaff sipper has snuck up on many victims with its surprisingly high alcohol content.*

1 ounce gin	½ ounce sweet vermouth
1 ounce orange juice	½ ounce dry vermouth
½ ounce Grand Marnier or similar orange liqueur	2 dashes orange bitters

Combine all ingredients in an ice-filled shaker. Shake vigorously for 25 to 30 seconds and strain into a stemmed cocktail glass.

NIGHTMARE

Calling all ghouls, goblins, and other diabolical creatures of darkness. Tonight is your time to lurk! Halloween's otherworldly beginnings date to Samhain, an ancient pagan harvest festival, when people believed that the worlds of the living and dead briefly intersected. Early Christians considered the ghostly celebration taboo, but by the Victorian era October 31 resembled the costume-wearing, prank-making, candy-eating, scary-story-telling, jack-o'-lantern-carving good time beloved by children and adults around the world. So grab a mask and get into the supernatural spirits!

No Halloween extravaganza is complete without a killer cocktail or two. The Nightmare, a classic gin tipple, origin unknown, has been served since at least the 1970s. It fits the bill with its eerie name and its strikingly ghastly, blood-red color. This citrusy riff on the Dubonnet Cocktail (page 142) is lush, herbal, bitter, and slightly fruity, making it the perfect party favor for a wide variety of sophisticatedly spooky palates. If that little devil on your shoulder convinces you to go extra hard tonight, you may find yourself communing with the dead—and feeling like you've joined them the next morning.

1 ounce gin
1 ounce Dubonnet
1 ounce orange juice

½ ounce Cherry Heering
2 dashes Angostura
    bitters

Combine all ingredients in an ice-filled shaker. Shake vigorously for 25 to 30 seconds and strain over ice into a double Old-Fashioned glass.

NOVEMBER

			1	2	3	4
			ALL SAINTS' DAY	DAY OF THE DEAD	CLICHÉ DAY	NATIONAL CANDY DAY
			St. Augustine	Juan Lockwood	Intro to Aperol	Sinners and Saints
5	**6**	**7**	**8**	**9**	**10**	**11**
NATIONAL HOT SAUCE DAY	SAXOPHONE DAY	HUG A BEAR DAY	NATIONAL HARVEY WALLBANGER DAY	CARL SAGAN DAY	AMERICAN FROG DAY	VETERANS DAY
Tequila Torchlight	Mercy, Mercy	Teddy No. 2	Freddy Fudpucker	Space Gin Smash	Connecticut Bullfrog	Special Forces
12	**13**	**14**	**15**	**16**	**17**	**18**
HAPPY HOUR DAY	SADIE HAWKINS DAY	INTERNATIONAL SELFIE DAY	STEVE IRWIN DAY	HAVANA, CUBA, BIRTHDAY	NATIONAL TAKE A HIKE DAY	NATIONAL PRINCESS DAY
Stay Up Late	Sadie Hawkins Sling	Adonis	Crocodile Cocktail	Little Havana	Falls Cocktail	Jasmine
19	**20**	**21**	**22**	**23**	**24**	**25**
INTERNATIONAL MEN'S DAY	NATIONAL ABSURDITY DAY	WORLD TELEVISION DAY	GO FOR A RIDE DAY	NATIONAL ESPRESSO DAY	CRYSTAL SKULL WORLD DAY	INTERNATIONAL HAT DAY
Gentleman's Buck	Trinidad Sour	Hollywood	Bicicletta	Irish Coffee	Skull Cracker	Raspberry Beret
26	**27**	**28**	**29**	**30**		
CASABLANCA DAY	THANKSGIVING	RED PLANET DAY	CUSTOMER IS WRONG DAY	WINTER WAR ANNIVERSARY		
French 75	Apple Cider Mojito	Warday's	86 Spritz	Hit Man		

ST. AUGUSTINE

Begone, evil spirits! Today honors a totally different kind of dead. In many Christian traditions, All Saints' Day celebrates the praiseworthy people whose acts of charity and kindness ostensibly made them super-stars in the celestial realm and the very real subjects of adoration for millions around the world. If you are still suffering from overdoing Halloween festivities and suddenly find yourself wanting to walk a holier path, you have literally thousands of examples to follow, including St. Bibiana of Rome, the patron saint of hangovers, epileptics, the men-tally ill, and torture victims.

But it's important to remember that not even saints are perfect. Before devoting his life to the Church, fourth-century bishop Augustine of Hippo famously partied harder than Keith Richards at an abandoned pharmacy. Maria Walley's savory, complex cocktail created in the saint's honor blends rum, beer, and coffee into a heavenly joy for martyrs and miscreants of all denominations. Have too many of these supercharged bad boys and you may find yourself firmly in the latter camp.

2 ounces rum

2 ounces stout

2 ounces cold brew coffee

1 ounce simple syrup

½ ounce heavy cream

In a large rocks glass, combine the rum, beer, coffee, and simple syrup. Fill with cracked ice and top with the cream.

Day of the Dead

JUAN LOCKWOOD

For those who celebrate el Día de los Muertos (Day of the Dead), the spirits of the deceased remain among us. A Mexican federal holiday loosely associated with 3,000-year-old indigenous rituals and the Catholic feast of All Souls' Day, today is for praying and acknowledging your ancestors by setting up altars with their favorite foods, drinks, flowers, and photos. You can't get down with the dead today without some mezcal or Tequila, Mexico's most popular additions to the booze pantheon. Both factor equally in the Juan Lockwood, an agave-fueled take on the Don Lockwood, created at Manhattan's Middle Branch in 2014. You can mix up this fitting ancestral tribute—mystically strong, smoky, and embellished with agave nectar and two kinds of bitters—in a jiffy. Which is good because, if the dead rejoin us only once a year, they're probably impatient, and you don't want to upset them.

1 ounce tequila reposado	2 dashes chocolate bitters
1 ounce mezcal	1 dash Angostura bitters
⅛ ounce agave nectar	1 orange twist, for garnish

Combine the tequila, mezcal, agave nectar, and bitters in an Old-Fashioned glass. Add ice and stir for five or six seconds. Garnish with the orange twist.

Cliché Day

INTRO TO APEROL

"Cat got your tongue?" "Woke up on the wrong side of the bed?" "Don't get your knickers in a twist because every cloud has a silver lining." Cliché Day celebrates these and countless other phrases that, while they have some truth to them, people repeat over and over until they lose their point through overuse. Not exclusive to our personal lives, clichés invade our workplaces with equal or greater frequency. Just ask any bartender who's had to muster the will to make several thousand Instagram-ready Aperol Spritzes during the first shift of the year that the temperature exceeds 50 degrees Fahrenheit. Yes, Cliché Day embraces the tired and trite, but it also gets it out of your system, which is why, instead of the dreaded and oh-so-#basic Spritz, you should try the Intro to Aperol, a much classier low-alcohol refresher from Pegu Club's Audrey Saunders. Brilliant, bitter, and an innovative example of the heights to which an aperitif can soar when not slathered in sparkles, it's "just the ticket" you need to "seize the day" (because, you know, YOLO).

---

2 ounces Aperol
1 ounce gin

¾ ounce fresh lemon juice
2 dashes Angostura biters
1 orange twist, for garnish

Combine the Aperol, gin, lemon juice, and bitters in an ice-filled shaker. Shake vigorously for 25 to 30 seconds and strain into a stemmed cocktail glass. Garnish with the orange twist.

SINNERS AND SAINTS

*Don't schedule that long-overdue dentist appointment today, sugar
freaks, because it's National Candy Day! It's a little weird to associate
artichoke-based Cynar with sweets, but when you combine this bold
amaro with floral St-Germain and champagne, the result is straight
out of a confectioner's recipe book—or Tom Richter's. The New York
City–based bartender combined those ingredients to give us Sinners
and Saints, a delicate yet slightly wicked low-ABV crowd-pleaser that's
as toothsome as anything that candy giants Mars, Hershey, or Haribo
can whip up. On the sweeter side but not overpowering, this easy-to-mix
indulgence will have you channeling your inner Willy Wonka in no time.*

1½ ounces St-Germain
¾ ounce Cynar

Champagne, to top
1 grapefruit twist, for garnish

 Combine the St-Germain and Cynar in a shaker. Pour into
a double Old-Fashioned glass filled with cracked ice. Top
with champagne. Garnish with the grapefruit twist.

TEQUILA TORCHLIGHT

Some like it hot. Some prefer their mouths scorched by flames from the deepest pits of chili-pepper hell. National Hot Sauce Day indulges the gnarliest spicy-food aficionados, the mealtime masochists who can't imagine a meal without gobs of glorious liquid fire. If hot sauce–infused food can't satisfy your diabolical cravings, plenty of spice-forward potations will do the trick. One of the most interesting, the Tequila Torchlight is a fascinating experiment in flavor from Benjamin Schwartz at Little Branch. Cholula hot sauce and honey syrup might not seem like the most logical combination, but the sweet, peppery, garlicky blend, enhanced by agave, citrus, and an extra kick of cayenne, tastes surprisingly well-balanced, each ingredient doing its best work. Save the boring spicy Margs for another day.

---

2 ounces tequila

1 ounce fresh lime juice

¼ ounce honey syrup

4 dashes Cholula hot sauce

1 pinch cayenne pepper

1 lime wedge, for garnish

Combine the tequila, lime juice, honey syrup, and hot sauce in an ice-filled shaker. Shake vigorously for 25 to 30 seconds and strain into a double Old-Fashioned glass over ice. Top with cayenne pepper. Garnish with the lime wedge.

MERCY, MERCY

We associate the saxophone's distinctive wail with jazz music, particularly the mid-20th-century bebop stylings of legends John Coltrane and Julian "Cannonball" Adderly. But the brass-made instrument's history goes back much further. Belgian inventor Aldophe Sax produced the first prototypes in the early 1840s. Consisting of nine specific types, the saxophone family remains a staple of marching and military bands, modern big bands, rock bands, and, of course, jazz ensembles, in which its uniquely expressive tone, both mellow and powerful, sounds unmistakable. English novelist Arnold Bennett wrote that "The saxophone is the embodied spirit of beer." But this booze-adjacent woodwind also serves as inspiration for several swinging mixed drinks, including Joseph Schwartz's Mercy, Mercy, which shares many funky attributes with a similarly named Cannonball Adderly Quintet tune from 1966. Appearing in 2006 at Little Branch—known for its live jazz performances—it's a nuanced, less bitter Negroni spin-off buoyed by equal parts Aperol and Cocchi Americano. Smooth and sultry like the finest saxophone solos, this insanely good, nimbly stirred sipper will make you feel like beautiful music.

---

2 ounces gin

½ ounce Aperol

½ ounce Cocchi Americano

1 lemon twist, for garnish

Combine the gin, Aperol, and Cocchi Americano in a mixing glass filled with cracked ice. Stir with a long-handled spoon for 30 seconds and strain into a stemmed cocktail glass. Garnish with the lemon twist.

TEDDY NO. 2

Celebrate today by giving a child the gift of a fuzzy, squishable protector or release your childhood teddy from storage and have a discreet cuddle sesh for old times' sake. We promise we won't tell anyone. As reassuring as hugging a teddy bear might feel, you probably don't want to make a public habit of it—unless you're a furry, in which case, let that freak flag fly. Either way, look for the same comfort in a Teddy No. 2, a bright, frothy take on the Teddy Bear, which first appeared on the bar menu at the Borough in Edinburgh, Scotland, in 2002. Zesty and silky, with notes of apple, pear, and vanilla, it's the liquid embrace you never knew you needed—until we just told you about it.

1½ ounces applejack	¼ ounce cane syrup
¾ ounce pear liqueur	1 egg white
¾ ounce fresh lemon juice	1 pinch freshly grated lemon zest,
¼ ounce Licor 43	for garnish

Combine the applejack, pear liqueur, lemon juice, Licor 43, cane syrup, and egg white in a shaker. Shake without ice (to emulsify the egg) for 10 seconds, then add ice and shake vigorously. Strain into a stemmed cocktail glass. Garnish with the lemon zest.

FREDDY FUDPUCKER

If you weren't around during its heyday, you might never have heard of this golden-orange sipper. Yes, the Harvey Wallbanger is a cocktail and not someone with a wacky, possibly adult film–related name. Southern California bartender Donato "Duke" Antone created the drink in the 1950s when he made a Screwdriver and simply drizzled a little Galliano atop the vodka and orange juice. That tiny change was inexplicably a huge hit, and by the 1970s the Harvey Wallbanger was the sweet and citrusy go-to of swinging cats and kittens everywhere.

You might be wondering why the Harvey Wallbanger merits its own holiday. If anything, it's a testament to simplicity and how cool you look pouring from Galliano's distinctive neon-yellow, outlandishly conical bottle. The Italian herbal liqueur isn't just for show, though. Even a small amount of the spirit adds vanilla, anise, citrus, woodsy, and herbal elements to whatever it graces, an alchemy perfectly illustrated in the Harvey Wallbanger and the Freddy Fudpucker, its younger sibling. Substituting vodka for tequila, which allows the botanicals to shine even more, it's one of the simplest concoctions for tricking people into thinking you're a mixological mastermind. Just make sure you drizzle the Galliano in front of them for added effect.

---

2 ounces tequila	¼ ounce Galliano
4 ounces orange juice	1 thin orange slice, for garnish

Combine the tequila and orange juice in an ice-filled shaker. Shake vigorously for 25 to 30 seconds and strain into a double Old-Fashioned glass over ice. Drizzle the Galliano. Garnish with the orange slice.

SPACE GIN SMASH

Some kids have their heads in the clouds. Carl Sagan's wasn't even on this planet. Though Sagan wasn't known as a prolific drinker, he probably would have loved a Space Gin Smash—and not just because of its out-of-this-world name. Adapted from a recipe by British bartender Angus Winchester, this supremely refreshing, gin lover's delight boasts a heaping helping of lemon juice and zest buoyed by favorite garden flavors mint, green grape, and green apple. Drinking one of these may not make you as smart as Sagan, but your friends will think you're a mixological genius every time you fix them one.

2 ounces gin
¾ ounce simple syrup
6 mint leaves
4 lemon wedges

2 seedless green grapes
1 green apple slice
1 sprig fresh mint,
    for garnish

Muddle the simple syrup, mint leaves, lemon wedges, grapes, and apple slice in a shaker. Add the gin, fill with ice, and shake vigorously for 25 to 30 seconds. Strain into a double Old-Fashioned glass filled with cracked ice. Garnish with the mint sprig.

CONNECTICUT BULLFROG

Most expert swimmers and divers will tell you that they're equally at home on land and in the water, but amphibians are the only creatures naturally suited to both habitats. With its frigid winters, Connecticut might not seem like an amphibian paradise, but the Nutmeg State boasts 11 species of frogs and toads, including the notoriously vocal American bullfrog. First appearing in the 1949 edition of the Esquire Handbook for Hosts, *the Connecticut Bullfrog is a puckeringly sour, slightly sweet potable with a finish as loud as its namesake. The potentially off-putting combination of gin and gold rum works marvelously well here, just like a frog's adaptation to wildly different habitats. Hop on down to your local liquor store and buy the ingredients to mix one of these sophisticated treats today.*

1½ ounces gin	½ ounce maple syrup
¾ ounce fresh lemon juice	2 dashes orange bitters
½ ounce gold rum	1 lemon wedge, for garnish

 Combine the gin, lemon juice, rum, maple syrup, and bitters in an ice-filled shaker. Shake vigorously for 25 to 30 seconds and strain into a stemmed cocktail glass. Garnish with the lemon wedge.

SPECIAL FORCES

In one of his famous Veterans Day speeches, President John F. Kennedy, a veteran of World War II, expressed his hope that one day there no longer would be a need for a military, that all countries would pursue only peace. Until that day comes, we can thank millions of personnel who served in the armed forces for their bravery, discipline, and unwavering sense of duty. Some of the best qualities of a great soldier, sailor, or flier include strength, balance, and ingenuity, all of which define Sam Ross's Special Forces. This souped-up, sophisticated take on an Army & Navy features a base of overproof gin and the nutty, crisp, saline properties of fino sherry. The sweetness of orgeat is mellowed beautifully by its citrus and absinthe components, a tactical decision resulting in an herbaceous dynamo that even intense rivals—like Marines and Navy SEALs—would join forces to enjoy.

1 ounce navy-strength gin

1 ounce fino sherry

¾ ounce fresh lemon juice

¾ ounce orgeat

1 dash absinthe

1 lemon twist, for garnish

Combine gin, sherry, lemon juice, orgeat, and absinthe in an ice-filled shaker. Shake vigorously for 25 to 30 seconds and strain into a stemmed cocktail glass. Garnish with the lemon twist.

STAY UP LATE

For the nine-to-five set, nothing's better than escaping office drudgery, heading to a watering hole with the homeys for happy hour, and filling up on reduced-price booze and appetizers. Most happy hours end around 7 PM, but there's no rule saying that the party must end then. For early evenings that unexpectedly turn into early mornings, fix a Stay Up Late for yourself and your like-minded posse of weeknight warriors. A slightly more involved take on the Gin and Soda, that bastion of two-for-one happy hour specials, this classic from Lucius Beebe's The Stork Club Bar Book *(1946) benefits from the lovely interplay of gin and cognac, with a proper dose of citrus and sugar to keep you perky for whatever the night or morning has in store.*

1½ ounces gin
¾ ounce fresh lemon juice
¾ ounce simple syrup

½ ounce cognac
Club soda, to top
1 thin orange slice, for garnish
1 brandied cherry, for garnish

 Combine the gin, lemon juice, simple syrup, and cognac in a shaker. Whip shake (no ice) and pour into a tall glass filled with ice. Top with club soda. Garnish with the orange slice and the brandied cherry.

SADIE HAWKINS SLING

Who says that men always have to make the first move? Certainly not Sadie Hawkins. During a popular 1937 storyline in Al Capp's classic comic strip, Li'l Abner, the homeliest spinster in the town of Dogpatch participated in a race—organized by her equally desperate father, Hekzebiah—in which she would chase the town's eligible bachelors, forcing whomever she caught to marry her. Dubbed "Sadie Hawkins Day," the event inspired hundreds of real-life reenactments on high school and college campuses throughout America. Today, kids who have never heard of Li'l Abner participate in Sadie Hawkins dances, where girls do all the inviting. No matter your gender, asking out a potential romantic partner always requires an uncommon amount of courage. The easiest way to drum some up is with a wonderfully tasty potation such as the Sadie Hawkins Sling. An adaptation of a recipe from New York City's Jbird Cocktails that's meant to be sipped by two lovebirds, this whiskey-meets-tiki marvel offers a cavalcade of diverse flavors—pineapple, apricot, pear, almond—that somehow all manage to make their presence felt and appreciated. If you see someone walking away with one of these, chase him or her down and ask who made it. It might be the start of a beautiful friendship.

---

2 ounces bourbon

1 ounce fresh pineapple juice

½ ounce fresh lemon juice

⅜ ounce John D. Taylor's Velvet Falernum

⅜ ounce pear brandy

¼ ounce apricot liqueur

¼ ounce demerara syrup

2 dashes Angostura bitters

1 orange slice, for garnish

Combine the bourbon, juices, velvet falernum, pear brandy, apricot liqueur, demerara syrup, and bitters in a shaker. Pour into a tall glass filled two-thirds of the way with crushed ice. Add a straw and top with more crushed ice. Garnish with the orange slice.

ADONIS

Find a spot with great lighting, turn on your camera's portrait mode setting, extend your arm, angle your phone slightly downward, strike a natural pose (no duck face!), and snap away. But you already knew that, right? Too much self-objectification is never good, but unless you've been living in isolation since 2005, you understand that the selfie is here to stay. If you're part of the infinitesimally small percentage of people who never have taken a selfie, join the party! For liquid encouragement, whip up a highly photogenic Adonis, a sherry-based Manhattan riff named for the gorgeous, ill-fated Greek god and created in honor of the 1884 Broadway musical of the same name. Brilliantly earthy, brisk, and refreshing, it's the perfect companion for all your self-portraits or, you know, just to drink.

1½ ounces fino sherry
1½ ounces sweet vermouth

2 dashes orange bitters
1 lemon twist, for garnish

Combine the sherry, vermouth, and bitters in an ice-filled mixing glass. Stir with a long-handled spoon for 30 seconds and strain into a stemmed cocktail glass. Garnish with the lemon twist.

CROCODILE COCKTAIL

If watching Animal Planet in the late 1990s and early 2000s kick-started your lifetime love of wildlife, you likely have Steve "the Crocodile Hunter" Irwin to thank. The late TV personality, zookeeper, and environmentalist enthralled millions of viewers with his up-close-and-personal encounters with dangerous critters, Down-Under diction ("Crikey!") and infectious enthusiasm. He never feared tangling with beasts of any species, but Irwin built his reputation (and nickname) on his passion for getting dangerously close to crocodiles. Inspired by his always cheery demeanor and maybe a bit of his recklessness, the Crocodile Cocktail is an exotic, floral, and sneakily potent Sidecar variation you'll want to jaw again and again. Highlighted by notes of melon and orange for a finish smoother than Irwin's Australian twang, it'll make you happier than the Crocodile Hunter knee-deep in a reptile-infested swamp.

1 ounce navy-strength gin

1 ounce Midori

1 ounce Cointreau

½ ounce fresh lemon juice

2 dashes Angostura
   bitters

Combine the gin, Midori, Cointreau, and lemon juice in an ice-filled shaker. Shake vigorously for 25 to 30 seconds and strain into a stemmed cocktail glass. Float the bitters.

LITTLE HAVANA

Age doesn't necessarily make something interesting. Unless you're a geologist, a million-year-old rock is simply a rock. Havana, Cuba, on the other hand, is both ancient and endlessly fascinating. Most deliciously, Havana also plays a major part in rum culture as the birthplace of the Mojito, reason enough to celebrate this beautiful seaside paradise! If you want a spirit-forward taste of the city's unique flavors, try the Little Havana, created by Matthew Linzmeier at Milk & Honey. Simple and elegant, with a slightly herbal finish, it's best enjoyed with Havana Club Rum, which, unfortunately, you can't buy in the United States. If you can't get your hands on a bottle of the excellent and elusive stuff, any good aged rum will do just fine.

2 ounces aged rum, preferably Havana Club Añejo 7 Años

1 ounce sweet vermouth
¼ ounce Fernet-Branca
1 lemon twist, for garnish

Combine the rum and sweet vermouth in an ice-filled mixing glass. Stir with a long-handled spoon for 30 seconds and pour into a stemmed cocktail glass rinsed with the Fernet-Branca. Garnish with a lemon twist.

National Take a Hike Day

FALLS COCKTAIL

Take a hike, pal. No, seriously, do it! Dust off your favorite pair of boots or sneakers and grab a walking stick, trail mix, and a water bottle for an exhilarating day in the great outdoors. Whether you're a lifelong urbanite or feel more at home in the sticks, hiking is one of the best ways to explore local surroundings and unfamiliar landscapes. It's perfectly fine to get your exercise with a few fast-paced trips around the block, but hard-core weekend warriors are footing terrain both challenging and gorgeous. Some of the most coveted hiking destinations—according to their frequent appearances on social media humblebrag posts—are waterfalls. It's unclear whether Meeyong McFalls-Schwartz took inspiration from these awesome natural features when she created the Falls Cocktail at Little Branch, but you'll want to pour this whiskey-based, gingery, and minty phenomenon down your gullet faster than a barrel over Niagara Falls, which runs along a popular trail.

2 ounces bourbon
¼ ounce fresh lemon juice
¾ ounce ginger syrup
4 dashes Angostura bitters

3 or 4 mint leaves
1 piece candied ginger,
 for garnish
1 sprig mint, for garnish

Combine the bourbon, lemon juice, ginger syrup, bitters, and mint leaves in an ice-filled shaker. Shake vigorously for 25 to 30 seconds and strain into a double Old-Fashioned glass over ice. Garnish with the piece of ginger candy and the mint sprig.

National Princess Day

JASMINE

National Princess Day celebrates the fantasies of millions of would-be Ariels and Meridas, encouraging participants to embark on a magical day of pampering, fabulousness, kindness, and ruffly dresses. It's also a great time to introduce all kids to strong, independent women such as Mulan or Xena, who refuse to follow fairytale stereotypes and prove that "happily ever after" can be anything you want. From 1992's Aladdin, Jasmine, the endearingly determined daughter of a sultan, rebels against her sheltered upbringing and ultimately succeeds in living her best life. A similarly self-willed gin sipper, Paul Harrington's Jasmine cocktail, from his influential 1998 book, Cocktail: The Drinks Bible for the 21st Century, *presents wannabe booze royalty with the opportunity to class up any drinking affair. Great as an aperitif before formal dinners or reckless magic carpet rides with thirst-inducing commoners, it's a sublimely dry, bitter, bright experience that, like your favorite childhood princess, is hard to forget.*

1½ ounces gin
1 ounce Cointreau

¾ ounce fresh lemon juice
½ ounce Campari
1 lemon twist, for garnish

Combine the gin, Cointreau, lemon juice, and Campari in an ice-filled shaker. Shake vigorously for 25 to 30 seconds and strain into a stemmed cocktail glass. Garnish with the lemon twist.

GENTLEMAN'S BUCK

Today's holiday celebrates gender equality and honors all who promote humanitarian values, regardless of how they self-identify. Making positive contributions to community and family, the pillars of International Men's Day, is what real masculinity is all about. We'll add another pillar: the ability to whip up a delicious cocktail. There's no better place to start than with a Gentleman's Buck, an easy-to-mix whiskey and ginger cooler that Michael Madrusan first served at Little Branch in 2009. Today's holiday puts a premium on self-improvement, and this brisk favorite of modern bartenders improves its predecessor, the Bourbon Ginger Highball, with an extra boost of citrus and bitters, resulting in a drink slightly sweeter and more complex. Salute the accomplishments of the good men in your life with a round of these tall glasses of constructive masculine energy. If your closest bros are truly gentlemen, they'll thank you kindly and help clean up.

---

2 ounces bourbon

1 ounce orange juice

¾ ounce ginger syrup

½ ounce fresh lime juice

2 dashes Angostura bitters

Club soda, to top

1 piece candied ginger,
   for garnish

1 thin orange slice, for garnish

 Combine the bourbon, orange juice, ginger syrup, lime juice, and bitters in a shaker. Whip shake (no ice) and pour into a tall glass filled with ice. Top with club soda. Garnish with the piece of candied ginger and the orange slice.

TRINIDAD SOUR

Forget about conventionality today, sheeple. Let's get weird! National Absurdity Day embraces the ridiculous and favors embarking on zany adventures. Over the years, drink-slingers have come up with thousands of seemingly illogical potables, with varying degrees of success. But none reaches the absurd heights of Giuseppe González's Trinidad Sour, first served at Brooklyn's Clover Club in the late 2000s. Featuring a full ounce of Angostura bitters as its base spirit—yes, you read that right— this eschewer of conventional wisdom tastes seductively rich, savory, and intense yet somehow still well-balanced. Complex and sassy, it's easy to see why this blood-red oddity has become a favorite of bartenders everywhere.

1 ounce Angostura bitters

1 ounce orgeat

¾ ounce fresh lemon juice

½ ounce overproof rye whiskey

Combine all ingredients in an ice-filled shaker. Shake vigorously for 25 to 30 seconds and strain into a stemmed cocktail glass.

HOLLYWOOD

In 1996, the United Nations declared today World Television Day to highlight TV's ability to "bring attention to conflicts, raise awareness of threats to peace and security, and sharpen focus on social and economic issues." So the next time you catch heat for an hours-long binge-watching session, explain that you're just being a conscientious global citizen. Chances are, you've heard someone (probably a parent who wanted you out of the house) say that "too much television rots your brain." Try telling that to the folks in Hollywood, where just about everyone's livelihood seems to depend on on-screen entertainment. Better yet, try the geographically motivated Hollywood cocktail, which first cameo'd at Los Angeles bars in the middle of the 20th century. With ingredients far more decipherable than the average true-crime mystery and easier to digest than your favorite reality show, this fruity, frothy number deserves your undivided attention tonight.

2 ounces white rum	**½ ounce pomegranate syrup**
1 ounce fresh grapefruit juice	**1 egg white**

 Combine all ingredients in a shaker. Shake without ice (to emulsify the egg white) for 10 seconds, then add ice and shake vigorously. Strain into a stemmed cocktail glass.

BICICLETTA

Celebrating the increasing freedom that developments in the transportation industry have given us, Go for a Ride Day also honors the achievements of inventors such as Mathias Pfatischer, who developed a prototype electric motor in 1904, or Carl Eliason, who received a patent for the snowmobile two decades later. Thanks to their ingenuity and the creations of those who followed in their footsteps, it's never been easier to get out and get moving. Sure, cars cover a lot of ground, but if you want your ride to be the total package—visually, mentally, athletically—it's hard to do better than a bicycle. Post-ride, nothing cools you down quite like a Bicicletta, which first appeared in Michael Madrusan and Zara Young's A Spot at the Bar (2016). A drier, airier take on the Americano, this low-alcohol marriage of French and Italian ingredients tastes quite bitter but, somewhat paradoxically, also extremely refreshing. It's a near-perfect energizer, regardless of your preferred method of transportation.

2½ ounces dry vermouth
1½ ounces Campari

1 ounce club soda
1 orange twist, for garnish

Combine the vermouth and Campari in a double Old-Fashioned glass. Add ice and stir for five or six seconds. Add club soda. Garnish with the orange twist.

IRISH COFFEE

*For some coffee cravers, a tiny café au lait can jump-start the morning.
If, to function, you need more caffeine than blood, a few shots of espresso
are just the ticket. This classic espresso-based tipple might not garner as
many Instagram likes, but it still tastes divine. Piping hot, earthy, nutty,
dark, and luxuriously creamy, this energizing, heartwarming marriage
of java and whiskey came to America in the 1950s courtesy of travel
writer Stanton Delaplane. His recipe allegedly came from a chef at Ireland's Shannon Airport, where it was a popular preflight beverage. It's
not the best option if you get jittery on planes, but as a cold-weather pick-
me-up, you can't go wrong with an Irish Coffee.*

4 ounces hot espresso	**2 teaspoons brown sugar**
1½ ounces Irish whiskey	**Hand-whipped cream, to top**

Place the sugar into a warm mug. Add the espresso and Irish whiskey.
Stir until the sugar dissolves. Float the whipped cream.

SKULL CRACKER

Most people's only knowledge of crystal skulls comes from the dreadful fourth installment of the Indiana Jones franchise, which is a shame, because the history of these controversial artifacts is far more interesting than two hours of crappy CGI. Hewn from quartz, the masterfully crafted, skull-shaped carvings—discovered in South America in the mid-1800s, and said to have pre-Columbian origins—exhibit mystical, psychic, paranormal, and even extraterrestrial qualities, according to New Agers. Set aside questions about the skulls' authenticity because, unless you can pull off an Indiana Jones–level heist, you're not going to be able to get your hands on one. But you might access their otherworldly abilities on the fourth Sunday of November with a Skull Cracker, created in collaboration with Michael Timmons at Little Branch on a particularly foreboding night around Halloween 2020. Spicy, fruity, herbal, nutty, and slightly astringent, the tiki-inspired oddball features a mind-warping combination of four high-proof spirits with just enough pineapple, lemon, and orgeat to mask its potency.

1 ounce fresh pineapple juice

¾ ounce spiced rum

¾ ounce Batavia Arrack

½ ounce absinthe (or Pernod)

½ ounce fresh lemon juice

½ ounce orgeat

¼ ounce 151-proof rum

1 pinch freshly grated cinnamon, for garnish

1 orange slice, for garnish

Combine the pineapple juice, rum, Batavia Arrack, absinthe, lemon juice, and orgeat in a shaker. Whip shake (no ice) and pour into a tall glass filled with cracked ice. Float the 151-proof rum. Garnish with the cinnamon and the orange slice.

RASPBERRY BERET

You can't have a bad hair day if you never take off your headwear, and International Hat Day is the perfect excuse not to! Break out your favorite baseball cap, fedora, sombrero, beanie or, if you're feeling especially retro, bonnet for a quirky, fashion-forward look or just some quality sun blockage. One of the most undoubtedly sophisticated and enduring head coverings is the beret, a round, flat-crowned cap beloved by everyone from artists and intellectuals to musicians and military masterminds. It was also the preferred headgear of an anonymous woman who caught Prince's eye and inspired one of the legendary musician's biggest hits. Named for both hat and song, the Raspberry Beret is a tall glass of romance highlighted by notes of raspberry, almond, and two types of citrus, "capped" with a duel base of gin and cognac. One taste and you'll be tipping your brim in admiration.

1 ounce gin

1 ounce cognac

¾ ounce orgeat

½ ounce fresh lime juice

½ ounce fresh lemon juice

¼ ounce pomegranate syrup

6 raspberries

Club soda, to top

Combine the gin, cognac, orgeat, juices, pomegranate syrup, and five raspberries in an ice-filled shaker. Shake vigorously for 25 to 30 seconds and strain into a tall glass filled with ice. Top with club soda. Garnish with another raspberry.

FRENCH 75

"Here's looking at you, kid."

When the romantic drama Casablanca *premiered on this date in 1942, Humphrey Bogart, who played the iconic role of expat nightclub owner Rick Blaine, wasn't the only one doing the looking. Set in Morocco during the early days of World War II, the film enjoyed a successful theatrical run and won Academy Awards for Best Picture, Best Adapted Screenplay, and Best Director. Primarily set in a bar during the heyday of classic drinking culture,* Casablanca *has been called the greatest cocktail movie of all time. One of the drinks ordered in the film is a French 75, a gin and champagne dandy popularized by Scottish bartender Harry MacElhone and named after the French Army's 75 mm guns used in World War I. Despite its military moniker, there's nothing belligerent about this bubbly, citrusy, effortlessly charming classic that's smoother than a line of Bogart dialogue and prettier than a Bergman pout. Whether you're a proprietor of a gin joint as notorious as Rick's Café Américain or a humble weekend warrior, the French 75 should be a staple of your drink-slinging repertoire.*

1 ounce gin
½ ounce fresh lemon juice
½ ounce simple syrup

Champagne, to top
1 lemon twist,
    for garnish

Combine the gin, lemon juice, and simple syrup in an ice-filled shaker. Shake vigorously for 25 to 30 seconds and strain into a stemmed cocktail glass. Top with champagne. Garnish with the lemon twist.

APPLE CIDER MOJITO

For some poultry fiends, just the freshly roasted scent of turkey makes the fourth Thursday in November a date over which to salivate. But you have plenty of other reasons—football, the National Dog Show, spending time with (select) relatives—that Thanksgiving is the most popular secular holiday in America. If you plan on getting lit first thing in the morning, ingest some healthy fruits and veggies to counteract the booze and the obligatory slice or three of pumpkin pie. The Apple Cider Mojito, a seasonal spin on an enduring rum classic, is chock-full of the good stuff, including a hardy dose of antioxidant-rich cider (duh), vitamin-filled lime juice, and indigestion-relieving mint. All immediately canceled by copious amounts of alcohol and sugar. You won't be doing your waistline any favors, but your taste buds will be giving thanks for this undeniably excellent liquid feast.

1½ ounces black rum,
   such as Goslings
1 ounce fresh apple cider
½ ounce applejack
½ ounce fresh lime juice

½ ounce simple syrup
1 small handful mint leaves
1 brown sugar cube
1 sprig fresh mint, for garnish
1 pinch freshly grated cinnamon,
   for garnish

Combine the rum, cider, applejack, lime juice, simple syrup, mint leaves, and sugar cube in a double Old-Fashioned glass. Gently muddle and fill the glass two-thirds full with crushed ice. Add a straw and top with more crushed ice. Garnish with the mint sprig and the cinnamon.

WARDAY'S

With all the hoopla surrounding Mars, it's important to learn a few handy tidbits about our celestial neighbor. That's the gist of Red Planet Day, which commemorates the 1964 launch of the spacecraft Mariner 4, *which came within 6,000 miles of Mars just 228 days later. Nowadays, it's about permanent residency. Named after the Roman god of war, Mars has held an ominous place in the human imagination, its glowing appearance in the sky often seen as a precursor to conflict. The Warday's, an equally perilous-sounding drink, is a fruity, herbaceous, volatile Martini that has sent many a tippler's head into orbit since appearing in 1930's* Savoy Cocktail Book *by Harry Craddock. As reddish-brown as the Martian soil, the combination of gin, calvados, green Chartreuse, and sweet vermouth begs to be sipped slowly, as this ultrapotent blend will have even the boldest cocktail adventurers soaring faster than rocket fuel.*

1 ounce gin
1 ounce sweet vermouth

¼ ounce apple brandy,
  such as calvados
¼ ounce green Chartreuse
1 lemon twist, for garnish

Combine the gin, vermouth, brandy, and Chartreuse in a mixing glass filled with cracked ice. Stir with a long-handled spoon for 30 seconds, then strain into a stemmed cocktail glass. Garnish with the lemon twist.

86 SPRITZ

To all the bartenders, servers, and retail workers who nearly have burst arteries after hearing that "the customer is always right," you have Marshall Field and Harry Selfridge to blame. The early 1900s retail magnates might have had an immediate hit with the catchy slogan, which in its entirety goes: "The customer is always right in matters of taste." But they failed to consider that, many times, the customer is wrong. Getting rid of a problematic customer is called "86ing," a term that originated at Chumley's, a longtime watering hole in Manhattan's West Village, where troublemakers (or those fleeing the police during Prohibition) were dumped unceremoniously at the bar's 86 Bedford Street entrance. You're not going to want to discard the 86 Spritz, created by Sam Ross for Las Vegas's Electra Cocktail Club in 2018. A fantastic low-ABV cooler enhanced by champagne and Amaro Montenegro's strong notes of bitter orange and vanilla, it's a great relaxation option after dealing with an unnecessarily rude scalawag. After you check your job's Yelp or GlassDoor reviews, you might need another round.

2 ounces champagne	Club soda, to top
1 ounce blanc vermouth	1 grapefruit twist, for garnish
1 ounce Amaro Montenegro	

Combine the champagne, vermouth, and Amaro Montenegro in a glass filled with cracked ice. Top with club soda. Garnish with the grapefruit twist.

Winter War Anniversary

HIT MAN

Soldiers often come back from war with extraordinary and sometimes greatly exaggerated tales of superhuman exploits and achievements. In the case of Finnish military sniper Simo "the White Death" Häyhä, legend and reality were one and the same. Protecting his country from Soviet invaders in subzero temperatures during the 1939 Winter War, Häyhä shot approximately 540 enemy combatants, single-handedly taking out 25 percent of an entire Soviet rifle division. His insanely good marksmanship made him the most prolific sniper in any major war and a source of terror for Soviet soldiers. One week before the Winter War ended, Häyhä was shot in the jaw and left for dead. When he awoke from a coma a week later, he read his obituary in a local newspaper. A rude awakening like that, even for a man with nerves of steel, demands a calming beverage, specifically the appropriately named Hit Man. An unusually funky potation highlighted by mezcal, Batavia Arrack (a spirit made from rice and sugarcane and popular in Nordic countries since the beginning of the 20th century), and maraschino, it's almost as complex as the inner workings of a sniper rifle—and far more pleasant. An automatic bull's-eye if you're looking to put a hole in your sobriety.

¾ ounce mezcal

¾ ounce Batavia Arrack

¾ ounce fresh lime juice

½ ounce maraschino liqueur

½ ounce ginger syrup

Combine all ingredients in an ice-filled shaker. Shake vigorously for 25 to 30 seconds and strain into a double Old-Fashioned glass over ice.

DECEMBER

					1	2
					ANTARCTICA DAY Fuzzy Penguin	NATIONAL MUTT DAY Invisible Gin
3 CUBA NATIONAL DOCTORS' DAY Dr. Funk	4 NATIONAL COOKIE DAY Karaoke Honeymoon	5 REPEAL DAY Scofflaw	6 NATIONAL MINERS DAY Coal Train	7 NATIONAL COTTON CANDY DAY Cotton Candy Margarita	8 WORLD PEAR DAY 41 Jane Does	9 INTERNATIONAL ANTI-CORRUPTION DAY Backroom Mob
10 HUMAN RIGHTS DAY, ANIMAL RIGHTS DAY Old Pal	11 INTERNATIONAL MOUNTAIN DAY Mount Fuji	12 INTERNATIONAL DAY OF NEUTRALITY Swiss Manhattan	13 NATIONAL HORSE DAY High Horse	14 MONKEY DAY Monkey Grip	15 INTERNATIONAL TEA DAY Jalisco High Tea	16 NATIONAL CHOCOLATE-COVERED ANYTHING DAY Chocolate Cocktail
17 PAN AMERICAN AVIATION DAY Pan American Clipper	18 UN ARABIC LANGUAGE DAY Rum Amandine	19 NATIONAL EMO DAY Black Barrel	20 NATIONAL SANGRIA DAY Suave Sangria	21 CAPRICORN DAY Saturn	22 GLOBAL ORGASM DAY Vesper	23 FESTIVUS Feats of Strength
24 NATIONAL EGGNOG DAY East New York Flip 31 NATIONAL CHAMPAGNE DAY Fortune Cocktail	25 NATIONAL PUMPKIN PIE DAY Headless Horseman	26 NATIONAL WHINERS DAY After All	27 NATIONAL FRUITCAKE DAY Mezcal Cobbler	28 NATIONAL CARD PLAYING DAY Poker Face	29 NATIONAL PEPPER POT DAY Old Pepper	30 FESTIVAL OF ENORMOUS CHANGES AT THE LAST MINUTE Corpse Reviver No. 2

DECEMBER 1
Antarctica Day

FUZZY PENGUIN

The 1959 Antarctic Treaty encourages scientific exploration and bans military activity on the borderless continent. Today's holiday, held on the anniversary of the signing of the international agreement, celebrates a wildly fascinating place better observed on television than in person. If you make the brave (totally insane) trek to Antarctica for research or tourism, prepare yourself for breathtaking glaciers, huge mountains, desolate beaches, and penguins—lots and lots of penguins. Seven species of the chonky, waddling birds, numbering some 12 million individuals, make their homes on the continent. They also inspired the Fuzzy Penguin, a tequila and spiced rum oddball that has been intriguing adventurous palates since the 1970s. Sharp, vegetal, and herbaceous yet supremely fruity and refreshing, it's as rare as a bird that swims but can't fly and lives on the most inhospitable landmass imaginable. And, of course, very icy.

1½ ounces fresh pineapple juice

1 ounce tequila

1 ounce spiced rum

½ ounce lime juice

¼ ounce curaçao

Combine all ingredients in an ice-filled shaker. Shake vigorously for 25 to 30 seconds and strain over ice into a double Old-Fashioned glass.

INVISIBLE GIN

When it comes to dogs, purebreds get all the attention. In a world of tele-vised kennel club shows, Lassie and Scooby Doo reruns, and skateboard-ing bulldogs on Instagram, it's rare to see a mutt in the spotlight. But the cocktail world loves a good mutt. Clever bartenders constantly combine and put their own spins on "purebred" classics, often to fantastic results. One of the oldest of these experiments, the Invisible Gin first appeared in Charles H. Baker's A Gentleman's Companion in 1939. This supremely satisfying mongrel mixes elements of several standards, including the Mule, Sour, and the tiki favorite Piña Colada. It's the perfect way to cel-ebrate a successful trip to the shelter or the canine pals already in your life, regardless of their genetics. Even if you're not a dog person, you're going to want to take the Invisible Gin home as a companion for good.

1½ ounces gin	1 dash Angostura bitters
1 ounce pineapple juice	Club soda, to top
¾ ounce ginger syrup	1 piece candied ginger,
½ ounce apricot liqueur	for garnish
½ ounce fresh lemon juice	1 orange slice, for garnish

Combine the gin, pineapple juice, ginger syrup, apricot liqueur, lemon juice, and bitters in a shaker. Whip shake (no ice) and pour into a tall glass filled with ice (preferably one long ice cube, known as a Collins spear). Top with club soda. Garnish with the ginger candy and the orange slice.

DR. FUNK

If you don't know anyone who's had yellow fever or, more likely, doesn't even know what it is, thank Carlos Juan Finlay. In 1882, the Cuban physician determined that Aedes mosquitoes were transmitting the disease and that the best way to eradicate it was to control the mosquito population. Held every year on Finlay's birthday, Cuba's National Doctors' Day honors his efforts, as well as the country's current crop of physicians, who, despite limited resources, have kept their health care system at the forefront of medical innovation, with one of the highest life expectancies and lowest infant mortality rates in the world. A Cuban-themed celebration would be incomplete without a rum-based potable, and, thanks to another 19th-century physician, Dr. Bernard Funk, we have just the drink. Arguably the first tiki drink, this simple remedy of rum, lime, pomegranate, and absinthe is a cure-all for everything from boredom to a broken heart. But use as directed, or you might be making a trip to the doctor's office sooner than you planned.

---

2 ounces white rum

¾ ounce fresh lime juice

¾ ounce pomegranate syrup

1 barspoon absinthe

Club soda, to top

1 lime wedge, for garnish

Combine the rum, lime juice, pomegranate syrup, and absinthe in a shaker. Whip shake (no ice) and pour into a tall glass filled with ice. Top with club soda. Garnish with the lime wedge.

KARAOKE HONEYMOON

If there was a competition for which holiday to celebrate every single day, we'd put our money on National Cookie Day. Milk might be the beverage most associated with cookies, but a few select potations perfectly mimic the aromatic flavors of the world's most popular dessert wafers. The best of these is Zachary Gelnaw-Rubin's Karaoke Honeymoon, a funky, fruity, tiki-esque swizzle that captures the essence of an entire patisserie in a glass. With a trifecta of rum raisin, gingersnap, and biscotti elements from two famously bold rums, fresh ginger, and, most saliently, biscotti liqueur, your inner cocktail Cookie Monster will feel right at home.

¾ ounce spiced rum

¾ ounce biscotti liqueur, such as Faretti

½ ounce Smith & Cross Jamaican rum

½ ounce fresh lemon juice

½ ounce orange juice

½ ounce ginger syrup

1 pinch freshly grated nutmeg, for garnish

1 thin orange slice, for garnish

Combine the rums, biscotti liqueur, juices, and ginger syrup in a shaker. Pour into a tall glass filled two-thirds of the way with crushed ice. Add a straw and top with more crushed ice. Garnish with the nutmeg and the orange slice.

Repeal Day

SCOFFLAW

For the most part, 1920 was a solid year. The Treaty of Versailles effectively ended World War I, women in America finally secured the right to vote, and Babe Ruth's homerun-hitting exploits launched baseball's popularity to stratospheric heights. But that year also marked the start of Prohibition, a dark 13-year period when alcohol sales were banned, honest American drinkers and bar owners suddenly became criminals, and organized crime skyrocketed. Prohibition was undoubtedly one of history's biggest buzzkills, but the era encouraged cocktail-making ingenuity. The Scofflaw, a nicely dry Rye Sour variant, takes its name from law-flouting entrepreneurs who made sure people still could get their drink on, even if it meant sacrificing their own freedom. This fine blend of whiskey, lemon, vermouth, and grenadine might not be worth doing jail time over, but it's still a perfect homage to a time when absolutely no one took a well-made tipple for granted.

1 ounce rye whiskey

1 ounce dry vermouth

¾ ounce grenadine

½ ounce fresh lemon juice

2 dashes orange bitters

Combine all ingredients in an ice-filled shaker. Shake vigorously for 25 to 30 seconds and strain into a stemmed cocktail glass.

DECEMBER 6
National Miners Day

COAL TRAIN

Mining is synonymous with dark, dirty, dangerous work because it's literally one of the darkest, dirtiest, most dangerous jobs around! Held on the anniversary of the worst mining disaster in American history— in which 362 people died in a 1907 mine collapse near Monongah, West Virginia—National Miners Day honors the sacrifices and backbreaking labor of the thousands who have participated in one of the United State's most historically important professions. In recent years, coal use has decreased, but 2019 alone saw the country consume nearly 540 million tons of it. Much of that runs on coal trains that often stretch for more than a mile, a sight nearly as impressive as the drink named after them. Eric Hosaka's Coal Train, first served at Las Vegas's Rosina Cocktail Bar in 2018, is a good, old-fashioned rye-based sipper embellished with both tiki and amaro elements as sweet and herbaceous as a breath of fresh air after a long day toiling underground. Even if straight whiskey is more your style, it's worth digging up all the ingredients to try this one.

1¼ ounces rye whiskey	½ ounce banana liqueur
¾ ounce aged rhum agricole	¼ ounce Amargo Vallet
	1 lemon twist, for garnish

 Combine the rye, agricole, banana liqueur, and Amargo Vallet in a double Old-Fashioned glass. Add ice and stir for five or six seconds. Garnish with the lemon twist.

National Cotton Candy Day

COTTON CANDY MARGARITA

If you prefer your candy to melt in your mouth and in your hand, today is your time to shine! Notoriously messy yet oh-so delicious, with a texture unlike anything else, cotton candy—also frequently referred to as spun sugar—has been a saccharine staple at amusement parks and fairs since 1897, when the unlikely duo of dentist William Morrison and confectioner John C. Wharton developed a spinning machine that created cotton candy in a matter of seconds. For many of us sweets sticklers, just a whiff of the cloudlike confection conjures immediate nostalgia for the carnivals, sporting events, circuses, and trips that formed some of our fondest childhood memories (and the cavity fillings that followed). If you crave a bag of cotton candy but not the sticky mess that comes with it, step your sweet tooth up another notch with a Cotton Candy Margarita. The name is self-explanatory, and the flavor is exactly what you'd expect: utterly sweet and scrumptious.

1 small handful cotton candy

1½ ounces tequila

1 ounce fresh lime juice

½ ounce Cointreau

Cream soda, to top

Fill a tall glass three-fourths of the way with cotton candy. Combine the tequila, lime juice, and Cointreau in an ice-filled shaker. Shake vigorously for 25 to 30 seconds and strain into the glass. Add ice and stir with a long-handled spoon until the cotton candy dissolves completely. Top with cream soda.

41 JANE DOES

Life isn't always apples and oranges. Pears need some love, too! Pear brandy traces its origins to 1700s France and reached peak popularity in the 19th century, but this fruit-infused, clear spirit has been making a comeback lately, particularly as a tasty modifier in cocktails. Toby Maloney turns the pear power up by using the brandy as a base spirit in his 41 Jane Does, a sublimely fruity and foamy Fizz first served at Milk & Honey in 2004. Also featuring pear's frequent cousin, apple brandy, this tall order of deliciousness tastes like an entire orchard in a glass.

1 ounce calvados or similar
   apple brandy
1 ounce pear brandy

¾ ounce fresh lemon juice
¾ ounce simple syrup
1 egg white
Club soda, to top

Combine the brandies, lemon juice, simple syrup, and egg white in a shaker. Shake without ice (to emulsify the egg white) for 10 seconds, then add ice and shake vigorously. Strain into a tall glass filled with ice. Top with club soda.

BACKROOM MOB

Goodfellas *makes for compelling cinema, but real-life criminality is nothing to cheer. Concerned about corruption "undermining the institutions and values of democracy, ethical values and justice, and jeopardizing sustainable development and the rule of law," the United Nations created International Anti-Corruption Day to raise awareness about this global threat. Unless you live in a dictatorship, most corruption occurs behind the scenes or in the guise of legitimacy. That allusion to secrecy inspired the name of the Backroom Mob, a lovely, effervescent cooler from Southern California bartender Alex Jaimes. Combining Mint Julep vibes with elderflower and fresh citrus, this ambitious twist on several classic flavors is as refreshing as a clean conscience. After a long day of fighting for truth, justice, and the American cocktail, this one hits just right.*

1½ ounces bourbon

¾ ounce elderflower liqueur

¾ ounce fresh lime juice

3 or 4 fresh mint leaves

Club soda, to top

1 sprig mint, for garnish

Combine the bourbon, elderflower liqueur, lime juice, and mint leaves in an ice-filled shaker. Shake vigorously for 25 to 30 seconds and strain into a tall glass filled with ice. Top with club soda. Garnish with the mint sprig.

Human Rights Day, Animal Rights Day

OLD PAL

Today's double dipper is well worth the effort. Since 1948, December 10 has been known as Human Rights Day, commemorating the release of the United Nations' Universal Declaration of Human Rights, a proclamation of the inalienable rights of people from all countries and ethnic origins. At more than 500 pages, it's the most translated document in the world. It also inspired activists to create Animal Rights Day, a time for highlighting the sad reality of animal abuse and exploitation while ensuring that no creature is treated as an inferior being, which is also something to celebrate! If you respect the rights of all your fellow earthlings—regardless of race, gender, age, or species—you'll never be short on friends. As far as cocktails go, it doesn't get any chummier than the Old Pal. A riff on the Boulevardier (itself a whiskey-forward tweak of a Negroni) first mixed by 1920s bartending icon Harry MacElhone at Harry's New York Bar in Paris, it's a lighter, zestier version of its more illustrious ancestors. This balanced, thoughtful, and refreshingly simple sipper is the perfect companion for championing any noble cause, from universal equality to getting your local bar to expand its happy hour specials.

1½ ounces rye whiskey

¾ ounce Campari

¾ ounce dry vermouth

1 lemon twist, for garnish

Combine the rye, Campari, and dry vermouth in a mixing glass filled with cracked ice. Stir with a long-handled spoon for 30 seconds and strain into a stemmed cocktail glass. Garnish with the lemon twist.

MOUNT FUJI

There's nothing like an exhilarating mountain adventure for tapping into some of the deepest and most profound parts of yourself. As Scottish-American naturalist John Muir beautifully put it, "You are not in the mountains. The mountains are in you." You don't have to climb a mountain to appreciate its spectacular topography, and you don't even need to be in sight of one to enjoy a delightful mountain-inspired cocktail such as the Mount Fuji. Named after Japan's tallest, most iconic peak, this Sidecar variation is a delicious potable at any elevation. Featuring French Cointreau and traditional Japanese sake—a clean-tasting, nutty, and slightly sweet brew made from the same kinds of rice that grow near Fuji's base—it's a fresh, citrusy sipper that had to cross continents and several mountain ranges to come together. This perfect, low-ABV treat won't leave your head in the clouds.

2 ounces sake
1 ounce Cointreau

½ ounce fresh lemon juice
2 dashes Angostura bitters
1 lemon twist, for garnish

Combine the sake, Cointreau, lemon juice, and bitters in an ice-filled shaker. Shake vigorously for 25 to 30 seconds and strain into a stemmed cocktail glass. Garnish with the lemon twist.

International Day of Neutrality

SWISS MANHATTAN

If you've ever tried (and failed) to avoid an argument between friends or coworkers, you know how hard it is to remain neutral in even a relatively innocuous situation. That's why it's incredible that Switzerland has kept its nose out of every major international conflict since 1815. Sometimes the most difficult conflicts arise within us, like which cocktail to drink after a tiring day of successfully evading controversy. No worries, just make yourself a Swiss Manhattan and feel the stress instantly melt away. This significantly drier take on the rye-based classic features calming notes of chocolate and almond with a clean, slightly bitter, cherry-tinged finish thanks to kirschwasser, a colorless brandy traditionally produced in Switzerland's German-speaking cantons. A few rounds of these powerful peacemakers and you're more likely to slip into dreamland than cause an international ruckus.

---

2 ounces rye whiskey

½ ounce dry vermouth

½ ounce kirschwasser

4 dashes chocolate bitters

1 brandied cherry, for garnish

 Combine the whiskey, vermouth, kirschwasser, and bitters in a mixing glass filled with cracked ice. Stir with a long-handled spoon for 30 seconds and strain into a stemmed cocktail glass. Garnish with the brandied cherry.

HIGH HORSE

In 2004, the US Congress designated December 13 as a day to celebrate the economic, historic, and cultural contributions that horses have made, an official recognition long overdue. Like 6,000 years overdue. From herding cattle and plowing fields to hauling goods and police patrols, there's no task too big for Earth's hardiest mammals, and there's no palate that the High Horse from Bobby Hicks at Lantern's Keep in Midtown Manhattan can't please. This agave-based modern classic boasts a fantastically well-shod combination of citrusy, sweet, smoky, and herbaceous flavors that's nothing to snort at. You'll want to sprint to your local cocktail spot faster than a thoroughbred approaching the finish line for one of these horses of a slightly reddish color.

1 ounce tequila	½ ounce pomegranate syrup
1 ounce Aperol	¼ ounce mezcal
1 ounce fresh lime juice	1 lime wedge, for garnish

Combine the tequila, Aperol, lime juice, and pomegranate syrup in an ice-filled shaker. Shake vigorously for 25 to 30 seconds and strain into a double Old-Fashioned glass over ice. Float the mezcal. Garnish with the lime wedge.

TURN THE PAGE TO
SEE THE ILLUSTRATION
FOR THIS DRINK.

High Horse
PAGE 421

Monkey Day

MONKEY GRIP

Stop monkeying around! Don't make a monkey out of me! No monkey business here!

Begun in 2000, Monkey Day was an immediate global success. Peter Jackson even coordinated the release of his 2005 blockbuster, King Kong, *on the holiday's fifth anniversary. It's unclear whether Australian bartender Cameron Parish had today's festivities in mind when he debuted the Monkey Grip at Melbourne's The Everleigh in 2018, but the nutty, bitter, gingery, and fizzy refresher is perfect for a tipple at crepuscule (which means twilight, when many species of simians are most active). Low on alcohol but soaring in flavor, it's more fun than a barrel full of, well, you know.*

1½ ounces fino sherry
¾ ounce fresh lemon juice
½ ounce Campari
½ ounce ginger syrup

2 dashes Peychaud's bitters
Club soda, to top
1 piece candied ginger,
   for garnish

Combine the sherry, lemon juice, Campari, ginger syrup, and bitters in a shaker. Whip shake (no ice) and pour into a tall glass filled with ice. Top with club soda. Garnish with the piece of candied ginger.

JALISCO HIGH TEA

If a simple drink can help cause a revolution, it's got to be good. International Tea Day, while celebrating the economic importance and cultural heritage of tea and promoting sustainable production practices, fails to recognize one of the best characteristics of this globally beloved beverage: It goes great with booze! Try it in this cocktail, the Jalisco High Tea, a delectable tipple from the not-so-mad scientists at Patrón Tequila. This sophisticated stimulator features an enticing blend of energizing lemon verbena, a pleasant hint of cherry, and the woodsy aromatics of aged tequila. Mix one of these and you'll agree that teatime will never be the same.

1½ ounces tequila reposado, such as Patrón

1½ ounces lemon verbena tea (chilled)

½ ounce simple syrup

¼ ounce Cherry Heering

¼ ounce fresh lime juice

Combine all ingredients in an ice-filled shaker. Shake vigorously for 25 to 30 seconds and strain into a double Old-Fashioned glass over ice.

CHOCOLATE COCKTAIL

*Oreos, potato chips, orange slices, waffles, and ants don't have much
in common, but you can dip them all (and more!) in melted chocolate.
For the folks behind National Chocolate-Covered Anything Day, that's
about as basic as it gets. There's nothing like chocolate wrapped around
an ice cube or two, in the form of Yoo-hoo, Nesquik, or any of the other
milk-based beverages that many of us enjoyed as kids. The unironically
named Chocolate Cocktail is a delightfully boozy take on these nostalgia-
inducing beverages. This complex, sweet and spicy sipper features subtle
hints of popular chocolate additives such as molasses, honey, almonds,
pepper, and sea salt, with odes to both the dark (bitters) and milk (cacao
and cream) varieties of everyone's favorite cocoa-based confections. It's
not the chocolate milk you remember, but it's the one you deserve.*

1½ ounces blackstrap rum

½ ounce crème de cacao (dark)

¼ ounce amaretto

1 barspoon honey syrup

2 dashes chocolate bitters

1 pinch sea salt

Hand-whipped cream, to top

1 pinch cayenne pepper,
    for garnish

Combine the rum, crème de cacao, amaretto, honey syrup,
bitters, and sea salt in an Old-Fashioned glass. Add ice and
stir for five or six seconds. Float the whipped cream. Garnish
with the cayenne pepper.

PAN AMERICAN CLIPPER

Now defunct, Pan American Airways began a scheduled airmail and passenger service between Key West and Havana in 1927 and ruled the Western Hemisphere's skies for decades. Countless world travelers made their first trips on Pan Am's top-of-the-line aircraft, including spirits author Charles H. Baker, whose Florida home stood a short distance from where the company opened the first international airport. An homage to that airline's pilots (with a recipe allegedly lifted from one of their notebooks), the Pan American Clipper is a deliciously fruity, slightly savory take on a Jack Rose that's ideal for settling the nerves before—or during—a long flight. If you prefer to remain firmly on the ground, mix one of these world-class sippers, sit back, and watch the planes go by.

2 ounces apple brandy	¾ ounce pomegranate syrup
¾ ounce fresh lime juice	1 dash absinthe

 Combine all ingredients in an ice-filled shaker. Shake vigorously for 25 to 30 seconds and strain into a stemmed cocktail glass.

UN Arabic Language Day

RUM AMANDINE

You know Arabic numerals, but can you speak the language? The folks at UNESCO, the United Nations' Educational, Scientific, and Cultural Organization, hope you give it a shot. We don't often associate the Arabic-speaking world with cocktails or booze in general, primarily due to the Islamic faith's heavy restrictions on alcohol consumption. But some of the most popular elements in Middle Eastern cuisine—almonds, cherries, orange blossom water—serve as excellent modifiers in countless concoctions. Those three flavor powerhouses blend spectacularly in the Rum Amandine, an old-school potation modeled after the nonalcoholic syrup of the same name. Featuring white rum for a nice kick and just enough absinthe to mellow its sweetness, it's the perfect reward for learning the beautiful twists and turns of Arabic.

2 ounces white rum

¼ ounce fresh lime juice

⅜ ounce maraschino liqueur

⅜ ounce orgeat

1 barspoon absinthe

3 dashes orange blossom water

1 brandied cherry, for garnish

Combine the rum, lime juice, maraschino liqueur, orgeat, absinthe, and orange blossom water in an ice-filled shaker. Shake vigorously for 25 to 30 seconds and strain into a stemmed cocktail glass. Garnish with the brandied cherry.

BLACK BARREL

Dust off your skinny jeans, studded belts, and liquid eyeliner and blast your favorite My Chemical Romance and Fall Out Boy CDs. To embrace the darkest aspects of your tormented soul while listening to your favorite emo tunes, you're going to need a drink equally brooding. The Black Barrel, a richer, darker take on an Old Barrel from Attaboy Nashville's Mitchell Taylor, is perfect for making your pulverized heart feel slightly less stabby—or more so, depending on how deep you want to get. Amaro Averna and amontillado sherry combine with rye to form a bittersweet, caramel-tinged concoction ideal for spirit-forward sensibilities but still weird enough to keep the normies away, which is just how emos like it.

2 ounces rye whiskey

½ ounce Amaro Averna

½ ounce amontillado sherry

2 dashes Angostura bitters

1 lemon twist, for garnish

 Combine the whiskey, Amaro Averna, sherry, and bitters in an Old-Fashioned glass. Add ice and stir for five or six seconds. Garnish with the lemon twist.

SUAVE SANGRIA

Wine is good, but it could be better. How, you ask? By adding fresh fruits, liquor, and spices to make Sangria, of course! We don't often think of tequila and red wine as having a particular fondness for each other, but the Suave Sangria proves otherwise. Created in collaboration with Sofia Present at Middle Branch on an unseasonably warm spring evening in 2014, this revitalizing cooler features a cornucopia of easily available fruits; a pleasant, agave-forward bouquet; and an egalitarian finish best realized with any slightly dry, light-bodied red wine, such as pinot noir or malbec. Fizzy and refreshing, bright and bracing, it's a svelte treat that's always in fashion, regardless of the climate.

- 2 ounces red wine
- 1 ounce tequila
- ½ ounce simple syrup
- 4 dashes Angostura bitters
- 2 halved strawberries
- 2 blackberries
- 1 lemon wedge
- 1 orange wedge
- 1 thin apple slice
- 1 brandied cherry
- Club soda, to top (optional)

Combine all ingredients except the club soda in a shaker. Gently muddle the fruits, then dump the shaker's contents into a large wine glass. Fill the glass with crushed or cracked ice. Top with club soda if desired.

DECEMBER 21
Capricorn Day

SATURN

According to the astrologically inclined, Capricorns can be emotionally cold, stubborn, impulsive, condescending, and pessimistic—and that's on a good day. December 21 marks the beginning of this notoriously prickly sign's time on the zodiac calendar and, to combat the negative stereotypes, offers a chance to celebrate its positive traits. The planet Saturn rules Capricorn, and while we aren't entirely sure what that signifies, we're certain that the Saturn cocktail will bring you the best celestial vibes, no matter your sign. Filipino bartender J. "Popo" Galsini invented this rare gin-based tiki potable in 1967, when it won the International Bartenders Association World Cocktail Championship, and author Jeff "Beachbum" Berry later rediscovered it. Straightforward, prudent, and balanced, like many Capricorns, it's also laid-back, fun, and fruity, as refreshing as a jungle stroll. After all, Capricorn is an Earth sign, whatever that means.

---

2 ounces gin
¾ ounce fresh lemon juice
¾ ounce passion fruit syrup
¼ ounce John D. Taylor's Velvet Falernum

¼ ounce orgeat
1 pinch freshly grated cinnamon, for garnish
1 brandied cherry, for garnish

 Combine the gin, lemon juice, passion fruit syrup, velvet falernum, and orgeat in a shaker. Pour into a tall glass or mug filled two-thirds of the way with crushed ice. Add a straw and top with more crushed ice. Garnish with the cinnamon and the brandied cherry.

VESPER

Few fictional characters have inspired more climaxes than James Bond. Originally appearing in novels by Ian Fleming, the dashing, intelligent, and powerful British Secret Service agent has been portrayed on-screen by some of the most ruggedly good-looking men in Hollywood, causing no small amount of multigenerational swooning. He's also known for his predilection for cocktails, particularly the Vesper, a sexy Martini riff he first ordered in the 1953 book Casino Royale *and which he named after equally alluring double agent Vesper Lynd. Featuring mostly full-proof spirits, it's strong enough to get the blood flowing, with enough honeyed sweetness from Lillet blanc to guarantee a supremely satisfying finish.*

1½ ounces gin
¾ ounce vodka

½ ounce Lillet blanc
1 lemon twist, for garnish

Combine the gin, vodka, and Lillet blanc in a mixing glass filled with cracked ice. Stir with a long-handled spoon for 30 seconds and strain into a stemmed cocktail glass. Garnish with the lemon twist.

Festivus

FEATS OF STRENGTH

"A Festivus for the rest of us!"

    *If you're familiar with December 23's most popular "celebration,"
you probably watched* Seinfeld's *season 9 episode "The Strike," in which
George Costanza's father, Frank, claims to have invented Festivus, after
a clash over a department store doll, to protest Christmastime commercialism. Highlights of this infamously horrendous festival include raising an unadorned aluminum pole (because "tinsel is too distracting"),
an "airing of grievances" directed at those who have disappointed you
over the past year, and the proclamation of easily explained events as
"Festivus miracles." Another important Festivus tradition, the "Feats
of Strength," occurs when the head of the household challenges someone
else at the Festivus celebration to a wrestling match. If you're not particularly dogmatic, try Michael Timmons's Feats of Strength cocktail for
a challenge to your palate. Featuring a who's-who of intense flavors, an
undeniably salty energy, and an alcohol content not for the faint of heart,
this acerbic dynamo might not be everyone's idea of a good time. But
if your tastes skew toward the extremely funky, it's a miracle of drink-making that lives up to the definition.*

1½ ounces Cynar

1½ ounces medium dry sherry

½ ounce Smith & Cross Jamaican
    rum

1 barspoon green Chartreuse

1 pinch salt

1 grapefruit twist,
    for garnish

Combine the Cynar, sherry, rum, Chartreuse, and salt in a
double Old-Fashioned glass. Add ice and stir for five or six
seconds. Garnish with the grapefruit twist.

EAST NEW YORK FLIP

It doesn't feel like the holidays if you aren't scarfing down reckless amounts of rich, sweet goodies. Few seasonal pleasures taste guiltier than eggnog, an utterly decadent mixture of cream, sugar, eggs, spirits (originally brandy or wine), and spices that has enchanted taste buds and expanded waistlines since the late 1600s, when it was a popular seasonal tipple among the English aristocracy. Flips are an obscure yet noble family of cocktails with cream and egg yolk components that wonderfully mimic eggnog's velvety texture. Perhaps the "noggiest" of these is the East New York Flip, created by José Gil at Milk & Honey in 2006. Its base of bourbon and fortified wine stays true to its early American predecessors, but this honey-sweet, spiced stunner is as timeless as it gets. Like other calorie-loaded bad boys, it can demolish months of health-conscious consumption in just a few rounds. No worries, though. Getting back in shape is what New Year's resolutions are for!

---

1 ounce bourbon

1 ounce port

¼ ounce honey syrup

¾ ounce heavy cream

1 egg yolk

1 pinch freshly grated nutmeg,
    for garnish

Combine the bourbon, port, honey syrup, cream, and egg yolk in a shaker. Shake without ice (to emulsify the egg yolk) for 10 seconds, then add ice and shake vigorously. Strain into a stemmed cocktail glass. Garnish with the nutmeg.

HEADLESS HORSEMAN

In recent years, pumpkin-flavored foods and drinks have taken a hit in the respectability department, mostly due to their unfortunate association with selfie-obsessed Millennials and Gen Z miscreants whose idea of individuality is buying a puffy vest in a slightly darker shade of blue. Thankfully, though, pumpkin pie always endures, and hooray for pumpkin beer! Hundreds of limited-edition, gourd-infused brews line supermarket shelves during the colder months of the year. These lagers and ales taste great on their own, but they're even better as the base of a seasonally scrumptious Headless Horseman from Rabbit Hole Tavern in Old Saybrook, Connecticut. Embellished and fortified by vodka, and with supple notes of spice and vanilla from Licor 43, this aromatic delicacy will enthrall holiday cocktail lovers rather than decapitate them. Give the pumpkin-spice latte a rest and make a spicy, icy glass of pumpkin perfection instead. It's just as Instagrammable and far less #basic.

12-ounce bottle of pumpkin beer, such as Schlafly Pumpkin Ale
1 ounce vodka
½ ounce pumpkin syrup
¼ ounce Licor 43
Freshly grated cinnamon, for rim
Sugar, for rim

Rim a tall glass with the cinnamon and sugar. Add the vodka, pumpkin syrup, and Licor 43 to the glass. Add cracked ice and top with pumpkin beer.

AFTER ALL

Here's an obvious statement: The holidays are stressful. As magical as it sounds to spend quality time with family and friends, events such as Christmas, Hanukkah, and New Year's Eve can prove unbelievably hectic and mentally exhausting. Today's your chance to complain about it. We all know at least one major-league whiner, a real-life Moaning Myrtle who can find faults in even the most joyous aspects of life, including a perfectly made cocktail. But it's nearly impossible to hate on the After All, one of the most soothing Prohibition-era tipples from Harry MacElhone's Cocktails and Barflies *(1927). Succulently fruity but noncloying—because most peach liqueurs taste surprisingly rather dry— it's powerful enough to calm the frazzled nerves of agitation-prone people and the even more unfortunate souls forced to listen to them.*

1½ ounces applejack	½ ounce fresh lemon juice
1 ounce peach liqueur	1 lemon twist, for garnish

Combine the applejack, peach liqueur, and lemon juice in an ice-filled shaker. Shake vigorously for 25 to 30 seconds and strain into a stemmed cocktail glass. Garnish with the lemon twist.

MEZCAL COBBLER

The phrase "nutty as a fruitcake" describes an exceptionally crazy individual, but today's holiday doesn't celebrate the clinically unwell. A lovely final step in many traditional fruitcake recipes suggests soaking the entire thing in scotch or brandy. If you'd rather skip the baking and go straight to the drinking, make a Mezcal Cobbler instead. Part of a pre-Prohibition family of drinks that takes its name from the pieces of ice over which they customarily were built, this modern crushed-ice version features a pleasantly smoky base and all the fresh fruits you can handle, minus the sugar added when they're preserved. A couple rounds of these provide an excellent source of plant-based nutrition, all conveniently canceled out by delicious booze.

2 ounces mezcal
½ ounce curaçao
1 lime wedge
1 lemon wedge

1 strawberry
1 blackberry
1 cherry
1 thin orange slice
1 cucumber slice

Combine all ingredients in a shaker. Muddle thoroughly and dump into a tall glass. Fill the glass two-thirds of the way with crushed ice and stir briefly with a swizzle stick. Top with more crushed ice. Garnish with whatever additional fruit pieces you have on hand.

DECEMBER 28
National Card Playing Day

POKER FACE

If you've spent any time watching card tables, you know that games can feel as intense as they are time-consuming. If you're looking for liquid refreshment while playing, you need a drink that doesn't take much time to whip up, such as the Poker Face. This mid-20th-century classic of indeterminate origins consists of only a few easy-to-find ingredients. It's got more than enough sugar-charged pineapple juice to keep you energized and focused, with plenty of tequila and Cointreau to give you the courage to make the biggest bets—and to ease the pain when you inevitably go belly-up.

---

4 ounces fresh pineapple juice

1½ ounces tequila

½ ounce Cointreau

1 thin orange slice, for garnish

Combine the pineapple juice, tequila, and Cointreau in an ice-filled shaker. Shake vigorously for 25 to 30 seconds and strain into a tall glass filled with ice. Garnish with the orange slice.

TURN THE PAGE TO
SEE THE ILLUSTRATION
FOR THIS DRINK.

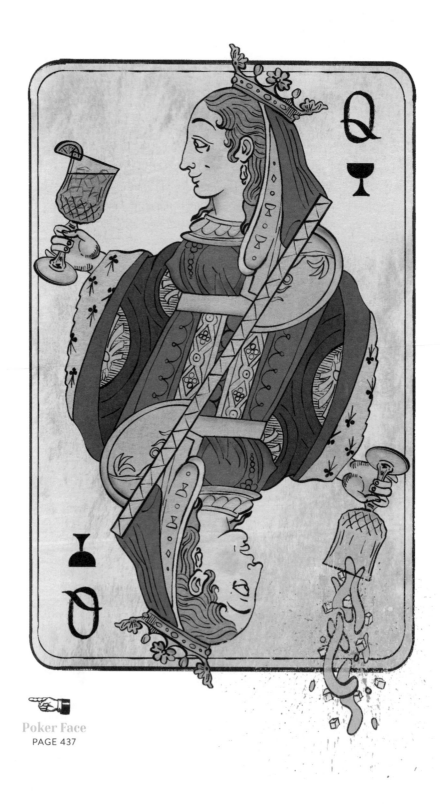

Poker Face
PAGE 437

National Pepper Pot Day

OLD PEPPER

Many a kitchen guru has laid claim to whipping up the world's greatest soup, but only one such dish changed the course of American history. During the harsh winter of 1777–78, George Washington and his Continental Army camped near Valley Forge, Pennsylvania. Farmers loyal to the British refused to sell their food to the troops, so Washington's head baker, Christopher Ludwick, concocted a spicy, savory stew featuring beef tripe, red peppers, peppercorns, and other zesty seasonings. Pepper Pot Soup, "the soup that won the war," not only warmed the soldiers and kept them alive but also boosted their morale. As a result, it became a popular Philadelphia street food beloved by generations of spice-loving patriots.

Peppery and savory flavors have become commonplace in cocktails, but the oldest of these spicy concoctions is still one of the best. A snappy addition to the 1939 edition of Charles H. Baker Jr.'s The Gentleman's Companion, *the Old Pepper is a funky Whiskey Sour spin-off perfect for warming up when the weather has you down. Taking advantage of bourbon's naturally peppery and oaky characteristics, this American classic turns up the heat with both hot sauce and the same cracked pepper that appears in Pepper Pot Soup, balanced by citrus and Worcestershire sauce.*

2 ounces bourbon

¾ ounce fresh lemon juice

¾ ounce simple syrup

4 dashes Worcestershire sauce

3 dashes Cholula hot sauce

3 thin cucumber slices

1 generous pinch cracked black pepper

Combine the bourbon, lemon juice, simple syrup, Worcestershire sauce, hot sauce, and cucumber slices in an ice-filled shaker. Shake vigorously for 25 to 30 seconds and strain into a stemmed cocktail glass. Garnish with the cracked black pepper.

CORPSE REVIVER NO. 2

In case you hadn't noticed, it's almost the end of the year. There's still time to cross an item or two off that to-do list you made in January, but you'd better snap to it! A not-so-subtle reminder to procrastinators, Festival of Enormous Changes at the Last Minute encourages everyone to take a long, hard look at the past 12 months and finish any tasks or self-improvement projects they've been meaning to complete while realizing that it's going to take a massive effort to get them done. If you started your New Year's revelry a day early, no worries. There's always next year!

Usually, the changes between similar-sounding cocktails are minuscule. For instance, an Aviation No. 2 is basically an Aviation No. 1 without crème de violette. But when it comes to the pre-Prohibition-era Corpse Reviver family—its chief purpose: to return morning-after sufferers to the land of the living—the differences are, well, enormous. The No. 1 version of the drink is a Manhattan-esque, cognac-based bracer. The No. 2 features gin, citrus, an aperitif wine, and orange liqueur. The latter's tart, heady, and deceptively strong bouquet (goodbye, hangover!) is an excellent reward for squeezing in one last iota of productivity before the calendar flips.

¾ ounce gin

¾ ounce Cocchi Americano

¼ ounce Cointreau

¾ ounce fresh lemon juice

1 dash absinthe

1 small lemon peel

Combine the gin, Cocchi Americano, Cointreau, fresh lemon juice, and absinthe in an ice-filled shaker. Shake vigorously for 25 to 30 seconds and strain into a stemmed cocktail glass. Express the oils from the lemon peel on the rim of the glass and discard the peel.

FORTUNE COCKTAIL

"Remember, gentlemen, it's not just France we're fighting for, it's Champagne!" Spoken somewhat in jest, that World War II–era quote from Winston Churchill underscores the passion that millions have for the world's most celebrated bubbly. Nothing sets another trip around the sun on the right track like a champagne toast. Take that good luck to even greater heights with Michael Madrusan's Fortune Cocktail, a superbly sippable celebrater inspired by the Serendipity, a similar drink served at Bar Hemingway in the Ritz Paris since 1994. A bountiful blend of citrus, apple, and mint that symbolizes the previous year's gains and the fruitful feeling of sharing a special night with like-minded company, it's your best bet for transforming a memorable time into an unforgettable one.

1 ounce applejack
½ ounce fresh lemon juice

½ ounce simple syrup
3 or 4 mint leaves
Champagne, to top

Combine the applejack, lemon juice, simple syrup, and mint leaves in an ice-filled shaker. Shake vigorously for 25 to 30 seconds and strain into a champagne flute. Top with champagne.

TURN THE PAGE TO
SEE THE ILLUSTRATION
FOR THIS DRINK.

Fortune Cocktail
PAGE 441

ACKNOWLEDGMENTS

Infinite gratitude is due to the many generous and supportive souls who made this book possible, including my agent, Rica Allannic; editorial director Ann Treistman, editors James Jayo and Michael Tizzano, and the entire crew at Countryman Press; and Matthew Linz, for the sensationally gorgeous art.

Big thanks to the dozens of bartenders whose creations appear in these pages, as well as the squad at Little Branch—especially Luis Gil, Michael Timmons, Courtney McKamey, and Victor Pereda—whose weary ears and palates bore the brunt of my experimentation.

And unending love to all the party people in my life who can turn the most mundane day into the wildest hullabaloo.

RECIPE INDEX